LOST WARRIORS

Seagrim and Pagani of Burma
The Last Great Untold Story of WWII

LOST WARRIORS

Seagrim and Pagani of Burma
The Last Great Untold Story of WWII

PHILIP DAVIES

ATLANTIC PUBLISHING

Above and right: Rangoon Jail, 1 May 1945, with 'British Here – Japs Gone' painted on the roof to alert Allied aircraft.

This is an Atlantic Publishing book
First published in 2017 by Atlantic Publishing
38 Copthorne Road, Croxley Green
Hertfordshire, WD3 4AQ, UK

© Philip Davies
Philip Davies has asserted his right to be identified as the author of this work in
accordance with the Copyright, Designs and Patents Act 1988.
For details of photograph copyrights see page 279

A catalogue record for this book is available from the British Library.

ISBN 1 978 909242 85 2
Printed in the UK

Contents

Foreword	7
Acknowledgements	11
Author's Note	15
Glossary	17
Prologue	19
Chapter 1: Eastern Catastrophe	21
Chapter 2: Brothers in Arms	26
Chapter 3: Behind Enemy Lines	46
Chapter 4: Grandfather Longlegs	62
Chapter 5: The Master of His Fate	86
Chapter 6: Walking with Destiny	101
Chapter 7: Lords of the Sunset	111
Chapter 8: Lord of the Far-Flung Battle Line	122
Chapter 9: Perilous Journey	134
Chapter 10: Undercover in the Jungle	142
Chapter 11: Dark Night of the Soul	151
Chapter 12: This Long War Beneath the Stars	160
Chapter 13: Death in the Forest	173
Chapter 14: He Who Would Valiant Be	190
Chapter 15: The Yank from Battersea	199
Chapter 16: Into Thy Hands I Commend My Spirit	210
Aftermath: Seagrim's Legacy	221
Chapter 17: Reaping the Whirlwind	222
Chapter 18: The Birth of a Legend	240
Epilogue	259
Appendix A	263
Appendix B Ian Morrison	265
Notes and Select Bibliography	268

For Hugh Seagrim and Roy Pagani and all those peoples of Burma who have suffered in their search for freedom. May they finally find peace.

Foreword

Many who read this book are likely to be too young to recall the dark years of the Second World War. Today, many may find it difficult to grasp the breadth and realities of that dreadful war in Asia, particularly in Burma (Myanmar). It might be useful to remind them of the enemy which the British Indian 14th Army, and so many others, valiantly faced.

The Japanese were a hated enemy, mostly because of the brutal treatment meted out to the people in the countries they conquered, what they did to our wounded who could not be recovered and the inhuman treatment of both military and civilian POWs. However, none can dispute the Japanese soldier's exceptional courage in battle, a ferocious enemy who never surrendered and fought to the death. It is said they were the most vicious and brave foe we British have fought.

This book depicts two quite different British soldiers. Each in his own way fought in isolation in enemy-occupied territory for over two years with no support, forgotten and lost within the main campaign. Roy Pagani and Hugh Seagrim came together for a short period and then continued on their different paths. I was most touched by the tough Pagani being so completely in awe of Seagrim and falling under the spell of his inspirational leadership. This stayed with him throughout his life and I am sure it helped him through the perils that lay ahead. I am somewhat surprised that after Pagani finally returned home more use was not made of his unique experiences by MI9 for instruction in escape, evasion and survival techniques rather than allowing him to sink into obscurity as an Army driver. To my mind, he was under decorated and deserved better.

Hugh Seagrim lived amongst the wonderful and courageous Karens, often in solitude for very long periods, in a debilitating climate, beset by hunger and killer diseases and continuously hounded by the Japanese military and kempeitai, but he developed an inner life which sustained him and inspired all those who he encountered. It is not always easy to be brave and bold when alone. The mind offers the easy way out and one has to be strong to counter this. Armchair warriors should be careful when dissecting Seagrim's decisions and actions and remember the circumstances in which he was living and the ruthless enemy he was fighting against. There is no doubt that his decision to sacrifice himself in the hope of saving the Karens from systematic torture and further abuse on his behalf was uppermost in his mind. He showed tremendous gallantry, knowing what would befall him in the hands of the Japanese.

I applaud Philip Davies who has taken great care over many years in amassing the subject matter and evidence in this book. Having visited Burma many times, he goes into great depth and detail, and in so doing, has uncovered the truth as far as humanly possible.

The Second World War still casts a shadow over Burma. It is fitting, and long overdue, that this book should have been written. Both men deserve to be remembered in the front rank of those who fought in that savage conflict.

I have visited the cemetery in Rangoon (Yangon) described by Philip Davies and walked amongst the lost heroes of many races and religions. They would be proud and honoured to lie alongside Major Hugh Seagrim GC, DSO, MBE, whom my father called 'a most gallant officer'.

SLIM
House of Lords
May 2017

Opposite: Map of Burma and surrounding countries

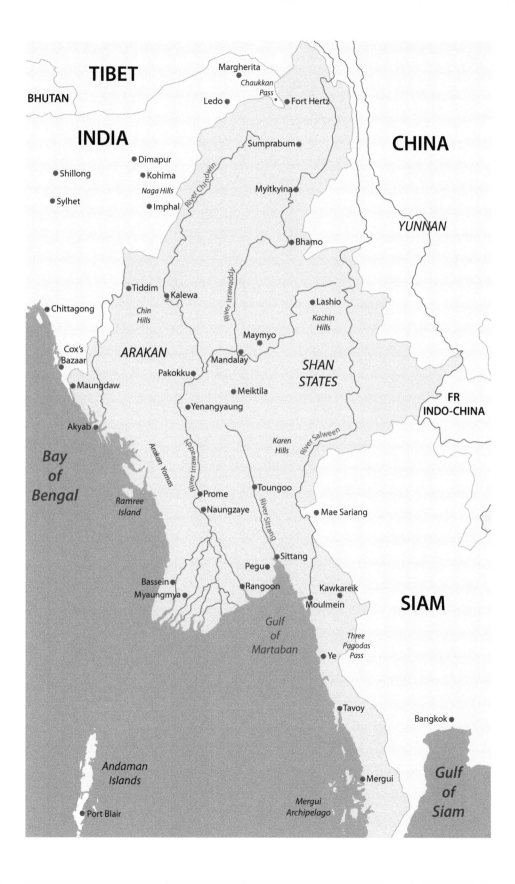

TIBET

BHUTAN

INDIA

CHINA

Margherita

Chaukkan Pass

Ledo

Fort Hertz

Sumprabum

Dimapur

Shillong

Kohima

Naga Hills

Myitkyina

YUNNAN

Sylhet

Imphal

Bhamo

River Chindwin

Tiddim

Kalewa

River Irrawaddy

Lashio

Chittagong

Chin Hills

Kachin Hills

Cox's Bazaar

ARAKAN

Maymyo

Maungdaw

Pakokku

Mandalay

SHAN STATES

Akyab

Meiktila

Yenangyaung

River Irrawaddy

River Salween

Karen Hills

Bay of Bengal

Arakan Yomas

Ramree Island

Prome

Naungzaye

Toungoo

River Sittang

Mae Sariang

Sittang

Pegu

Rangoon

Kawkareik

SIAM

Bassein

Myaungmya

Moulmein

Gulf of Martaban

Three Pagodas Pass

Ye

FR INDO-CHINA

Tavoy

Bangkok

Andaman Islands

Gulf of Siam

Mergui

Port Blair

Mergui Archipelago

Acknowledgements

This book, the outcome of fifteen years' research in Britain, the United States, Burma, Australia and France, would not have been possible without the unstinting support of many people in many countries, to all of whom I owe an immense debt of gratitude.

First and foremost, I would like to thank Michael and Catherine Seagrim for allowing me unrestricted access to the family's papers, photographs and remaining letters, and above all for continuing to have faith in my commitment to the book in the face of so many unexpected setbacks and diversions.

Thanks, too, to the late Anne Seagrim for sharing her childhood memories of her intrepid cousins, and also to Derek and Antoinette Seagrim for showing me their records and copies of family photographs.

Similarly, I would like to thank Cheb Campbell and Michelle Wells, Roy Pagani's daughters and their families, for sharing their family records and memorabilia with me, and both families for reading and correcting the drafts, suggesting amendments and for never tiring of my endless questions over a long period of time.

In Edinburgh, Harry and Carol Nimmo extended me a warm welcome and hospitality and provided copies of their family records and photographs of Jimmy Nimmo for my use.

I am also extremely grateful to Viscount Slim for his enthusiastic support and for providing the foreword.

For a story which is now over seventy years old, I have had to rely heavily on the eyes and ears of Ian Morrison, who unearthed so much material at the end of the war for his book *Grandfather Longlegs*, published in 1947, shortly before his death in Korea in 1950. Faber and Faber have been immensely helpful in allowing me to use photographs of some key characters and selected quotes from Morrison's book.

Roy Pagani's own typescript of his life and wartime adventures – *I Did It My Way* – is the principal source of material for his experiences, along with surviving records in the National Archives and the Australian National War Memorial. I am hugely grateful to Cheb and James Campbell for allowing me to use Pagani's own words, wherever possible, and to quote extensively from his typescript, which was published virtually verbatim in

1988 in the late Robert Hamond's book *The Flame of Freedom*. Thanks, too, to Leo Cooper and Pen and Sword Books for their full co-operation.

Many libraries and institutions offered assistance and guidance, and tolerated my incompetence when interrogating digital catalogues and other reference material with patience and equanimity. Particular thanks are due to the staff of the British Library, the Newspaper Library, formerly at Colindale, *The Times* newspaper archives, the London Metropolitan Archives, the National Archives at Kew, the Imperial War Museum, the National Army Museum, the School of Oriental and African Studies, the Centre for South Asian Studies, Cambridge, the Royal Military Academy, Sandhurst, the RAF Museum, Hendon, the Green Howards Museum in Richmond, Yorkshire, Sedbergh School, and Andrew Curtis and his staff at King Edward VI School, Norwich.

Outside the UK, the Missions Etrangères de Paris, the Department of Veterans' Affairs in Canberra and the National Archives of Australia were also consistently helpful, the latter providing a copy of Lionel Hudson's diary and a letter from Roy Pagani from his time in Rangoon jail. In Burma, Andy Heyn and Andrew Patrick, the past and current British ambassadors, and the staff at the British embassy in Rangoon offered help, support and guidance during my various visits, in particular Fergus Eckersley and Joe Fisher. Friends and colleagues at the Yangon Heritage Trust were, and remain, unfailingly helpful, especially my good friend Thant Myint-U, as well as Moe Moe Lwin, Zunetta Herbert and Jane Brooks.

It is a testament to the respect and admiration in which Hugh Seagrim was held that so many old Burma hands and ex-PoWs were prepared to share their harrowing memories and experiences with me in the evening of their lives so many years later. Most have now passed away. I would like to thank Diana and Carnig Thomasian in New Jersey, John Reid and Donald Eastgate in Australia, and Don Lomas, Alec Gibson, Denis Gudgeon, Ken Spurlock, Clifford White, George Leggatt, William Matthews, Alex Bourne and Neville Hogan in the UK. Matt Poole in the USA was a tower of strength, selflessly offering hours of his time checking references and copying transcripts for me. Terry Hissey and Steve Snelling both shared their own research material with me.

Thanks, too, to the Burma Forces Welfare Association and that wonderful organisation Help for Forgotten Allies, which works so tirelessly to succour that dwindling band of Karen veterans who survive in Burma and the refugee camps in Thailand, often in conditions of great hardship. Their work has done something tangible to redress the Karens' betrayal by the Attlee government in 1947. I would particularly like to thank Lieutenant Colonel Sam Pope, Sally McLean and Peter Mitchell. Thanks, too, to Ben Rogers, Denis Gray, the late Mark Fenn and the indefatigable David Eubank of the Free Burma Rangers, who continue to highlight the sad plight of the Karens.

Many people in Whissonsett selflessly shared their memories and records with me, in particular Joan Mason, Lesley Pegg, Shirley Drew, Ann English, Buss Jackson, Ruby Knight, Eric Minister, Rodney Hill and the Reverend Robin Stapleford. Georgina and Charles Holloway, who reside in the old rectory, proudly showed me the Seagrims' childhood home, where little has changed.

A particular thanks to my sister, Margaret Carlyle-Lancaster, for reading the manuscript and for making numerous constructive suggestions and to Roderick Bailey, Alan Ogden, Pauline Davies, Mary Miers, Ayako Collins, Sue Woods, Richard Aldrich, Chris Young at the *Telegraph and Argus* in Bradford and Madeleine Compagnon in Paris for their help.

A huge thanks to Kate Moore, who provided invaluable advice and guidance on the structure of my early drafts and who imposed editorial rigour and focus when my enthusiasm for the story got ever wider.

Finally, this book would not have been completed without the help and guidance of my friends at Atlantic Publishing, in particular Greg Hill, Murray Mahon and Christine Hoy, and also constant prompting from friends and family, who have been equally moved by the story, in particular the late William Bingley, my wife, Ann Farrell-Davies, and my incomparable daughter, Anya.

Thanks to them all for repeatedly guiding me back onto the path time and again when my stamina flagged and for sustaining my spirits from afar during long absences deep in the jungles of Burma in search of England's forgotten heroes.

PHILIP DAVIES
London, 2017

'Man is but a pebble thrown into the pool of Life. But – the ripples of influence he leaves go on widening and ever-widening until they reach the farthest bank.'

JEFFERY FARNOL

'These heroes are dead. They died for liberty – they died for us. They are at rest. They sleep ... under the flag they rendered stainless ... They sleep beneath the shadows of the clouds, careless alike of sunshine or of storm, each in the windowless Place of Rest. Earth may run red with other wars – they are at peace.'

ROBERT G. INGERSOLL

Author's Note

Throughout the book generally I have used the names and spellings in popular usage at the time. Sometimes this seems illogical, but it reflects common wartime parlance used in official reports and documents. Hence the use of England rather than Britain, Burma and Rangoon rather than Myanmar and Yangon, and Siam rather than Thailand. The latter was known as Siam until renamed by the pro-Japanese fascist dictatorship in 1939. After the war it reverted again to Siam before adopting Thailand as the official name in May 1949.

Unless acquainted with the country, Burmese names can be confusing for the general reader. San Po Thin, 'the Tiger of the Delta' is a different person from Saw Po Thin, who helped Ras Pagani escape into the hills to join Hugh Seagrim. Many Karens also adopt English versions of their names, such as Saw Henry or Saw Darlington, which can add confusion to their inherent charm.

Any mistakes or inaccuracies are entirely the responsibility of the author. Every effort has been made to obtain permission to quote from other books and material. Any omissions should be brought to the attention of the publisher for correction in future editions. The author would welcome information from relatives of those mentioned in the book so that their stories can help enrich future editions.

Part of the proceeds from this book have been dedicated to the erection of a memorial plaque to Hugh Seagrim in Holy Trinity Anglican Cathedral, Rangoon.

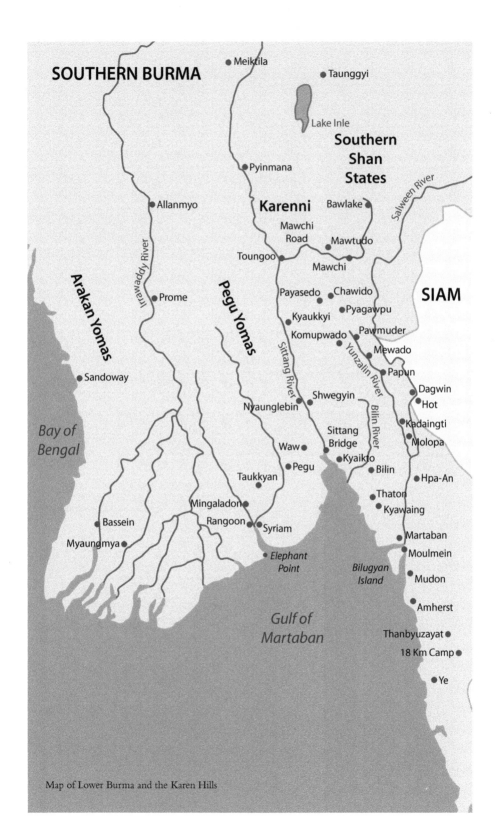

SOUTHERN BURMA

Meiktila

Taunggyi

Lake Inle

Southern
Shan
States

Pyinmana

Karenni   Bawlake

Allanmyo

Mawchi
Road   Mawtudo

Salween River

Toungoo

Mawchi

Irrawaddy River

Pegu Yomas

Prome   Payasedo   Chawido

SIAM

Kyaukkyi   Pyagawpu

Komupwado   Pawmuder

Arakan Yomas

Sittang River

Mewado

Yunzalin River

Papun

Sandoway   Dagwin
                                      Hot

Shwegyin

Nyaunglebin   Kadaingti

Bilin River

Molopa

Bay of
Bengal

Sittang
Bridge   Kyaikto

Waw   Hpa-An

Pegu   Bilin

Taukkyan

Thaton

Mingaladon   Kyawaing

Bassein   Rangoon
                  Syriam   Martaban

Myaungmya   Moulmein

Elephant
Point   Bilugyan
               Island   Mudon

Gulf of   Amherst
Martaban
                    Thanbyuzayat

                    18 Km Camp

                                      Ye

Map of Lower Burma and the Karen Hills

Glossary

Beri beri	Vitamin B deficiency disease
Betel	Areca palm nut which when chewed stains mouth and teeth red
Bren	Standard British light machine gun
BIA	Burma Independence Army
BNA	Burma National Army
Bofors	40mm anti-aircaft gun
Burman	Majority ethnic group of Burma
Changkul	Mattock, or short trenching tool
Chattri	Indian style pavilion
Coolie	Unskilled native labourer
Dah	Long-bladed knife, like a machete, for slashing vegetation
Dakota	Transport plane
DFC	Distinguished Flying Cross
Dhal	Thick stew of lentils and pulses
Dhobi	Washerman
DSO	Distinguished Service Order
Force 136	Common name for Special Operations Executive (SOE) in the Far East from 1944
Fundoshi	Japanese style undergarment or loincloth
GC	George Cross
Havildar	Indian Army Platoon Sergeant
ISLD	Interservice Liaison Department, or Secret Intelligence Service
Jaggery	Coarse form of sugar from sugar cane
Jemadar	Indian Army platoon commander
Kempeitai	Japanese security police
Lance Naik	Indian Army Corporal
Levies	Locally raised guerrilla forces
Longyi	Cloth worn by men and women around waist similar to a sarong
MBE	Member of the Order of the British Empire
MC	Military Cross, awarded to officers
MM	Military Medal, awarded to other ranks
NCO	Non-commissioned officer
Nga pi	Burmese fish paste
OBE	Officer of the Order of the British Empire
Oozie	Elephant driver or mahout
Padi	Semi-aquatic rice fields
Pagri	Turban
Pongyi	Buddhist monk
PoW	Prisoner of War
Punji	Pit of sharpened bamboo stakes
Sahib	Master or owner
Sampan	Small Oriental boat
Saw	Karen prefix equivalent to Mr in English
Sawbwa	Literally, sky lord; a hereditary Shan chief
Sepoy	Indian Army private soldier
SOE	Special Operations Executive
Sten	Mass-produced British sub-machine gun
Subedar	Indian Army Company second in command
Taungya	Slash-and-burn system of cultivation
Tenko	Japanese word for roll call
Thakin	Literally, lord or master, but used by Burmese radicals in 1930s
Towkay	Chinese or Oriental merchant
VC	Victoria Cross
Yomas	Hills, or mountain ranges

Prologue

'Show me a hero
and I will write you a tragedy.'

F. SCOTT FITZGERALD

Whissonsett, Norfolk

The villages of England are enigmatic places, haunted by the ghosts of those long since passed. All too often, beneath their quiet repose lies a hidden web of connections to the furthest reaches of the earth. Through chaste memorials of stone and polished brass, their churches and burial grounds offer a melancholy record of the deeds of their sons: lost far from home in the service of king, queen and country. Whissonsett is such a place.

Shortly after midsummer, on the warm Saturday afternoon of 29 June 1985, a remarkable ceremony took place in this most English of villages. The occasion – the unveiling of a village sign – was nothing unusual: the sort of small ceremony that many places arrange to display pride in their local community. But this was different. For among the gathered guests was a colourful group of people from the remote hill tracts of eastern Burma – the Karens – who had come to pay their respects to a child of Whissonsett; to a legendary Englishman whose name is still revered in the villages and forests of those far-off hills. His name was Hugh Seagrim. He stands depicted on the village sign, complete with topee, alongside his older brother Derek – the only members of the same family to win Britain's two highest awards for gallantry, the George Cross and the Victoria Cross.

As the villagers assembled that afternoon, a third surviving brother, Jack, spoke of his long-lost siblings; how their memory was treasured not only by those who once knew them, but by so many since who had been inspired by their deeds. Also present that day was another exceptional individual, the only surviving Englishman to have fought under Hugh Seagrim so long ago and far away, who had come to pay tribute to the greatest man he had ever had the privilege of knowing. One of the most intrepid and daring escapees of the entire war, his name was Roy, or Ras,

Pagani, a pugnacious bulldog of a man, and the only European to have escaped successfully from the fearful 'Death Railway' in Burma.

Over seventy years ago, two great empires – the British and the Japanese – fought to control this vast, peaceful land. Each was determined to prevail as this somnolent, dream-like place was turned suddenly into the cockpit of Asia. It was a time of war in a place of peace; a time when ordinary men were called upon to do extraordinary things in the forgotten corners of a forgotten land.

This is their story.

Chapter 1

Eastern Catastrophe

'These are the times that try men's souls.'
THOMAS PAINE

On 11 December 1941, just four days after Pearl Harbor, the Japanese invaded Burma. Transported by sea from Saigon, a detachment of troops landed west of Bangkok, seized the railway and swooped south to Victoria Point, the southernmost tip of the long arm of Burma, cutting the narrow land link to Malaya. Dominating the skies, the main invasion force streamed along the overland route from Indo-China ravaging everything in its path.

It was two days before Christmas when their planes came to Rangoon, bearing their gifts of death. High in the heavens above, a tiny silvery-white object faded and reappeared, flickering moth-like around the glaring midday sun – insolent, inquisitive, insignificant to all but the most trained observer, gliding silently in circles over the capital. On the teeming streets far below, Chinese and Indian traders stopped their haggling to gaze skywards. Burmans roused themselves uneasily from their reverie and shook off the stupor of the noonday heat. Europeans wandered lazily out from the shops and offices lining the elegant downtown city. With their hands shielding their eyes, they stared quizzically at the alien, spectral shape as it shimmered and hovered far above in the cerulean sky.

To some, the reconnaissance plane was a novelty: an impudent intruder to be dismissed as nothing more than a transient curiosity; a topic perhaps for discussion at the club later in the day. Others were more apprehensive, but reassured themselves that this was nothing that the RAF could not handle from its base at nearby Mingaladon. But for many that day, it was the angel of death.

Halfway along Phayre Street, just outside one of the elegant colonial bank buildings, an RAF officer glanced eastward. His trained eye suddenly spotted something far more ominous.

A wave of thirty huge, twin-engined Japanese bombers loomed out of a gap between two towering banks of cloud – heading straight for the heart of the most beautiful garden city in Asia. As the yellow-brown shapes droned closer there was a moment of stunned silence, then pandemonium reigned as people ran for their lives. Coolies and pavement vendors fled down the narrow streets, desperately searching for cover in the dense maze of alleys off the main boulevards. Europeans drew back into the shelter of their great banks and halls of commerce, few of which had bothered with any air-raid precautions.

After the initial surprise, batteries of Allied anti-aircraft guns opened up, hurling high explosives and molten metal far into the air. A Bofors gun blazed away from a ship moored in the harbour, pockmarking the sky around the enemy bombers. A great shout went up as a raider was hit: one wing wheeled away from the fuselage, which then slowly rotated in ever-decreasing circles. Flames licked along the length of the doomed remains as it hurtled earthwards, destined to explode in a great mushroom of yellow-black smoke. Four white gossamer parachutes blossomed out as the plane went down. Two drifted clear, with black blobs suspended beneath, but two others failed to open and hurtled faster and faster towards the ground.

Suddenly, the RAF was among the enemy planes, weaving and arcing across the sky, spitting lines of orange tracer fire from their wings. A Tomahawk from the American Volunteer Group (AVG) shredded another bomber, which plummeted down in flames, incinerating its crew.

On and on they came, nearer and nearer. The city was deafened by the roaring crescendo of approaching aircraft: pitiless, remorseless and unyielding. And, as they came, they unloaded sticks of fat bombs, each pregnant with the promise of death, destruction, desolation and horror. Horror from which no one in the city could escape.

Entire buildings burst and collapsed into the street. Others disappeared in great columns of orange flame. Tiny brick-and-canvas pavement shelters, where poor street vendors eked out their livelihoods, were blown to smithereens along with their occupants. A hideous shower of blood and charred flesh rained down on the rubble that was once their homes. Lethal glass shards scythed through the air, maiming, blinding and killing indiscriminately. Splinters shorn from roadside trees impaled people where they stood. Telegraph poles and electricity cables crashed to the ground in showers of sparks, crushing and electrocuting those beneath. Subterranean fountains erupted as the water mains burst. Parked cars were reduced to blazing wrecks, many with their owners still inside transformed into flaming human torches.

Among the obscene dismembered remains of the dead were people seemingly uninjured, who had been killed by the capricious effects of blast. The streets of the city were choked with dust and debris, the injured and the dead. In just seconds, shops, offices, flats and even a hospital were reduced to rubble. From the far eastern side of the city to the sacred golden Sule Pagoda, the bombs wreaked havoc, destroying and mutilating everything in their path. Along the riverfront and docks, a congested mass of vehicles, guns and supplies, intended for relief to China via the famous Burma Road, was obliterated.

Not content with pulverising the city with high explosive, the Japanese then strafed the sheltering masses of civilians. Staccato bursts of machine-gun fire raked a huddled crowd of terrified men, women and children who were sheltering in a park. Their cowed ranks were decimated, leaving hundreds dead. Nearby, a solitary Japanese pilot, who had floated to the ground on a parachute, killed himself with his dagger – before he was set upon by the incensed crowd and tossed contemptuously onto a funeral pyre.

As the sun dipped into the western sky, a pall of acrid smoke and flames cast a ghastly refulgent glow across the city. Firefighters did their best to stem blazes at dozens of city buildings. Ambulances wailed through blocked streets, desperately ferrying the injured to overloaded hospitals. Corpses were left where they fell – food for the city's rabid pi-dogs, who scavenged and tore ravenously at severed limbs, greedily consuming unidentifiable gobbets of human flesh. Romantic Rangoon, the cosmopolitan city, feted by Somerset Maugham, H. G. Wells and Pablo Neruda, would never be the same again.

They came again on Christmas Day, and again after that: waves of bombers from the east, heralded by the dull repetitive throbbing of their engines, their wings marked with the blood-red sun of Nippon. This time, the defending RAF and AVG pilots were better prepared, and the damage was less. Over 1,250 people had been killed in the first raid, and more than 600 died of wounds later, but by the time of the third, just sixty were killed and forty wounded. The Japanese lost over forty planes. Anxious to avoid further losses and damage to the docks, railways and other potentially useful infrastructure, the Japanese switched their attention away from the city's heart to RAF Mingaladon and other military targets.

The nights were the worst for those struggling to survive in this post-apocalyptic world. The city was plunged into darkness. In one place, according to George Rodger, a press photographer on the scene who was later quoted in *Burma: The Longest War*, 'a temple wall had collapsed, and a row of twenty Buddhas, twelve feet high, glowed red-hot against the darkness'.[1] On Christmas night, parts of the city resembled a charnel house. Military and police patrols did their best to keep order in the midst of a nightmare. Arson and looting were widespread. Mobs rampaged through the streets, stripping the homes of the wealthy, settling old scores and setting houses ablaze. To add to the chaos and terror, bands of convicts released from the prisons ran amok alongside inmates freed from the asylum. Reeking of smoke, dust, death and charred flesh, Rangoon, the pearl of Asia, was now a city of the dead.

After the first day of bombing, over 100,000 people took to the roads as refugees: the beginning of a vast civilian exodus westwards towards India and safety, each man, woman and child desperate to escape the onslaught. Many were ethnic Indians, part of an expatriate community of over one million, who had played an important role in the economic life of the country as merchants, traders and shopkeepers, but whose lives were not rooted in Burma. There was little love lost between them and the Burmese. Just three years earlier, simmering tensions had flared into open communal violence. Few Indians regarded Burma as their home. When the bombs began to fall, they fled with all possible speed.

Burma was vulnerable because it had been milked of trained personnel for the European theatre of war. The Far East came fourth in the list of British priorities for reinforcements and equipment after Europe, the Middle East and Russia. Regarded as a backwater with natural protection from its seemingly impenetrable jungle-clad hills, Burma was also at the bottom of the list there after Singapore, Malaya and India. Starved of resources and faced with a lightning strike by a merciless enemy, many brave souls did a fine job in impossible circumstances.

As the Japanese switched their attacks to RAF Mingaladon, under-equipped and outnumbered, the British struck back against insuperable odds. RAF Tomahawks, Brewster Buffaloes and Hawker Hurricanes could be seen heading off to meet the enemy. Obsolete, battered Blenheim bombers flew away to hit back as best they could at the invading Japanese, many never to return.

Watching this aerial combat unfold over Mingaladon was a tall, young British officer attached temporarily to the RAF but with very clear, unorthodox views of his own on how to fight the Japanese – views which he had not hesitated to express to his superiors for years before the war. Dismissed as an eccentric, if charming, crank, he was destined to become one of the most charismatic guerrilla leaders of the entire Second World War. His name was Hugh Paul Seagrim.

Above: Hugh Paul Seagrim

Chapter 2

Brothers in Arms

'Into my heart an air that kills
From yon far country blows:
What are those blue remembered hills,
What spires, what farms are those?
That is the land of lost content,
I see it shining plain,
The happy highways where I went
And cannot come again.'

A. E. HOUSMAN

There is a certain breed of solitary Englishman whose destiny can only be fulfilled in the deserts or jungles of Africa and the East. For generations Britain has produced a remarkable number of intrepid individuals who have had a profound impact on world history, each impelled by a raft of different and often conflicting motives. Many came from the ranks of the lesser gentry, or were the younger sons of the clergy. The *beau idéal* of the British gentleman hero was the saint militant, the chivalric Christian knight *sans peur et sans reproche*, imbued with boundless self-confidence and strong moral convictions. The Indian Army officer and future Field Marshal Sir Neville Bowles Chamberlain wrote: 'A horse and a sword were all that were needful, and one never gave a thought as to danger. Not that there was any levity in facing death; it was simply that one was possessed of a light heart to meet anything that came. There was nothing but God above and duty below.'[1]

These ideals of muscular Christianity were inculcated into generations of young men through the public schools' system. With an unshakeable faith in God, Duty and the Empire, these young Sir Galahads could look death in the face, sure in the knowledge that those who fought the good fight could expect everlasting life. Englishmen were expected to adhere to a higher standard of behaviour than others and to set an example in all aspects of their conduct. This was not from any innate notion of superiority, although often it was misconstrued as such, but driven by a

26

profound sense of duty and mission. One must simply never let oneself or the side down. Quiet, understated heroism, sang-froid, self-restraint and making light of intense personal suffering set a moral standard to which all aspired.

Many of those imbued with such values in the Army and Colonial Service dedicated themselves selflessly to the well-being of those for whom they had charge. Supremely confident and incorruptible, these were men whose word was law. To the modern observer in a more cynical age, one of the more surprising motivations of those who devoted their lives in such a way was a sincere belief in Christianity. This inner conviction sustained many through appalling suffering and hardship. When they died, some were even deified and their graves worshipped by their devoted followers.

By the early part of the twentieth century, faith in both God and the Empire had been shaken severely on the battlefields of the First World War, but the qualities that had supported so many throughout the carnage remained a crucial part of the English belief system and an immense national strength. Courage, fortitude, endurance and selflessness, understatement, humour, self-deprecation and stoicism – all qualities that have continued to influence the behaviour of subsequent generations in extremis to this day.

Hugh Seagrim was just such a man, and raised to believe in just such values. The youngest of five brothers, he was born at Ashmansworth, Hampshire, on 24 March 1909 into a close-knit family of old India hands with a long and noble tradition of military and public service. Hugh's father, the Reverend Charles Paulet Conyngham Seagrim, was born in 1864 in the foothills of the Himalayas, just six years after the end of the Indian Mutiny. At well under five feet tall, Charles was intellectually gifted but plagued by a delicate constitution. After studying law at Cambridge, he forsook a promising career as a London barrister, took holy orders and left for life as a missionary in Basutoland and the Cape. Restless, and suffering from ill health, he returned to England in 1895 to become a curate at Hamble in Hampshire. Three years later he moved on again, to Dinant in Brittany, as the local Church of England chaplain, where he met and married Amabel, the daughter of James Skipper, a retired Norwich lawyer.

Thirteen years younger than Charles, Amabel was a good-looking, complex woman, who had been heartbroken when her parents rejected a union for her with a young French army officer on the grounds that he was a Roman Catholic. Soon after, she married Charles Seagrim on the rebound, perhaps to escape her parents, or her unhappy love affair, or both. It was a curious match – he the rather unworldly diminutive priest and she the tragic beauty.

After several years back in England and shortly after the birth of Hugh, the couple's fifth child, a post became vacant in the remote Norfolk village of Whissonsett-with-Horningtoft, at the head of the Wensum valley, midway between Fakenham and Dereham. The family settled in the rectory at Whissonsett in 1909, and the house, set in the picturesque rolling countryside of East Anglia, became the rock upon which a secure home was built for their five ebullient children: Charles, Cyril, Derek, John – known as Jack – and Hugh. The large rambling rectory still survives at the edge of the village: a plain but handsome late Georgian house surrounded by a sprawling garden overlooking open fields. The gatehouse, which once guarded the gravel drive, may have gone, but the

Above left: Amabel Seagrim with her five sons and their dogs (from left to right) Cyril, Charles, Jack, Hugh and Derek c.1915.

Above right: Hugh and Jack Seagrim playing with their toy yacht c.1915.

Left: The family home – The Rectory, Whissonsett.

house remains much as it was in the Seagrims' day – the perfect place to raise five high-spirited young boys.

As the local rector, Charles Seagrim was well liked. Tom Bunnett, who lived in the village, remembered him as 'a little old man who always looked blue in the face because he had a weak heart', helping the poor and sick as best he could, if not always the most tactful soul.[2] His neighbour Mary Rush recalled: 'Rev. Seagrim was all for King and Country, and when the First War broke out he went round the village telling the young men they ought to volunteer to fight.' Not surprisingly, 'He was much abused by some.'[3]

He was prone to the most bizarre antics – a mischievous quality later inherited by Hugh. Once he went out to buy his wife a winter coat, but returned with a Macaw parrot, which caused mayhem in the house, squawking loudly and chasing the family around the kitchen. This eccentric streak in the rector, and a stubborn refusal to heed advice, was to have dire consequences, however. Even after his bank manager pleaded with him to think again, he ploughed ahead with a reckless business venture in Canada and lost his wife's entire family fortune. Overnight a genteel, well-bred lady with substantial capital was reduced to penury – and the family rendered virtually destitute. With only a rector's stipend to fall back on, life was hard. Thomas Makins, whose wife cleaned at the rectory, frequently saw the five brothers running around the village 'barefoot like a lot of gypsies' to save their shoes for term time.[4] All too often the half-crown a week his wife was paid was a long time coming.

Hard times forced the five brothers to make their own amusements. They kept a veritable menagerie of animals, including a couple of ponies on the glebe, and pumped their own water from a well in the yard. But for all five brothers it was an immensely happy childhood full of opportunities for devilment. Long summer holidays at a converted windmill at Horning were spent fishing and paddling, or sailing on the Norfolk Broads, interspersed with wild forays across the countryside in search of mischief, the games they played honing their skills and self-reliance for the more serious adult challenges that lay ahead. In summer there was cricket; in winter rough shooting, riding or village football, at which Hugh excelled as goalkeeper.

In spite of the family being hard up, the rectory was the centre of village life. Fetes and garden parties were held on the lawn, with candles in coloured glass jars placed around the gardens. Dora Robbins, whose sister Daisy was a maid at the rectory, recollected fondly: 'We used to trim up the gardens with fairy lights and the Fakenham town band played for dancing … If we had a dance in the house, the Seagrims would go to bed and we could play the piano and have the run of the whole ground floor.'[5] Village upbringing instilled a deep-seated sense of community and provided an excellent grounding for regimental life, although – paradoxically – all five boys were seen as rather aloof, perhaps the product of a certain lack of warmth from their parents.

As the youngest and most boisterous of the five, Hugh was nicknamed 'Bumps'. Some say this was because he fell out of his pram at an early age; others, that it was his totally fearless attitude towards anything and anybody. An incorrigible prankster and practical joker, he was forever getting his brothers into trouble. On one occasion when the Bishop of Norwich, who for some reason he actively disliked, was due to visit the rectory, he joined forces with his brother Jack and ambushed the unsuspecting prelate by careering down the staircase on a tea tray and sending the Bishop crashing to the floor while his parents looked on aghast. With both wide-eyed children professing their total innocence in the unfortunate accident, the Bishop had no alternative but to forgive them – much to their lifelong amusement.

Despite the family tensions, it was a happy childhood for the boys. Later, Jack confided in his son Michael: 'Our upbringing was very austere, even harsh. Your generation has no inkling of what it was like to have lived through two world wars and the deep economic depression between them. Survival was all we really hoped for, much of the time.'[6] Given the parlous state of the family finances, it was fortunate that the two elder sons, Charles and Cyril, both won scholarships to Gresham's School in nearby Holt, and thence to Woolwich. Charles was commissioned into the Royal Artillery, and Cyril, the most intellectually gifted of the five, into the Royal Engineers. The three remaining sons – Derek, Jack and Hugh – went to King Edward VI School in Norwich, which then catered for around 200 pupils including 50 boarders. Illustrious past alumni included Horatio Nelson, who was reared in a similar local rectory at Burnham Thorpe in Norfolk, and the charismatic adventurer James Brooke, the first White Rajah of Sarawak. As Heads of House, the names of the Seagrim brothers are still inscribed on the school memorial panels. Each showed early signs of his leadership qualities, but in very different ways.

At school Hugh and Jack were inseparable. They shared a study and even put their beds together. Along with their older brother, the triumvirate were known to the masters as Seagrim major, Seagrim minor and Seagrim tertius. Both Derek and Hugh made a lasting impression at school, but for very different reasons. Derek, known as Bunny on account of his protruding front teeth, was not much of an academic, but he was an extremely good athlete, and a noted half-miler and cricketer. A subsequent headmaster, Andrew Stephenson, who was a contemporary, recalled: 'There were nearly 300 of us in the school, but Seagrim was outstanding. I remember him vividly. He was self-possessed in all circumstances – never lost his head. He was captain of the soccer team, was in the first cricket eleven, and he had his rowing colour.'[7] By a stroke of good fortune, the cost of Derek's education was met from the sale of a forgotten family heirloom discovered by his father – a letter from Sir Francis Drake to Queen Elizabeth that belonged to Amabel – which he sold at Sotheby's for the colossal sum of £500. This also covered Derek's subsequent training at Sandhurst, where he scraped in only after last-minute withdrawals by two other candidates.

Evidence of his coolness in a crisis was demonstrated very eloquently in 1919 when the school caught fire. The boys were in danger of being trapped, but Derek led them down the stairs to safety. Thanks to his imperturbable nature and presence of mind, no one was hurt. Another master, Douglas Liddell, remembered a particular cricket match. 'The school was in a tight corner until Seagrim began bowling. He rapidly took five wickets for seven runs. That is the sort of thing he would do. He was always the right chap to have with you in an emergency. Whatever he put his hand to, he finished.'[8] A faded copy of his schoolboy exploits, as recorded in the *Eastern Daily News*, remains in the school archives, pasted into the front of his copy of John Buchan's *Greenmantle*. At a much more personal level, Derek also made a huge impression on his cousin Anne. She fell hopelessly in love with him at the age of sixteen. He was her 'first pash', and she adored him to the point of hero worship even much later in life: 'He was very attractive, very good-looking, and so full of fun and life, very elegant and stylish.' In spite of his practical jokes, Bumps she found 'more reserved, a quiet and thoughtful person', perhaps already showing a growing awareness of the deeper meaning of life.

Hugh enjoyed a reputation rather different from his older brother's, being habitually mischievous – Anne reminisced nostalgically of an extended holiday with Derek, with Hugh misbehaving: seeing how far he could spit cherry pips[9] – and perpetually challenging authority. He was notorious for his pranks. When the school matron reported him for misbehaviour, for which he was caned, he got his revenge in the dead of night by threading a bar of soap on a piece of string, leaning out of the window of his room and knocking repeatedly on her window directly below. Already of a nervous disposition, she was convinced that the building was haunted, handed in her notice and left at the end of the half term.

Being dyslexic, Hugh did not shine academically and preferred the sports field to the classroom. At six feet four inches tall, with an extraordinary reach and formidable goalkeeping skills, he had trials for Norwich City reserves. In 1927, his last year at school, the boys' father died. Their aunt – Amabel's twin sister, Mrs Douglas-Lane – then supported both Jack and Bumps through school and, later, Sandhurst. The family could not afford to send Bumps to university, putting paid to his ambition to become a doctor. With four sons in the Army thought to be enough, he was initially encouraged to try for special entry to the Royal Navy, but he failed at the outset: the preliminary medical examination found that he was partially colour-blind. So, in September 1927, Hugh, too, was packed off to Sandhurst.

While his brothers were serving overseas, Bumps periodically returned home. His underlying compassion and empathy for others made a lasting impression. Ruby Knight, a local girl, recalled how after her father had an accident 'Hugh Seagrim used to come and see my father and sit with him. I used to think what a huge tall man he was. He was very kind. He used to come to the school with his Great Dane dog, which he harnessed to a cart that he had made for collecting food for his rabbits.'[10] Awed by his sheer height, the village girls took great delight in riding pillion on his motor bike. He towered over his diminutive father. Monica Nelson remembered that when Hugh visited the village reading room, 'he never opened the gate, he just jumped over it from the road'.[11]

Hugh did not exactly shine at Sandhurst, finishing 137th out of 154 in his class. Nevertheless, he can be seen looming confidently over his classmates of No. 4 Company in the college photograph of December 1928, and he flourished on the sports field keeping goal for the Academy soccer team. His reputation for eccentric pranks continued unabated – a trait that did little to endear him to his superiors. On one occasion, he and his friends hauled a ceremonial Napoleonic cannon from the front of the college across the playing fields and into the lake. On another, he organised an armada of potties, which he set sail across the lake with candles burning in them – a sight that he thought looked very pretty. There was little to suggest that he was destined to become one of the most inspirational guerrilla fighters of the Second World War.

Like many of his contemporaries, on leaving Sandhurst in 1929 Hugh joined the Indian Army, drawn by the prospect of action and adventure. Initially he was attached to the Highland Light Infantry at Cawnpore, the scene of the grisly massacre of British men, women and children during the Indian Mutiny, through which his paternal grandfather had served. It was not a particularly demanding existence for Hugh. During his frequent leaves, he made two trips high into the Himalayas: one to Sikkim and another, with just a few native porters, into the mountains around Everest, where he met up with an expedition returning from a failed ascent. After borrowing a few more porters, he pressed on, but was forced back by bad weather. The photographs that he took, and that still survive in a family album, show that he reached a considerable height. Later, in 1938, he led another expedition to Nun Kun and reached 23,000 feet. Almost ninety years ago these achievements were no mean feat, and a testament both to his powers of endurance and his solitary nature – a characteristic family trait.

Late in 1931, at the age of twenty-two and after a year in India, he was posted to the 1st/20th Burma Rifles, who were stationed temporarily at Taiping in Malaya. Soon after arriving with his regiment, in 1932, the 1st battalion mess was discussing the scandal of the Vicar of Stiffkey in Norfolk.[12] As a result of his efforts to save vulnerable girls from a life on the streets of Soho, the hapless vicar had been found guilty of immoral conduct and defrocked. As a Norfolk man, Seagrim pointed out that the local pronunciation of Stiffkey was 'Stookey'. As is the way at school and in the Army, there and then he was dubbed 'Stookey' – a nickname that was thought hilarious by all. The name stuck long after its origins had been forgotten. Before returning to Burma, he took three months' leave and travelled to Japan to tour the country. With war looming in the Far East, this experience was to stand him in good stead as he gained a rare insight into the Japanese national psyche at a dangerous time. He liked and admired the Japanese and, unlike most of his compatriots, did not underestimate their military capabilities.

On arriving in Burma, Seagrim was dazzled by the exotic beauty of the country and its engaging people. Burma resembles the fingers of an outstretched hand, with the wrist at Rangoon. It is divided by a network of vast rivers running from north to south, which drain into the brilliant blue waters of the Andaman Sea. For centuries these were the main highways – the Chindwin, which joins the Irrawaddy near the pagoda-studded plain of Bagan, and further east the moody Sittang and the tempestuous Salween, one of the longest rivers in Asia. Defiant, tortuous and untamed, the Salween churns its way along the Siamese border through precipitous limestone gorges thousands of feet deep; it is unnavigable, other than for the last few miles where it disgorges into the Gulf of Martaban, close to melancholic Moulmein. Between the Sittang and the Salween lies the heart of Karen country.

Like many British officers commanding native troops, whether Gurkhas, Jats, Sikhs or Pathans, Seagrim developed a deep bond with the Karens in his company. He astonished his tutors by mastering spoken Burmese in just five weeks, his linguistic expertise doubtless aided by his dyslexia, which forced him to memorise facts and information. The Karens are a fiercely loyal, honest people, who had rendered invaluable service to the British since the first Anglo-Burmese War between 1824 and 1826. From early on they recognised that the British offered an unprecedented opportunity to break free from perpetual subservience to the Burmese. The Karens' loyalty and martial qualities were extolled by a Dr Vinton, an American Baptist missionary, who wrote: 'Under their own officers, and commanded by men they trust, the Karens will go anywhere, and do what no other troops can do. You could put ten thousand such men in the field for little more than the cost of one sepoy regiment; but they must be led by men.'[13] Hugh Seagrim was just such a man. He loved them with a passion, and it is easy to see why.

The Karens claim to be the original inhabitants of Burma. Dispersed across the country in various tribal groups, they retain a distinct racial and cultural identity. The two largest groups are the Sgaws and the Pwos, but others include the Red Karens, the Striped Karens, the Bwes in Karenni and the famous Padaungs, or 'giraffe-necked women', who elongate their necks with coils of wire that depress the shoulder blades. Whether ethnologically correct or not, the Karens' belief that they are the original inhabitants has been a foundation stone of their folklore and national aspirations. With a long oral history passed down in mournful songs, one of their most potent legends is that of their ancient hero, Taw-Mei-Pa, who led them towards the Promised Land. The Karens remain convinced that one day he will reappear to lead them to the Promised Land of Peace and Plenty.

Early Karen foundation stories bear such a remarkable resemblance to the Old Testament that early missionaries believed they must be one of the lost tribes of Israel. Monotheistic, the Karens believe in an omnipotent God called Y'wa, who made the world in seven days. He made man and woman, and tempted the woman in the guise of a snake. Prophetically, in another messianic story, the Karens foretell of a 'young white brother' who will come from over the seas bearing the Book of Y'weh, a lost Book of Gold, to usher in a golden age of peace and contentment. With such a resonance between their ancient tribal beliefs and Christianity, in the first half of the nineteenth century many Karens were converted by the American Baptist missionary Adironam Judson in the most successful exercise ever undertaken by Christian missionaries. Paradoxically, alongside belief in a single, omnipotent God, the Karens still retain a complex system of spirit-worship and animism.

This nexus of beliefs generated a strict moral code. Parents take responsibility for their children's physical, mental and moral well-being. In return, the younger generation care for their elders. Partners are expected to be faithful, respectful, loving and devoted. Chastity, honesty, sobriety, hard work and sincerity are celebrated as inherent virtues creating communities that are compassionate, tolerant and mutually supportive in times of adversity. Neighbours are regarded as extended family. Deep within the Karen psyche is a remarkable ability to offer simple undying loyalty to others. To a Karen, the basis of this fidelity is 'to put a thing in the heart': 'Only when they know a man well will they open their hearts. To a man they know and trust and love they will remain faithful till they die.'[14]

A symbiotic relationship evolved between the Karens and the British, which was to withstand the most fearful tests in the coming struggle. In a direct fulfilment of their messianic prophesies a 'young white brother' from across the seas was destined to come to their aid in their hour of need – Hugh Seagrim.

★★★

35

Until 1937 Burma was ruled from India as a province of the British Raj. It had been acquired in a series of conflicts over a period of sixty years. As a result of the first Anglo-Burmese War between 1824 and 1826, which had been triggered by Burmese aggression in Assam, the British took control of the coastal states of Arakan and Tenasserim. Round two followed in 1852, which ended with the annexation of Rangoon, Bassein and the whole of Lower Burma. For a while there was little interest in further expansion, even when in 1879 the new Burmese king, Thibaw Min, massacred his extended family in a palace bloodbath, but in 1885 French machinations in Indo-China prompted the British to invade and then annexe Upper Burma. Under the subsequent British administration trade flourished.

Across the central plains and the predominantly Burman core of the country, where there had been the greatest resistance and where the hereditary chiefs were not to be trusted, the British ruled directly through a network of local District Commissioners. The remote hill states belonging to the Chins, Nagas, Shans, Kachins and Karens remained largely autonomous. Rarely, if ever, subject to Burman royal rule, they guarded their cultural identity and independence fiercely. At the outbreak of war in 1941, just forty-four dedicated British officers exercised a loose suzerainty over three million people and 125,000 square miles of territory: a light touch that the tribes valued.

In the 1930s, Burma was a backwater of the British Empire where nothing much happened. Away from the mainstream of imperial life in Calcutta, Bombay and Delhi, it enjoyed none of the glamour of the North-West Frontier of India, with its opportunities for swashbuckling adventures against the warlike Pathans on the Afghan border, but it had its compensations – not least the cosmopolitan elegance of Rangoon, one of the most beguiling cities in Asia.

Despite its many attractions, city life held little allure for Seagrim. He spent his periods of leave cutting loose from regimental life and the suffocating hierarchy of colonial society by exploring the breathtaking country that is Burma. He was much more at home by a campfire deep in the forests. Often alone, or with just one other officer and perhaps a dozen or more of his beloved Karens, he ventured deep into the wildest tracts of the hills, exploring the remote jungle-clad terrain and learning more about the culture and ways of the people under his command. He revelled in the excitement of his expeditions into the wilds. He identified strongly with a favourite quote from Kipling about wood-smoke:

'A whiff of it can take us back to forgotten marches over unnamed mountains ... to day-long halts beside flooded rivers in the rain; wonderful mornings of youth in brilliantly lighted lands where everything was possible ... and, above all, to that God's own hour, all the world over, when the stars have gone out and it is too dark to see clear, and one lies ... and waits for a new horizon to heave itself up against a new dawn.'[15]

Never a particularly fluent Karen speaker, Seagrim communicated with the hill people he met in English or Burmese. Experiences shared with the men under his command instilled a deep mutual respect and affection, which he believed an essential prerequisite for effective leadership.

In the cold weather of 1933 to 1934 he took one expedition across the Lower Salween and the eastern fringes of Burma up to Kawkareik on the borders with Siam, which led to a particularly fateful meeting. Noel Boyt, a forestry manager for Steel Brothers, was at his jungle camp at Kawkareik when he saw a tall, unkempt, bearded white man trekking up with a young Karen carrying a knapsack and shotgun. Boyt thought he was some stray drifter or n'er-do-well. He was astonished when he introduced himself as Captain Seagrim of the Burma Rifles. He explained to Boyt that he was travelling through Karenni and living with the local people to understand the country, learn their ways and do a spot of shooting. He spent a single night with Boyt and his wife. Like many others, she thought him an amusing guest but found his solitary nature and intensity rather peculiar. But both Seagrim and Boyt were destined to meet again in much more demanding circumstances.

On another expedition a year later, Seagrim ventured far into the Chin hills in the largely unexplored north-west of the country, the haunt of head-hunters – wild areas which were to witness ferocious fighting in the years to come. It was expeditions such as these that gave him rare experience of the possibility of living and fighting in the jungle, insights which were to stand him in such good stead in the coming years. There was a strong element of the explorer in Seagrim. This seems to have been a metaphor for a much deeper personal quest on which he had embarked, as if by exploring and understanding the unknown areas of the physical world around him he would gain greater insights into the numinous – the unknown spiritual world that was slowly unfolding within.

He was certainly in the right country in which to explore his inner self. In Burma the unseen is the cause of the seen, the ethereal ever-present. Every rock, every tree, every river and every hill has its own resident spirit, which must be propitiated. Alongside Buddhism lie older, atavistic beliefs – thirty-seven nats – a pantheon of the spirits of those who have died a violent death, which remain in a perpetual state of limbo, haunting people and places as evanescent green ghosts. Across the country, gilded white pagodas perched on moss-green hills proclaim the inner world of the spirit, each suffused with the intoxicating aroma of incense, flickering candles and sacred offerings.

On his long, strength-sapping treks through dense jungle, something profound was being forged. Seagrim was testing his powers of endurance, but also honing his inner self and exploring his nascent spiritual beliefs. In his own private anthology is a quote from Oscar Wilde, which he treasured:

'I am conscious now that behind all this beauty … there is some spirit hidden of which the painted forms and shapes are but modes of manifestation, and it is with this spirit that I desire to become in harmony. I have grown tired of the articulate utterances of men and things. The Mystical in Art, the Mystical in Life, the Mystical in Nature – this is what I am looking for. It is absolutely necessary for me to find it somewhere.'[16]

This was a man in search not just of himself, but of the very meaning of life. One of his brother officers, who knew him well, thought 'he was groping for the answers to things'.[17] Undoubtedly, in his own rather peculiar, unconventional way, he was. The twin poles of his personality – warrior and martyr – were already being forged. On another occasion, he spent two months in quiet meditation in a remote Buddhist monastery in Tenasserim, beside the sapphire waters of the Andaman Sea. At other times he stayed with the Delta Karens in the flat, flooded estuary of the Irrawaddy river, or high in the hills in the steaming jungles along the Siamese border. This was certainly not the normal behaviour of a regular Indian Army officer.

It was not surprising that other, more conventionally minded souls found him odd. An aloof, eccentric loner, he was not a naturally sociable person, preferring his own company, or that of his men, to the clubbable atmosphere of the regimental mess. He tended to shun formal social occasions – the dances, parties, soirées and mess nights that constituted the conventional social life of a young regimental officer in colonial Rangoon, but on the rare occasions when he did join in, his innate good humour and natural charm made him excellent company. He was easily the best-liked officer in the mess, with a brilliant sense of humour. A comrade reminisced: 'He was one of the most amusing talkers I have ever known. To listen to him for five minutes was a tonic. He could be very funny. The thing that always used to strike me about him was his unfailing good humour and his ability to make anything amusing.'[18]

In truth, though, Seagrim was far happier on the playing field than in the mess. With his goalkeeping prowess, he played in both battalion and regimental teams. Later, in 1937, he was the only European in an All-Burma side, which defeated the visiting Islington Corinthians. It was typical of his sense of fair play and his reaction to the rigid social mores of colonial life that, on being appointed captain of the team, he refused, insisting that the Karen centre-half take his place. Neville Hogan, a redoubtable ex-Chindit, half-Irish and half-Karen, lived in a house at the foot of the hill beneath Sale Barracks. Over sixty years later, he remembered Seagrim well. 'He was an excellent goalkeeper; tall, clean-looking; and he spoke the language of the Karens. He loved the people and was a brilliant officer and sportsman.'[19] Seagrim cared little for the brittle racial and class nuances that were the hallmark of pre-war colonial life. An accomplished rider, he eschewed polo, disdained the snooty horsey set and referred to the cavalry as 'horse wallopers'. He was his own person, a lateral thinker, athletic, but quiet and introspective; cranky, perhaps. Caring little for what others thought, he made a great impression on all who met him.

In 1934 Seagrim befriended Harold Braund, a young recruit at the colonial trading company Steel Brothers, which specialised in shipping rice, oil, timber and other commodities and for which Noel Boyt also worked. Seagrim and Braund met up regularly for a drink and supper in his rooms after evensong at the Anglican Cathedral. For Braund, Seagrim was 'the most unforgettable character I have ever met ... a dynamic, infectious character. We always got involved in discussion, sometimes religious, sometimes not, but usually serious – despite which, Stookey's manner of arguing promoted laughter sooner or later.'[20]

Above left: Hugh with his mother, Amabel (left), on his last leave before departing for Burma in 1931, and (above right) aged 27, with his paternal grandmother at the wedding of Jack and Camilla in 1936.

Home leave was every three years. In 1936 Hugh returned to be best man at his brother Jack's wedding to his fiancée Camilla at St Thomas's Church, Greatford, near Stamford. Although none realised it at the time, this was to be the last occasion on which all five brothers would be together. They enjoyed one another's company in an old open four-seater car, which they christened 'The Rusty Bullet'. Camilla later recalled: 'Granny Seagrim rented ... a beautiful converted windmill ... where they could moor a small yacht if they wished to sail, but they also were in much demand for tennis parties and dances. Life was very different to what it is now.'[21] At the end of their leave, Derek and Hugh parted outside the Cumberland Hotel at Marble Arch. Each went his own way in a taxi. They never saw each other again.

Shortly after returning to Burma, at the age of twenty-seven, Hugh felt that perhaps he should follow his brothers and find a wife. He wrote home to his mother, saying that he felt he 'ought to get married'. Perhaps mindful of her own heartbreak, she immediately replied that that was the worst possible reason to marry. Tall, tanned and striking, with an alluring personality and an engaging manner, there must have been no shortage of eligible matches for him. However, Hugh found the local memsahibs and their shallow preoccupations both tiresome and restrictive, so for a time he went out with an Anglo-Burmese girl, something frowned upon by conventional colonial society, which maintained rigid racial barriers. The Burmese, for instance, were not allowed to join the fashionable Pegu Club, which Seagrim knew well. Today, the carved teak ranges of the club buildings lie empty and decaying, haunted by the ghosts of generations long since passed, architectural flotsam left stranded on the receding tide of Empire.

Like many young people, Seagrim was a creature of sudden intense enthusiasms. Plagued by regular bouts of dysentery, for a while he tested a series of experimental diets. During one period of leave in England, he existed for almost a month on water, fruit juices and milk. On his return to Burma, he tried to introduce vegetarian meals into the mess, an innovation given short shrift by his fellow officers. All of this added to his reputation as a charming, if contrary, eccentric. Music was a perpetual joy, while fast cars and motorcycles were another distraction from the dull routines of Army life. At various stages he owned a three-litre Bentley, then a Norton motorbike, followed by Ariel Square-Fours, which had large Austin Seven engines – and then, rather incongruously, a tiny Austin 'Bug'. One afternoon Ann Purton, a fellow officer's wife, was taking tea on the veranda of her house in Mandalay when she was surprised to see the 'Bug' screech through the driveway entrance and skid to a halt outside her bungalow. She recalled:

> 'The driver uncoiled himself, as he emerged, to a height of six feet four inches. I knew at once who he was. I had never previously met him, but he was a close friend of Humphrey's and I had heard a great deal about him. He was Paul Seagrim, alias "Stookey"... We had tea together and established an immediate rapport. When he left our bungalow that day, it was with the promise to come and spend a leave with Humphrey and me as soon as possible. I looked forward to that with real pleasure. He was one of the nicest men I have ever met. It was amusing to see him compress himself into the seat of his little "Bug". Then away he drove through the gate and along the road outside the compound, one huge hand thrust out of the window, waving cheerfully until he was out of sight.'[22]

Seagrim fulminated against the old-school-tie approach to army promotion through seniority, which he thought simply enabled dead wood to float at the expense of the natural leader in any group. His outspoken disdain for Army convention upset his superiors in the Burma Rifles and elsewhere, but he didn't care. Once, he remarked that he would sooner be a postman in Norfolk than a general in India. He held trenchant views on the way to fight the coming war. He was highly critical of the ponderous tactics that dominated the conventional thinking of his fellow officers. These were a throwback to the tactics of the First World War, he believed, obsessed with drill, formal manoeuvres and defensive deployments around fixed positions and bunkers. They fostered a cautious, defensive mindset totally unsuited to future threats. Hill tribes like the Karens, he argued, had a natural talent for flexible, hit-and-run guerrilla warfare. Their instinctive skills were wasted in endless drills along conventional Indian Army lines.

Seagrim's unconventional thinking was displayed during pre-war exercises. On one occasion he was sent with his company to Pegu, some fifty miles north-east of Rangoon, with the task of trying to move south to attack Mingaladon. In typical maverick fashion, Seagrim procured some Burmese buses, laid his men on the floor and got a number of local women to sit on the seats. The buses sailed through the defences unchallenged and ended up in the middle of the objective. This was viewed by the staff officers as not at all playing the game. When Seagrim argued that this was exactly what the Japanese would do, he was – much to his irritation – sent back to try again in a more conventional fashion. But he was soon to be proved right.

The ossified official approach to soldiering extended to recruitment, which was carried out from fixed posts to which potential recruits could report, rather than more dynamic peripatetic tours up country led by men whom the locals could trust. By early 1939 there was a growing awareness of the need to expand the local defence forces, and Seagrim was given his head. He led a recruiting expedition on foot across some 500 miles of the Karen hills. At that time, however, when the likely adversary seemed to be Germany, his heart was not in it. He thought it manipulative and dishonest to enlist simple hill people for a far-distant war they could never begin to comprehend. Later, when the threat from Japan was only too clear, he changed his mind and was perfectly placed to raise the hill tribes of eastern Burma against a ruthless common enemy.

★★★

Heroism can be obedience to the secret impulse of an individual. For Seagrim, his impulse was the growing quest for spiritual enlightenment and a peculiar sense of his own destiny. The search for a deeper understanding of the meaning of life, and the actions contingent upon it, took priority over everything else. This was the hidden dynamic of his life, fed from a multiplicity of sources – his upbringing, his enquiring mind, his restless desire to get to the root of things and an emerging sense of his own personal destiny. The evidence for this dynamic is not hard to find.

Throughout the 1930s Hugh voraciously consumed works of spiritual philosophy, history and politics. He was apt to sound off to all and sundry on a whole range of subjects. He would talk long into the night about 'finding the real essence of truth' or 'beauty'. For a while he would delve into Nietzsche, then Tagore, Kahlil Gibran, Santayana and Schopenhauer. This was a man embarking on the lonely path of spiritual awakening while absorbing the mystical traditions of the East, which lay all around him. For Seagrim, this was not some abstract intellectual exercise, but the forging of a code of conduct and belief that was to be lived and followed in every aspect of his daily life.

Among regular military officers, who all too often viewed local culture and spiritual beliefs with disdain or suspicion, this intense interest made him very unusual indeed. He was not a religious man in the conventional sense; he avoided church parades whenever he could, and professed to despise the dogma and formalities of organised worship. Rather, he sought meaning through a deeper understanding of comparative religions from a wide variety of backgrounds and traditions, all of which, he began to realise, were simply different paths to the same source. Paradoxically, he considered the Bible 'the finest literature in the world'. Later, it became an unending source of inspiration and comfort to him.

With the outbreak of war in Europe in September 1939, greater emphasis was put on officer training. Early in 1941, Seagrim was dispatched to Staff College at Quetta, in India, where he bristled at the blinkered, defensive mentality of his superiors and argued passionately in favour of flexible irregular forces that could harass the enemy and live off the jungle and its abundant resources. Outspoken, critical and uncompromising, he openly dismissed the staff as 'odds and sods', and their teaching as irrelevant. He frequently lectured his fellow staff officers in breaks between the formal lectures. On one occasion he treated eighteen of his colleagues to an impromptu session on tactics, dismissing two heckling cavalry officers as 'donkey-wallopers' and wagging his finger reproachfully at the others, but his points hit home. At Quetta he met and befriended Ralph Griffith, a future commanding officer of the legendary Queen Victoria's Own Corps of Guides. Of the eighteen officers who listened to Hugh that day, Griffith was one of only three who were to survive the war.

Over time Seagrim had collated and typed out two very personal anthologies of poetry and prose, which he believed offered real insights into the meaning of life. He took them with him wherever he went. He kept one set on a lectern in his room, where, as a relief from military theory, he used to declaim in a loud voice to all and sundry to vent his inner feelings. Anyone passing was invited to take part. Quite what his fellow officers made of it all is anyone's guess, but in December 1941, when on the outbreak of the war in the Far East, he was rushed back to Burma, he asked Griffith to take charge of the collection. When Griffith was then later posted to Iraq, he placed it with the rest of his kit, where it lay forgotten. Many years later, as an old man, he had it bound, and after his death his widow finally presented it to the Seagrim family. In the preamble to this version of the collection, written years later, Griffith asks for forgiveness that he never sent it on to Seagrim's mother. Hugh sent the second version to his mother, and it arrived in time for Christmas 1941. To read both anthologies is profoundly moving. They shine a light deep into his soul. The poems and prose express the finest spiritual ideals and reflect the diverse facets of this enigmatic and complex man.

Two passages in particular, both by Giovanni Papini, the Italian essayist and poet, explain precisely why Seagrim decided not to marry. It would have come between him and the freedom to pursue his own destiny.

'The man who would lead and change others may not tie himself for life to any one being. He would either be unfaithful to his wife or his mission. His sense of universal brotherhood is too strong to allow him to love one of his sisters only. A hero is a solitary being ever. Solitude is at once his penalty and his greatness. He renounces the joys of marital affection indeed, but the love that is in him is multiplied infinitely and he communicates it to all men in a sublimation of sacrifice that surpasses all earthly ecstasy. The man who has no woman is lonely but free; his soul, that is not weighted with common and material considerations, can soar the higher. He begets no children according to the flesh, through him the children of his spirit are reborn to a second life.'[23]

Another passage on 'Greatness' develops this idea further and argues that the responsibilities of a wife and children are so onerous that they impede more serious obligations.

'Whosoever would devote himself entirely to a great work must condemn himself to chastity. No one can serve both humanity and a single individual. The man who has a difficult mission to accomplish, which demands all his time down to the last hour, may not tie himself to a woman. Marriage implies the dedication of self to another being, but he who would be a Saviour must dedicate himself to all humanity. The union of two souls is not sufficient for him, and it would but render more difficult, perhaps even impossible, a union with all other souls.'[24]

It is very clear from these and other passages in the collection that he sensed his own destiny. For him, to be a Saviour was the highest mission in life. Another piece, an extract from Captain Scott's diary of his fateful expedition to the South Pole in 1912 records the legendary last hours of Captain Lawrence Oates, who sacrificed himself in a vain attempt to save his comrades.

'He was a brave soul ... We knew that Oates was walking to his death, but though we tried to dissuade him, we knew it was the act of a brave man and an English gentleman. We hope to meet the end with a similar spirit, and assuredly the end is not far ...'[25]

Chapter 3

Behind Enemy Lines

'Unhappy is the land in need of heroes'
BERTOLT BRECHT

The Japanese had prepared well for their lightning attack on Burma and South-East Asia, gleaning information and intelligence about the burgeoning nationalist movement from a network of sleeper agents. In May 1940 a journalist for the Japanese newspaper *Yomiuri Shimbun* arrived in Rangoon under the name of Minami Masuyo. This was a cover. He was, in fact, Colonel Suzuki Keiji of the Imperial General Headquarters, charged with finding out whether dissident Burmese could be used to close the Burma Road, the principal supply route to China, where the Japanese had been fighting a brutal race war since 1937. Paradoxically for a culture that prided itself on conformity, Suzuki was a swashbuckling maverick with an abiding belief in Burmese independence and very clear views of his own. The outstanding cadet of his year, he had served on the Russian border during the First World War and acquired a reputation as a man of action and drive. While there was a stream of good naval intelligence from Burma, army intelligence was woefully inadequate. With the blessing of the Army General Staff, Suzuki set up a clandestine operation which had its roots within Burma itself, and personnel straight from the history books.

In the 1930s, Rangoon University had been a hotbed of nationalist sentiment. Prominent among the student leaders was a young activist, a rather moody and unpredictable young man, called Aung San, who was destined to become the godfather of modern Burma, and the father of Aung San Suu Kyi. In 1932 he entered Rangoon University and soon made a name for himself in the febrile world of nationalist student politics. Six years later he joined the Dohbama Asi-ayone, literally the 'We Burmese' organisation. Rather pretentiously, the members adopted the prefix Thakin, or Master, in a deliberate subversion of the honorific term used for the British. Like many of his fellow students, Aung San had left-wing ideals, but, unlike them, he was a pragmatist prepared to pursue any course that would secure independence.

In 1940 Aung San led a Thakin delegation to India, where he met both Gandhi and Nehru. With his customary wisdom, and given the inevitable complications that would ensue, Nehru advised strongly against seeking help from a foreign power. On returning to Burma, Aung San found there had been a wave of arrests of nationalists. Forced to flee to China with a fellow activist, he stowed away on a Norwegian freighter smuggling contraband and opium to the international settlement of Kulangsu at Amoy (now Xiamen), where, without any papers, he was stranded, destitute, disheartened and ill. Suzuki seized his chance. He arranged for the Japanese secret police, the kempeitai, to bring the two Thakins to Tokyo, train them as fifth columnists and send them back to Burma as infiltrators. Disconcertingly, the two erstwhile left-wing firebrands suddenly found themselves befriended by fascist Japan.

While Hugh Seagrim was becoming ever more disenchanted with the out-of-date British military tactics and teaching at the British Staff College at Quetta, the Japanese were burrowing deep into the fabric of Burmese society. In February 1941, they set up the Minami Organ – a covert intelligence operation to subvert Burma, with its operational centre in Bangkok. At a stroke, Aung San and the Thakins were poised to get the training and support that other dissident Burmese factions had failed to acquire. It put them in pole position to influence the future of Burma, but also on a collision course with the communists, who were ideologically opposed to any help from fascist Japan. Ever the pragmatist, Aung San thought that they should get help from whatever source they could, but he was supping with the devil. Later that month he slipped back into Burma disguised as a Chinese seaman to convey to his comrades the offer of Japanese arms, money and support and to seek volunteers for training on Hainan Island.

Suzuki established a real rapport with the Thakins. Disingenuously, he circulated a spurious story that he was the grandson of a Burmese prince. In a blood-letting ceremony on Hainan Island with the 'Thirty Comrades', they each took dramatic Burmese names. Suzuki became Bo Mogyo, or 'Thunderbolt'. Aung San became Teza, meaning 'Fire'. Each man slit a finger until blood dripped into the bowl. This was then mixed with alcohol, and the bowl passed around. Each man drank in turn. All then swore an oath to be indissolubly bound together by the bond of blood when fighting the British.

While the Japanese were busy raising a fifth column of Burmese dissidents, the British finally woke up to the need to prepare for an impending war with Japan. It was not an auspicious time. Being engaged in a war of national survival in Europe and the Middle East, few resources were available to bolster Britain's Far Eastern colonies. In May 1941, a group of senior officers from the newly formed Special Operations Executive (SOE) was dispatched from London to Singapore to plan underground operations and subversive propaganda in the event of war with Japan. Code-named Oriental Mission, it was put in place in case the Far Eastern colonies were attacked, or worse, occupied. Operating independently from the Secret Intelligence Service (SIS), SOE had been formed a year earlier, in a merger of different departments of the War Office and the Ministry of Economic Warfare. Initially, its primary focus was on Nazi Germany and Italy, but as the political situation deteriorated in the Far East, it turned its attention to the Orient.

With the collapse of France in June 1940, and with Britain under threat of imminent invasion, politicians all over the East saw an opportunity to exploit the situation to their own advantage. The Japanese cabinet met in July 1940 to review the sudden transformation in the new world order. It resolved to seize the moment, with a southern advance against the British and Dutch colonies in South-East Asia to grab their rich supplies of oil and other natural resources. The British responded by using public propaganda to bolster the image of British power in the Far East and boosting the concept of an impregnable 'Fortress Singapore'. While this may have reassured home and colonial audiences, it did not fool the Japanese. Privately, many in London acknowledged Britain's military weakness in the Far East, but hoped that the military bluff, which had sustained Britain's Empire for so long, might pass unchallenged. Oriental Mission was put in place in case it did not.

The Mission was led by Valentine St John Killery, a former managing director of ICI in China. Resourceful and astute, Killery was a bright young man with considerable political nous and an excellent network of political and commercial contacts throughout the Far East – but he faced an impossible task. In September 1941, he was joined by a second unit, India Mission, under Colin Mackenzie, a one-legged businessman and veteran of the First World War. Mackenzie was sent out to Meerut, north-west of Delhi, with a similar objective of cultivating resistance movements in Persia, Iraq and Afghanistan in case the Germans overran the Middle East. These units, later combined, were to form the cadre of future British SOE operations in the Far East code-named Force 136. Oriental Mission was intended to assist military operations as soon as war broke out – by sabotaging key infrastructure and industrial facilities, and deploying local irregular forces of levies led by 'left-behind parties'. These would remain behind enemy lines to garner intelligence, build resistance and harass enemy lines of communication. However, from the outset, the Mission faced internal wrangling and even outright opposition from sections of the Army and the colonial government, who were irritated by civilian meddling.

Since 1939 the idea of raising the hill tribes of Burma as potential guerrillas against the increasingly combative Japanese had been current among officers of the Frontier Service. By far the most enterprising of these was Noel Stevenson, the thirty-seven-year-old Assistant Superintendent at Kutkai in the northern Shan states, a brilliant linguist, and the author of several books on the country's ethnic groups, including the seminal work *The Hill Peoples of Burma*. Early in 1941, fearing that the Chinese province of Yunnan might defect to Japan and pose an immediate threat to the Kachin people of north-east Burma, Stevenson had begun training Kachin guerrillas, who had a natural aptitude for such work. He received strong support from the Commissioner of the Shan States, who encouraged others in the Frontier Service to start raising levies among their own charges and peoples – in particular, the Karens and the Lahus.

Stevenson's training methods and ingenious booby traps were commended to the recently arrived Governor of Burma, Sir Reginald Dorman-Smith. As a consequence, in December 1941 – and in the face of open resentment from several senior staff officers – Stevenson was summoned to Rangoon and put in touch with the newly arrived officers from Oriental Mission to organise a nationwide network of levies: a resistance force of men from the hill tribes, who could provide intelligence and, at the right point in time, come together as an effective fighting force behind enemy lines. With little experience of Burma, and minimal equipment and resources, Oriental Mission had struggled, but with similar aims and enthusiasms, Stevenson and the officers hit it off brilliantly. Stevenson had the local knowledge, and Oriental Mission had what little funding, arms and equipment were available.

Hugh Seagrim was Stevenson's first recruit. He knew the country like the back of his hand, and for years had been advocating a radically different approach to the rigid defensive thinking which prevailed among the upper echelons of the Army. With his experience of the Karens and the hill tracts – garnered during his pre-war expeditions through Karenni, the Chin Hills and Tenasserim – he was the obvious candidate to lead a guerrilla force of Karen levies and organise covert resistance to the Japanese. On returning to Burma from his staff course at Quetta in December 1941, as soon as Seagrim heard that moves were afoot to raise Karen levies, he volunteered.

Like so many others who met him, Stevenson was deeply impressed. Tall, thin and with penetrating, deep-set brown eyes and a determined jaw, Seagrim had great personal presence. He was 'an ascetic type, very dark. He looked as if he might have been a monk',[1] but what impressed Stevenson most was Seagrim's detailed knowledge of the Karens and their home in the wild hills on the eastern borders with Siam, and his unswerving belief in their abilities to form an effective force of irregulars. For a month or so Seagrim was forced to kick his heels on temporary attachment to the RAF at Mingaladon, where in impotent frustration he witnessed the bombing of Rangoon and endured the continuous Japanese bombing raids on the airfield. Unlike the Army, he held the RAF, with its emphasis on individual ability, initiative and skill, in high regard and rather wished he had joined it.

Early in January 1942 Stevenson was dispatched to report to Major General 'Jackie' Smyth VC, the commander of the 17th Indian Division, which was guarding the eastern approaches to Burma. Unfortunately, Stevenson and Smyth did not see eye to eye on the value of levies. After a blazing row, Stevenson returned to Rangoon seething and highly critical of Smyth. Never the diplomat, Stevenson's outspoken criticisms permanently soured the Army's opinion of him. Forever after, he was regarded with suspicion by many at Army headquarters as a meddling civilian who knew little of military affairs. It soon became clear that if there was to be the remotest chance of success, the levies required much more support from a hitherto aloof and indifferent Army command. At a stroke the newly arrived commander-in-chief, General Alexander, transformed the fledgling outfit, sanctioned an increase of fifty officers, and brought the organisation directly under Army command, with Stevenson commissioned as a lieutenant colonel responsible for their activities.

With the Japanese Air Force strafing Burmese towns and cities at will, Stevenson was keen to hit back at the Japanese immediately, but, frustratingly, a bold plan for a surprise counter-strike on the poorly defended Japanese airfield at Mae Sariang in Siam using Karen irregulars was vetoed. Stevenson immediately ordered Seagrim to raise Karen levies in the hills overlooking the strategically vital Kyaikto-Thaton-Moulmein railway line, a task that offered Seagrim full rein for his unorthodox thinking. This was just the moment for which he had been waiting and honing himself: the chance to recruit, train and lead a guerrilla army of his beloved Karens and show his superiors just what they could achieve. But following the unholy bust-up between Stevenson and Smyth, the latter re-assigned Seagrim to reconnaissance work, a task at which he was extremely successful, but which delayed his recruitment and organisation of the levies by several crucial weeks – weeks that never seemed to end. For Hugh, it was exasperating.

Demoralised, Seagrim believed that British prestige in the hills was reaching rock bottom, and that the Karens' morale had deteriorated so much that it was now too late to do anything. He returned to Rangoon from his reconnaissance work disconsolate, thinking that his big chance to prove the value of his innovative tactical thinking was in danger of slipping through his fingers. But he was wrong. After discussions with key officers from Oriental Mission, Seagrim volunteered to go up into the Karen hills. At a conference with Smyth, the commander gave him permission to organise a force of irregulars around a nucleus of fifty-five members of the Salween District military police. Smyth advised him to consider soberly the enormous risks he was taking. The Japanese were ferocious enemies, with a reputation for savage brutality. If caught, Seagrim could expect no quarter. He would face merciless torture and summary execution by beheading. But he was resolute. Nothing would deter him from his goal. His orders were to keep watch on what were likely to become the crucial Japanese supply routes into Burma – the Moulmein–Pegu–Rangoon road and railway corridors – to mount lightning raids upon them, and to feed back to Rangoon a stream of intelligence about Japanese movements using a civilian wireless transmitter at Papun.

On 20 January 1942, Seagrim loaded up in Rangoon with a ragbag of weapons that Stevenson had managed to purloin, including some tommy guns and grenades. Accompanied by Lieutenant Ronald Heath from Oriental Mission, he drove up into the hills along the only road: a tortuous ribbon of dusty red earth that wound its way through precipitous jungle-clad hills to the capital of the Salween district. Over the next two and a half years, Papun would become the eye of the storm for his guerrilla operations. Surrounded by endless impenetrable forests that roll in great swathes across emerald green mountains along the border with Siam, in 1942 Papun was – and in fact still is – just a small, ramshackle town of mostly timber and palm thatch buildings on the banks of the Yunzalin river, a tributary of the tempestuous Salween. Trees soar over 200 feet high, forming a continuous, undulating canopy that pullulates incessantly to the threnody of countless exotic birds and insects. Lashed by the south-west monsoon, between May and October each year Papun was virtually cut off, the only access being a twelve-day journey upriver against the engorged current. Although predominantly Karen, some Burmans, Gurkhas, Shans and a smattering of Indian and Chinese traders made a modest living there.

Seagrim made his base in a small public-works department bungalow. His only British companions were the local deputy commissioner and district superintendent of police, George Chettle, and his wife. They had lived there for four years, and Chettle's authority was widely respected. He epitomised old-style British paternalistic rule at its best: the 'father and friend of his people', and a man whose word was law. He thought Seagrim 'a most unusual person, but a good soldier and a very stout fellow', who believed that the Japanese would go through Burma like 'a dose of salts, but did not seem at all depressed at the prospect'.[2] Papun received few European visitors. The only other Europeans present at the time were two French Catholic priests: Father Loizeau, who had established a mission there in 1921, and his assistant, Father Calmon, who had come out to join him in 1935. Both were destined to play important roles in the years ahead.

On arriving in Papun, Seagrim was in his element. He issued a string of commands. Immediately, he requested a further supply of rifles, automatics, ammunition and equipment. Heath returned to Rangoon, then came back in a convoy of small Jeeps with a Captain Stephenson and two other Oriental Mission officers carrying over 200 obsolete Italian rifles, some shotguns and several thousand rounds of ammunition. Stephenson planned to make the journey again and return with more supplies, but on his way back to Rangoon he just made it through before the road was cut by the Japanese. Seagrim would have to make do with what he had. Shortly afterwards, the civilian wireless transmitter was withdrawn from Papun, leaving Seagrim with no direct means of communicating with the outside world.

Heath, who later went on to work with the legendary Chindit leader Orde Wingate as a jungle-training officer, was both intrigued and inspired by Seagrim. He saw in the two men similar unorthodox qualities: 'Both Seagrim and Wingate were determined men who knew their own minds. They could analyse a situation, take a decision and act on it without consulting others.'[3] The latter quality, of course, was one that could drive the more conventional military mind to distraction, but it was ideal for guerrilla warfare where initiative and self-reliance were essential for survival. Both Wingate and Seagrim were charismatic leaders who never asked their men to do anything that they would not themselves do. Heath recalled: 'Any of the Karen boys would have done anything for [Seagrim]. He had a terrific sway over those lads.'[4]

While Seagrim was busy setting up his base at Papun, Oriental Mission found two more brave men to work in Karenni with Seagrim. Their purpose was to coordinate resistance and intelligence in the districts

Above left: Father Jean Calmon and (above right) Father Loizeau on graduating from his seminary in 1898.

north of Papun. They were both civilian forestry managers, who were at home in the wilds – strong, self-reliant individuals accustomed to lonely forest life far from the company of other Europeans. Though lesser men could be driven insane by the suffocating isolation and the alien sounds emanating from the teeming jungles that surrounded them, these thrived on the challenge. Tough men who knew the jungle and their peoples, they formed the core of the special forces that were recruited to operate alongside regular officers like Seagrim.

The first was Noel Boyt of Steel Brothers, the tough, no-nonsense, timber manager from Pyinmana, with whom Seagrim had stayed years before on his pre-war foray to Kawkareik. The other was Cecil Smith, the Conservator of Forests for the Sittang Circle, who knew the forests like the back of his hand. A few weeks later, Stevenson seconded three more officers, including an enterprising young man called Eric McCrindle, who would play a key role in future guerrilla operations with Seagrim. They were to form a strong presence in the district alongside some good Burmese officers. The jobs were divided up: Smith was to organise and train levies north of the vital Toungoo–Mawchi road; and Boyt, based at Mawchi, would do the same for the area south of the road, including liaison with Seagrim – who was out on a limb even further south at Papun.

Above left: Lieutenant Eric McCrindle and (above right) Noel Boyt at Pyinmana in 1929.

On 26 February 1942, Boyt and Smith set off for Toungoo. Despite their explicit orders from Stevenson, being civilians they were roundly dismissed by the local army officer as 'boy scouts' and sent packing. On returning, however, they were commissioned on the spot by the divisional commander, Brigadier Curtis, and sent off to raise the tribes. Like Seagrim, they were phenomenally successful. Within two weeks they had raised more than 3,000 Karens to the Allied cause. Smith had organised his area into twenty-two circles, each with a circle leader and NCOs (non-commissioned officers). For Smith, 'the appeal for recruits met with a great response. The patriotic fervour and loyalty shown by the Karens, especially the Protestants, reminded me of the atmosphere I have experienced at Armagh, Northern Ireland on Orange Day, July 12.'[5] Meanwhile, to the south, Seagrim was becoming increasingly isolated. In a conversation with a fellow officer at Kyaikto shortly before leaving for Papun, he made it very clear that as a 'question of principle' he was determined to stay behind, even if the British retreated from Burma. Before the war, he had made himself unpopular with his superiors by expounding that the British deserved to lose the war because of their general lack of principle. He was determined to set an example.

The Siamese frontier lay only twenty miles from Papun. Chettle had fifty-five armed police and over 200 civil police to resist cross-border raids. A month earlier, occasional sniping between border guards had escalated into an all-out raid by the Siamese, who had attacked a local police station and killed the Karen inspector. In the temporary lull which ensued, Seagrim arrived with his modest supply of arms and ammunition to join Chettle and raise the levies. He leapt into action, immediately recruited over 200 Karen volunteers and embarked on a crash-training programme. The mornings were spent in rifle practice, and the afternoons rehearsing ambushes and forest tactics, such as digging camouflaged punji traps of sharpened bamboo canes designed to impale any hapless enemy that fell into them. In the evenings training continued on the local football field. There was none of the square-bashing or drill so ingrained into the British and Indian armies. Seagrim avoided being too didactic, preferring to nurture the Karens' natural abilities as guerrilla fighters. He let his men adopt whatever firing position they found most comfortable on the basis that they would shoot better that way. As on the North-West Frontier, and elsewhere in the East, this was usually squatting rather than prone, a technique advocated by Orde Wingate for the Chindits. Unfortunately, their obsolete Italian rifles were chronically unreliable and repeatedly misfired. Many Karens preferred the crossbow, deadly up to seventy-five yards and ideal for eliminating Japanese sentries in total silence, with a limitless supply of ammunition from the surrounding forests.

However, while Seagrim was preparing his guerrilla army in the hills, Stevenson and Oriental Mission were busy planning for the worst. Just a month after landing at Victoria Point, the Japanese had seized the key ports of Mergui and Tavoy, aiming to break out into the heartlands of Burma via the long flat coastal road through Moulmein, Bilin and Pegu to Rangoon, over which Seagrim was keeping watch. Unremitting and pitiless, they swept all before them. In their wake came Colonel Suzuki, Aung San and his cadre of 300 dissident young Burmese Thakins marching under the banner of the Burma Independence Army (BIA). As the Japanese advanced, the BIA attracted all manner of chancers, opportunists and riff-raff, including thousands of criminals released from the jails, who saw an opportunity for plunder and to settle old scores. It was a toxic mix, which rapidly sowed the seeds of communal violence and murder. The British were forced back to the formidable river crossings over the Salween, Bilin and Sittang rivers. At each they hoped to stem the relentless Japanese advance. But it was not to be.

The Japanese were a savage enemy, schooled from an early age by a militaristic government to drill, march and prepare for war. Under its bushido code, every soldier was expected to be prepared to die for the Emperor. To die in battle was to die at the moment of perfection, like cherry blossom in spring. There was no expectation of returning home. Capture was the ultimate disgrace. An Order of the Day found on the body of a dead Japanese officer in Burma read: 'If your hands are broken, fight with your feet. If your hands and feet are broken, use your teeth. If there is no breath left in your body, fight with your ghost.'[6] This was a fanatical foe, who struck fear and dread in all those who stood in its way.

The apocalyptic climax came on the very borders of Karen country – at the Sittang river. It was the decisive turning point, and a defining moment for the British Empire in Asia. In mid-February 1942, the famous 17th Indian Division withdrew from a mauling at the Bilin river towards the strategic crossing over the Sittang – and disaster. With the 16th and 46th Indian Brigades still retreating in good order towards the bridge, on 20 February the Japanese attacked the bridgehead, causing mayhem, exacerbated by friendly fire from RAF and AVG pilots and lethal Japanese air strikes. Starved of supplies and equipment, the British were ill-prepared for invasion. Major General 'Jackie' Smyth later commented:

'It was a crashing disadvantage to me … that I hadn't got a wireless set which could contact Rangoon. Believe it or not, the only thing I could do was tap into the railway telegraph line and get the babu in the Post Office in Rangoon to try and persuade him that it was vitally important for me to be put through to Air Force Headquarters.'[7]

As British troops and transport retreated towards the river and the bridge, time after time they were outmanoeuvred by the Japanese, who simply percolated through jungle tracks and paths, and attacked their flanks and rear. These sudden unexpected onslaughts were only repelled by ferocious hand-to-hand fighting – among some of the worst experienced during the entire Burma campaign.

As Hugh Seagrim had predicted, British pre-war planning was hopelessly inadequate. Stymied by the conviction that the jungle was impenetrable, the troops' lack of jungle training was a fatal strategic mistake. For the British, the jungle was a fearful place – alien, claustrophobic, terrifying, full of strange sounds and dreadful insects, spawning fatal diseases like scrub typhus, malaria, dysentery and dengue fever; the very heart of darkness made infinitely worse during the drenching monsoon rains, when the endless green growth turned into a foetid swamp. It was to be avoided at all costs. For the Japanese, the jungle held no such fears. Lieutenant Teruo Okada later commented: 'I liked the jungle. It didn't have the fear [for me] it seemed to have had for some of the Allied soldiers. It was a friendly place where it was dark and you could cover yourself and camouflage yourself.'[8]

At 5.30 a.m. on 23 February 1942, three gigantic explosions rent the early morning air, the sound rolling like thunder across the plain and far up into the hills where Hugh Seagrim was watching and waiting. Great steel girders were hurled skywards like matchsticks as the retreating British blew the Sittang bridge to deny its use to the advancing Japanese. It was one of the most controversial decisions of the entire Far Eastern war, leaving over two brigades of the 17th Division – some 5,000 men – stranded on the east bank. For two or three minutes, absolute silence reigned. Then the Japanese realised what had happened. Machine-gunned, mortared, shelled and bombed, the tired but undaunted British battalions had fought their way to the river bank – only to despair that their escape route had been destroyed by their own side to prevent it falling into Japanese hands.

Swollen to one and a half miles wide by the incoming tide, the river posed an intimidating barrier to those desperate to escape. Some attempted to cross the river by swimming, or lashing together rafts of discarded petrol cans and bamboo as flotation aids. For those left trapped on the eastern bank, like Captain Bruce Kinloch of the 1st/3rd Gurkhas, it was a demoralising blow. 'Our hearts fell down into our boots,' he recalled; 'I was bloody angry'.[9] Neville Hogan, who had witnessed Seagrim's goalkeeping prowess in pre-war Rangoon, was then a private with the 2nd Burma Rifles:

'I felt devastated and lost … Chaos reigned all that day. We started to make rafts out of bamboo and big earthenware jars, because the Gurkhas could not swim. We were organised in two parties of twenty or thirty to swim the river. I had my boots round my neck, my pistol on its belt, and a pair of shorts. About three-quarters of the way across I felt a blow on my thigh, and thought I had collided with a Gurkha, but it turned out that I had been hit by shrapnel.'[10]

Hogan was one of the lucky ones. Having reached the west bank and survived, he faced a forty-two-mile walk along the railway line to Pegu.

The carnage was described by one officer as 'a party, which made Dunkirk look like a picnic'.[11] Another, who swam across with his men, spoke of nobility and gallantry alongside which anything else he witnessed throughout the entire war paled:

'Wave after wave of Japanese Navy fighters emptied their guns on the target. The water was a mass of human debris. Wounded were helped. The few swimmers supported the non-swimmers. Contrary to what has been said, many were helped across the river by friendly Burmans and Indian villagers from upstream. Hundreds were killed. Many drowned. Not a few died at the hands of dacoits and traitors. Those who lived were truly heroes. May those who died never be forgotten. Men of the Empire!'[12]

For months afterwards, survivors woke in terror with the screams of dying and drowning British soldiers ringing in their ears.

Following the disaster at the Sittang bridge, it was not just the front door to Rangoon and Burma that lay wide open, but the high road to China and the whole security of the Burma Road. All too late, the British High Command realised that however disastrous symbolically the loss of Singapore might have been in February 1942, it simply meant the loss of a naval base. The loss of Rangoon threatened the whole South-East Asian theatre and the imperative of keeping China in the war. On 1 March 1942, the Governor, Sir Reginald Dorman-Smith – disparagingly referred to as 'Dormouse-Smith' or 'Dormant-Myth' – held a last supper at Government House in Rangoon before retreating northwards. After desperate British resistance, Pegu fell on 7 March. On the same day, the new commander-in-chief, General Alexander, ordered the evacuation of Rangoon.

Thus began the long road of sorrows for so many refugees, terrified by tales of atrocities committed by the advancing Japanese. Just two weeks earlier, after the fall of Singapore, the Japanese had run amok through the Alexandra Hospital, bayonetting more than 250 patients in their beds and even on the operating table. Over 400 survivors had been crammed into three foetid rooms with no water and little air. Those who had not died from suffocation were machine-gunned, their mutilated bodies bundled unceremoniously into a mass grave. Stories like these quickened the feet of the refugees as they trudged westwards through the jungles of Burma in a desperate bid to reach India and freedom.

Almost 300,000 made the overland journey to India successfully,. No one knows how many tens of thousands died en route. The eleven-year-old Stephen Brookes became inured to death:

> 'a huge black cloud of flies rose up in front of me and a foul stench hit my nostrils. Before I could prepare myself, my eyes had taken in the awful sight of a bloated brown thing covered in a thick mass of wriggling white maggots. It had once been a human being, but now looked like any decomposing animal. The distended belly heaved and moved with insects; stiff mouldy limbs stuck up through the weeds, glistening with black flies.'[13]

As the Japanese surged up the Irrawaddy and Sittang valleys and across the plains of central Burma, a tidal wave of humanity welled before them – a great diaspora of men, women and children moving to the north and west as people trekked along the few tortuous escape routes to India, preyed upon by dacoits, renegade Chinese soldiers and hostile locals, and strafed by the advancing Japanese.

The jungle held many terrors. Poisonous snakes, scorpions, leeches and venomous spiders took their toll on many whose reserves of strength and endurance were depleted by malnutrition and disease. For John Beamish, an Anglo-Burmese officer, the worst horror had ten legs:

'In the fading light I was vaguely aware of a slight movement a few yards ahead. I peered down at the track. Scuttling over it at right angles to my line of march was a huge spider. I knew it for the venomous "pangu", the snake-killer. Three inches long, its squat belly covered with red hairs, the pangu has ten legs with hooked claws, a scaly case not unlike that of a tortoise, and in its mouth are two deadly black fangs. Its peculiar pleasure lies in hunting the serpent, climbing on its back and sucking out its brains …
I shuddered to think that I might have stepped on that hairy, swollen body.'[14]

Cholera, typhus, malaria and blackwater fever were rife. Many dropped dead from sheer exhaustion under the unrelenting, scorching sun. But the prospect of freedom in India, just over the distant hills on the western horizon, gave many the willpower to endure the most appalling privations. Whatever the hardship, whatever the perils, whatever the suffering, it was preferable to falling into the hands of the dreaded Japanese.

For thousands, the heartbreak and horror of being forced to leave mothers, fathers, sons and daughters to die alone and frightened in the jungle traumatised them for the rest of their lives. Few ever spoke of it again. Years later, the young Stephen Brookes remembered both the fear and the shame. 'We were the last of the Empire's children, fashioned for a world of certainties but living in a world in transition. What an awful, frightening mess. I put my hands up to hide my eyes because I knew that men did not cry. But, oh God, how I cried inwardly.'[15] It was not just civilians who suffered. Wounded British soldiers were left behind to sell their lives dearly.

But not all Japanese troops were unfeeling. Major Misao Sato, for one, came across a handsome, eighteen-year-old British soldier who had been shot through the abdomen. He realised that he must be suffering intense pain, the bullet having ruptured his intestines. With compassion, Misao

Sato talked with him of his parents, held his hand and sat quietly with him until he died. The Japanese soldier recalled:

> 'As I looked at him closely I saw a thin stream of tears coming from his eyes. I understood he was enduring pain with all his might, his young pale face contorted. Ah! His attitude was really dignified. He was doing his best to maintain the pride of the Great British Empire while his life was ending. Unconsciously I cried and held his hands. I would never forget the last minutes of that young British soldier! At that time, I really discovered the origin of the strength of the British Empire.'[16]

Despite a bitter fighting retreat up the Irrawaddy valley, it proved impossible for the British to check the Japanese advance. High in the hills of eastern Burma, Hugh Seagrim and his newly mobilised levies were outflanked, cut off and dangerously exposed.

Chapter 4

Grandfather Longlegs

'I loved you so I drew these tides of men into my hands
and wrote my will across the sky in stars.'

T. E. LAWRENCE

Early in March 1942 Seagrim prudently moved his small headquarters of less than a dozen trusted men further into the hills to Pyagawpu, about thirty miles to the north-west of Papun. Nestling in the bottom of a flat valley, surrounded by rolling hills and accessible only via mountain tracks, it was a safe haven with ample warning of potential enemy intruders. With the military situation deteriorating day by day, he took the opportunity to write to his family. Only two of his letters survive as he disappeared behind the bamboo curtain, but his voice is very clear.

On 2 March he wrote to his brother Jack, who was at Staff College in Quetta. Characteristically, he penned across the top of the first: 'Don't become Staff College minded. I am sure they are wrong, together with most of the students who are utter blockheads.' He continued:

'Dear Bro,

What do you think of the Staff College and what do you think of the show over here? When I was there, they neglected utterly anything to do with the Far East and the peculiar conditions of warfare over here. I knew exactly that this would happen and frequently told fellow students, who laughed and thought I was a fool!

I see no way out of things here. If I wrote what I think, I would without doubt be censored. I once told Colonel Armstrong that if I gave a lecture on Burma the opinions I expressed about certain senior gentlemen would not be acceptable at the Staff College, but those opinions of mine were true, hence the present show.

I am no longer with the Army, but on my own. I was first of all on the aerodrome near Rangoon (for a month) and got thoroughly used to being bombed, which is not nearly as bad as might be imagined. It's hair razing [sic] to begin with, but then gradually one becomes a fatalist and bothers no more. During the Moulmein battle I was on the other side of the river so only heard and did not experience the battle. Since then I've been roaming with some odds and sods, which may come to a lot or may fizzle out, depending largely on whether we can get arms or not.

How do you like Staff College? Don't take it too seriously. One needs common sense much more than a lot of the stuff they teach there. I think our whole system of discipline is wrong. It is a massed affair built on a foundation which is dead and out of date. We need, I think, tremendous personal discipline, based on a creed or philosophy of life which each must work out. In this jungle fighting, one must be an individual and not a machine. Everyone must think; those who wait for ideas are dead men and those who wait for rations will starve.

Give my wishes to Col. Armstrong and the Commandant. We all worshipped Col. Armstrong. Also please give my Salaams to Col. Waring and tell him the Enemy have done what was considered impossible. They would have been idiots to do anything else since what was impossible for us, was only impossible because we were too unimaginative to do what was possible but not orthodox. Best wishes to Camilla and the brats. Please pass this on to Mrs S. I have not written for a long time to her.
Bumps.'[1]

The second letter, also to Jack on the same day, is much more formal and refers to his own spiritual anthology. Unspoken, but implicit, is the thought that he may not return, but that for those closest to him its publication might offer some insight into his true self.

'Dear Jack (Captain J. H. Seagrim),
If you are at the Staff College, will you please do this for me.
Write to Capt. R. Griffiths, 12 Frontier Force Rifles (he was on the course with me). He has with him a typewritten manuscript of an anthology, which I am anxious to get printed. It has taken many years to compile.

Will you ask him for the manuscript and, having got it, have thirty copies printed. It will cost about R200, which I will pay.

I have no chequebook here and am miles away in the blue with a gang of men. If I return, it will only be on very rare occasions, so will you forward this letter to A. Scott & Co., Bankers and Shipping Agents, Burma (they have moved to India, Calcutta probably) and ask them to use this letter as the authority for payment of the printing.

H. P. Seagrim, Capt.'[2]

In another letter to his mother at this time, he told her of his decision to stay behind and explained that there was a chance he would get through, but if he didn't he wanted to leave a memory with the Karens. In another he admitted: 'How long we can survive depends on how much ammunition and arms we can capture.' He closed the letter on a note of fatalism: 'It is not this life that matters, but the next.' Tragically these letters and much other correspondence were lost in a fire after the war, but bound into the front of Hugh Seagrim's personal anthology is an undated typed copy of a heart-breaking letter (Appendix A). The family believe it to be his last letter home. In fact, it is not, although it is profoundly moving and infused with understated patriotism and pride – at once a thanks, a farewell and an expression of faith in the Divine purpose of life. Uncannily, it encapsulates precisely Hugh Seagrim's own beliefs and those of a generation of Englishmen who fought for the highest ideals.

★★★

On 10 March, two weeks after the disaster at the Sittang bridge and in danger of being outflanked, the 2nd Battalion Burma Rifles marched through Pyagawpu in good order, retreating north to Kyaukkyi and Toungoo. They made an impressive and colourful sight: a long swaying train of ninety-three elephants carrying all their stores and equipment. Several days later, the deputy commissioner and superintendent of police, George Chettle, arrived en route to Kyaukkyi. He stayed the night with Seagrim, who was 'cheerful, but not betting on his chances'.[3] Shortly after, Father Loizeau, the French missionary priest, appeared. He was the last European to move through. Seagrim was now alone, and increasingly out of touch with the melancholy events unfolding elsewhere across the country, but charged with setting up an effective left-behind party to harass the Japanese, he was determined to stay and lead his beloved Karens.

Seagrim lived in a house on the east bank of the river belonging to Saw Ta Roe, a prosperous Karen villager who was to become a firm friend and staunch ally in the testing times ahead. Around him was assembled a ragbag of Gurkha stragglers cut off on the wrong side of the river when the Sittang bridge had been blown, and about twenty sick Karens of the 2nd battalion Burma Rifles, who had been struck down with fever. They were cared for by Ta Roe's sister-in-law, a teacher, who knew a little nursing.

At his new base, Seagrim set about raising and training local recruits and organising a command structure. In the first week alone over 800 volunteers streamed in to report for duty. Given the chronic shortage of arms and ammunition, most were sent back to their villages after having registered their names. The most promising 350 were organised into sections of a dozen or so men, usually armed with a couple of rifles, a few shotguns, a tommy gun and sparse amounts of ammunition. Each was given a distinguishing armband with the letter K for Karen embroidered on it and then taken out for regular tactical training in the surrounding forests by Karen ex-Burma Rifles section commanders. Each section was ordered to help cut-off soldiers, to protect villages from marauding bands of dacoits and Burmese, and to pass intelligence by runner to Seagrim. Lookouts were placed on all the jungle tracks with an outer and inner screen and a mobile central reserve, which could be deployed rapidly wherever the need arose. Overnight Seagrim had become the de facto ruler of his own private fiefdom, a white sawbwa, a romantic hero straight out of a Joseph Conrad novel seeking his own personal salvation in the sweltering wilderness of the Burmese jungle.

He appointed three dependable Karen lieutenants. The lantern-jawed Saw Digay at Pyagawpu was an influential local timber contractor and elephant driver, with eighteen sections under his command. In the centre around Papun, with twenty sections, was Saw Darlington, a piratical old rogue and womaniser with a pronounced squint; a man of many talents, he was variously a carpentry teacher at the local Wesleyan mission school, a former military policeman and a contractor. In the south around Kadaingti, with nine sections, was the dependable Saw Willie Saw, a striking-looking forest ranger with a bushy head of hair. Having organised his levies,

Seagrim's next priority was to secure more arms and ammunition. With only about thirty rounds per rifle, and many of the rifles unreliable, he sent Ta Roe fifty miles north to solicit more arms and ammunition from Noel Boyt at Mawchi. Boyt passed on what little he could spare – 150 12-bore shotguns and 100 cartridges, fifty 410s and 500 cartridges, plus a couple of boxes of grenades. With the help of seventy local villagers, Ta Roe carried the much-needed supplies back to Pyagawpu.

Working the area north of the Mawchi road, Cecil Smith continued to encourage the local Karen elders to mobilise levies for intelligence and guerrilla warfare, albeit in his view 'at least a year too late'. Armed pickets were placed on all the tracks leading into the hills. On a march to Loikaw, Smith selected an area at the headwaters of a stream in the most inaccessible part of the Karen hills as a refugee camp for displaced Karen women and children: a final redoubt, which the levies could defend at all costs. He then moved on to Yado on the borders of the Shan States, a hotbed of pro-Japanese dissidents. With the British in full retreat, on 24 March Smith was ordered by Stevenson to get out to avoid being completely outflanked by the Japanese. He was wracked with guilt at leaving and felt that he was 'deserting [the Karens] in their hour of need', but thought he might be of better use to them outside the hills, where he could intercede on their behalf. He wrote later:

'They implored me to do all I could to ensure that for their loyalty, they would never again be dominated by the Burmese. Feeling against the Burmans, whom they despised as traitors, was very bitter and the Karens were almost as keen to keep the Burmans out of

Far left: The swashbuckling Saw Darlington showing his pronounced squint.
Left: Saw Digay standing with two of his elephants and their oozies.

their hills as to keep out the Japanese. With the invasion and the raising of the levies the Karens really thought that a new era had begun for them and it was significant that the badge chosen for the levies and which was handmade by their womenfolk represented a Karen drum against a rising sun.'[4]

To the south at Mawchi, Boyt was working at full stretch to organise his own levies and to liaise with Seagrim even further south, and also with the Chinese, who had been tasked with the defence of the whole of the Allied Eastern Front in Burma with an Advance HQ at Toungoo. With fighting taking place just a few miles south of the town, the levies were of immense potential value to the Chinese, who were anxious to make good use of them. But communication was difficult: interpretation relied on two young Chinese students, whose English was confined to politely offering cups of tea, while on the British side the Chinese Liaison Mission seemed shy of the Chinese General. Nonetheless, what help could be offered was received with gratitude. Guides and information were supplied and various local informers were seized and shot. Unfortunately, in the confusion, a number of Karen levies were also killed by mistake when trying to bring in information to the Chinese. On top of all this, there was little communication between the two local Chinese armies. Neither had made adequate arrangements for the defence of the crucial Mawchi road, so the levies stepped in. And here, for the first time, they justified Hugh Seagrim's faith in their fighting capabilities in a full-bloodied confrontation with the battle-hardened Japanese.

On 30 March 1942, the Chinese blew the Paletwa bridge over the river leading to the Mawchi road. Although they had prepared demolitions along the road to the east, as the situation became ever more precarious they proved unwilling to provide troops to cover setting them off. As the Japanese advanced along the road, they were watched by Karen levies perched high in the trees. Tipped off as to the enemy's location, on 2 April Captain Arthur Bell Thompson, until recently a Steel Brothers man, and a company of 150 Burma Rifles moved forward to meet and harass the enemy, lay booby traps, carry out the necessary demolitions and crater the road to impede the Japanese advance. By driving all night from Mawchi, Boyt and his levies joined Thompson in the nick of time to launch a ferocious ambush on the unsuspecting enemy. A hail of machine-gun and rifle fire tore through the enemy ranks. The Japanese did not know what had hit them. They thought they had run into the spearhead of the entire Chinese army.

The Japanese vanguard of 700 to 800 men was stopped in its tracks. Their armoured cars and lorries ground to a screeching halt, lacerated by a storm of rifle and machine-gun fire. Bullets splattered and ricocheted off the armoured cars and sent the Japanese diving for cover. Lorries and motorcycles were reduced to flaming wrecks as grenades and booby traps exploded beneath the column. Some of the slower-footed Japanese soldiers were skewered silently by Karen crossbow bolts. Soon the hollow crump of mortars signalled that the Japanese had rallied and were fighting back, which unnerved some of the less experienced Karens. Thompson was transfixed when a mortar bomb landed between his legs. By some miracle it was a dud and failed to explode. Boyt was blown up by another, but only slightly injured. Both Boyt and Thompson, who just two months earlier had been civilians, had narrowly escaped death. Thompson was later awarded the DSO and Boyt the MC.

After an hour and a half, Thompson ordered a fighting retreat, leaving a brave levy officer, Lieutenant Ba Thein, to carry out the demolitions. As he made his way back, at each twist of the road Thein blew bridge after bridge and laid some nasty surprises for the unsuspecting enemy. Like Boyt and Thompson, Ba Thein was a recently commissioned civilian, having only weeks beforehand been a forestry assistant with Macgregor and Company. After repeated withdrawals, Thompson reached Mawchi, having proved the value of the levies. It had been a fierce firefight. Over eighty Japanese lay dead. Crucially, it gave the Chinese eight extra days to prepare their defences at Mawchi, where they fought stubbornly, inflicting heavy casualties. Stevenson's and Seagrim's faith in guerrilla attacks had been vindicated in full. As long as there was a cadre of trained troops led by good officers, the loyalty and courage of the Karens could be counted upon. However, as the enemy broke through, and the Chinese armies retreated, Stevenson ordered Thompson, Boyt and Seagrim to follow Smith and get out fast. The levies were ordered to remain in their home villages to minimise the risk of reprisals against their families, and to hide their arms and equipment pending the return of the British.

Before leaving Mawchi, Boyt had received letters from Seagrim in which he explained that he had set up an extensive network of levies, which could provide an invaluable source of intelligence, and a highly effective guerrilla force – just the sort of left-behind party that Stevenson and Oriental Mission had envisaged. But the letters also revealed just how isolated Hugh had become. Sent along obscure jungle tracks by runners, letters took days to arrive. All too often they never arrived at all. Completely unaware of the wider strategic situation, Seagrim had heard wild rumours that both Rangoon and Moulmein had been recaptured by the British. In his final note to Seagrim, Boyt told him of a little-known escape route to southern Yunnan so, should he choose to do so, he could make his own way out. With considerable skill, Boyt managed to extricate most of his stores, arms and explosives and eventually he arrived with them at Lashio on 20 April.

Far to the south, Seagrim never wavered for a moment. He resolved to stay and fight alongside his Karen levies. They were the sole left-behind party operating in Burma.

★★★

Thompson, Boyt and the handful of other Force 136 and Oriental Mission personnel in eastern Burma did not realise at the time the orders to withdraw were given quite what a desperate undertaking it would turn out to be. While the main body of the British Army withdrew in planned and ordered formations, isolated groups like the Force 136 officers in Karenni were on their own with no back-up, no supplies and no certainty about anything. In just a few months, the familiar civilian world they had known had collapsed around them. They were now pitched into a struggle for their very survival.

Having stemmed the Japanese advance along the Mawchi road, Thompson and around sixty soldiers of the 1st Battalion Burma Rifles became separated from the main body of the Army. Initially, as they withdrew northwards, their aim was to regain the British frontline, but this proved ever more elusive. On 29 April 1942, Lashio, a key strategic town on the Burma Road to China, fell. On 8 May, it was Myitkyina. By mid-May the last British rearguard had passed over the border into Assam. In just five months, the Japanese had swept across the country and expelled the British. All over Burma, the blood-red rising sun of Japan was in the ascendant. For Thompson, Boyt and the other Force 136 men, it soon became clear that the only possible escape route was a 900-mile trek to safety in Assam, travelling over appalling terrain, some of which had never been explored by Europeans. Fighting despair, disease and despondency, hotly pursued by the vengeful Japanese, and suffering from starvation and unimaginable physical hardship, their plight was desperate.

However, Thompson was fortunate to have in his party a number of outstanding men, both British and Karen, who were destined to play a seminal role in Seagrim's guerrilla campaign later in the war, in particular two British officers, Jimmy Nimmo and – for a while – Eric McCrindle. They would need all their wits to survive the gruelling four-month trek that lay ahead of them. Among the Karens were two loyal stalwarts. One was Subedar Ba Gyaw, the only surviving platoon commander. Slightly built, but a man of great character, he was later to become Seagrim's trusted companion. The other was Subedar-Major Kan Choke, a stout-hearted old warrior and one-time footballing friend of Seagrim. He formed the rock-hard centre of his unit, an inspiration to all ranks. At one point on their hideous journey, Thompson was reduced to crawling on his hands and knees, his back a suppurating mass of jungle boils

'that seemed to merge into one vast area of pus and inflammation … I could see with astonishing clarity and detachment … I was going to die. I was going to die on the track in the same way I had seen so many other people die in the past, and I was in despair; not because of death, for that seemed a pleasant release from my present condition, but because of waiting for death to come.'[5]

It was Kan Choke who rescued him, cajoling and supporting him as they inched their way forward to catch up with their comrades.

After sixteen weeks of footslogging through the jungle, wracked with hunger and weak from exhaustion, the emaciated party staggered into the

tiny settlement of Fort Hertz (now Putao), so remote and so far north that it was never occupied by the Japanese. Thompson, sporting a filthy three-inch-long beard, had lost four stone in weight. Seagrim's mentor, Noel Stevenson, who had reached Fort Hertz earlier, had built a rudimentary landing strip. In mid-August, they managed to attract the attention of a low-flying Hudson aircraft with their only Verey signal flare. The next day sacks of food were showered down upon them. Eventually, on 26 August, the party was rescued by a Dakota and flown back to India.[6]

Seagrim's closest contact, the tough Noel Boyt, was part of another disparate group. Having reached Myitkyina in northern Burma in May 1942, his party set out on a six-week trek to India via the remote Chaukkan Pass. Largely unexplored, to attempt to cross this territory at the beginning of the monsoon season was little short of suicidal. With Boyt were Lieutenant Colonel Ritchie Gardiner, a former forest manager from Macgregor and Co., later the head of Force 136 in Burma; Major Peter Lindsay; Captain Cumming and Corporal Sawyer of Oriental Mission; and Lieutenant Eric McCrindle, who had managed to join up with them after separating from Thompson's party. Their epic journey is another remarkable testament of human endurance. The leeches were a particular

Above: The Chaukkan Pass party: Noel Boyt fourth from left at rear with pipe, Ritchie Gardiner to his left with a pipe and large Burmese dah across his chest, and Eric McCrindle to the extreme right of the group.
Opposite left: Captain Arthur Bell Thompson in Fort Hertz after his epic four-month trek to safety and (opposite right) Jimmy Nimmo.

nightmare. Gardiner caught one crawling up his urethra – just in time. They assailed every part of the body: the neck, the head, the crotch and ears. Gardiner recalled: 'I woke up one night to find one in the roof of my mouth. I was dreaming that I had just got a succulent morsel of meat, and my disappointment can well be imagined.'[7] The ragged party finally staggered into Margherita after an epic journey of fifty-five days, aided in no small measure by a search party led by Gyles Mackrell, an heroic Assam tea planter. On his own initiative he saved over 200 refugees in one of the most inhospitable regions on earth for which he later received the George Medal for gallantry.[8]

The previous jungle experience of Boyt, Gardiner and McCrindle proved crucial to their eventual survival, confirming Seagrim's long-held belief that it was essential for fighting troops to be able to live off the jungle indefinitely. Knowing how to navigate through impenetrable forest, how to improvise, what to eat and what to avoid, and how to construct the most basic shelter were essential survival skills. Gardiner concluded: 'Without it, we would not have got through.'[9]

★★★

Meanwhile, far to the east and south in the Karen hills, things were going from bad to worse. As the Japanese and their BIA allies consolidated their hold on the country, lawless bands of the BIA roamed the Burmese countryside and up into the hills, raping, looting and pillaging. Seagrim was determined to fight back.

On 21 March 1942 an unruly mob of about 150 turned up in Papun under Boh Nya Na, one of the original 'Thirty Comrades', the fifth column that had been trained by the Japanese with Aung San in Hainan. With him was Boh Tun Hla, a disreputable local rogue, as his second in command. Two days later they summoned the Karen elders, announced their intention to take over the administration and ordered the surrender of all arms. When few were forthcoming, they locked up seventeen elders and sent the others out to the villages to make it clear that they meant business. After accusing the Karens of collaborating with the British, they plundered their houses for loot. Incensed, the Karens hit back. On 4 April Boh Nya Na was ambushed on the road outside Papun and killed, along with his companions. The following evening, in retribution, his lieutenant Boh Tun Hla lined up the seventeen Karen elders. They stood, bewildered and frightened, in front of a firing squad. All seventeen were machine-gunned. Two who remained alive were then bayonetted. Among the dead were three teachers, an ex-policeman and various prominent community leaders. It was an appalling atrocity, and the signal for internecine warfare.

When word got back to Seagrim, he immediately dispatched 200 levies to support Saw Darlington, his squint-eyed local levy commander, to drive the BIA from the hills. The attack was only partially successful, but it freed a number of prisoners. In retaliation, the BIA herded together as many Karens as they could find and kept them under armed guard, while making occasional forays into the surrounding countryside, burning down villages and molesting the women. One poor woman, who watched her husband killed in front of her, was forced to eat part of his body. After several skirmishes, Seagrim planned another full-scale attack on Papun, but realising that they had stirred up a veritable hornet's nest, the BIA slipped away to Bilin during the night, murdering several Karen hostages on the way. The levies sent the villagers into the safety of the forest, and then torched Papun, using scorched-earth tactics to deprive the BIA of any prospective shelter should they attempt to return. Papun lay a smouldering, skeletal ruin – the destruction not, for once, at the hands of the Japanese, but from bitter communal violence between fellow Burmese.

It was a similar pattern further south around Kadaingti. There the BIA openly invited people to kill the local Christians. Again, Seagrim leapt into action. After an initial attack under Saw Willie Saw failed, he dispatched six sections of levies to help. By attacking at noon during the hottest part of the day, they caught the BIA by surprise. Seagrim and the levies forced them to flee, raking their ranks with a hail of bullets and crossbow bolts. Despite these occasional victories, however, by the spring of 1942, the Karen hills were in a sorry state, the people short of food and living in temporary huts scattered throughout the forest. Petty feuds began to break out. The redoubtable French missionary Father Calmon worked tirelessly to keep his flock together and unite the rival factions, but increasingly they split on religious lines. Buddhists, Baptists, Catholics and Animists, who had once lived so contentedly side by side, were all at one another's throats.

If matters were bad in the hills, they were even worse among the Karens far to the south in the Irrawaddy Delta, where an escalating spiral of communal violence around the town of Myaungmya led to genocide: 152 Catholic men, women and children were massacred and their priest burned alive by the BIA in the clergy house. The rampaging mob then sated their blood lust by hacking to pieces with their dahs a group of terrified young Karen orphan girls, including a six-month-old baby. It took the arrival of disciplined Japanese troops before order could be re-imposed on the lawless BIA, the frightened Karens being warned by Colonel Suzuki to behave themselves. An uneasy peace then ensued, brokered by two influential local Karen leaders: Shwe Tun Gya, known as the 'Tiger of the Delta', and San Po Thin, a former Barnum and Bailey circus performer and erstwhile graduate of the Central School of Arts and Crafts in London.

It was the classic tragedy of Empire, repeated time and time again from Burma to Cyprus, and from India to Palestine. Once central authority and the rule of law were removed, ancient animosities resurfaced. Minorities that had once had the protection of an impartial civil power were suddenly exposed to horrifying abuse. It generated hatreds that have cast a very long shadow, one which has darkened the entire post-war history of Burma.

★★★

Completely cut off from Allied support, Seagrim was frustrated by a chronic lack of equipment, particularly money, arms, ammunition and medical supplies, and, above all, a wireless receiver/transmitter, which as a former battalion signals officer he had been trained to use. Contact with Boyt had dried up completely weeks before. Unaware how rapidly the military situation had deteriorated, and that British forces had withdrawn far to the north, in mid-April 1942 he resolved to travel to Mawchi to track down the long-vanished British Army headquarters and secure supplies. Before leaving Pyagawpu, he told the elders not to lose heart and reassured them that he would return soon – as indeed, he promised, would the British.

Having left strict instructions not to attack the Japanese for fear of reprisals, he set out in force. After a couple of days' trekking, he left most of his men at the village of Lermuti, pending his return. He carried on with just three trusted Karens – Ba Din, Po Gay and Tha U – and a local guide. On arriving in the hills overlooking Mawchi, he cautiously scanned the town through binoculars. The Japanese were swarming all over the place. Undaunted, he decided to proceed further north to Taunggyi, deep in the Shan states. Before crossing the Mawchi road, Seagrim insisted that the party kneel and silently pray. The journey took seven days along obscure jungle tracks, the guide scouting ahead to check every track and every village for signs of the enemy. Dogged by fever, first Tha U fell ill and had to be left behind, then Seagrim succumbed, but after resting for a while he carried on. By this time he was wearing native dress – a Karen tunic and woollen cap, khaki trousers and shoes, all bought in a local village bazaar. Adopting Karen dress made good sense. It was far better adapted to the climate and made him slightly less conspicuous. It also demonstrated very visibly his solidarity with the Karens. He carried no rifle or revolver, just a pair of grenades and his two beloved Bibles.

As they moved between villages, local elders and pastors provided food, shelter, hospitality and guides. Wherever he received help, he left behind testimonial certificates. To be found with one by the Japanese was a death sentence, but after the war, a couple came to light. To one pastor, Thra Shwe Laye, he left the following testimonial:

'This is to certify that Thra Shwe Laye has assisted the British Government during the period February–April 1942. He has given invaluable service in helping to raise Karen volunteers and has helped individual officers to return to their units. He has persuaded the Karens of the Mawchi area to remain loyal to the British.

This man, by remaining loyal, has endangered his life. Being a Karen leader, the Japanese have offered a big reward for his capture. He could run away but is afraid that if he did so other Karens would suffer at the hands of the Japanese. He therefore prefers to remain with his people and accept the consequences.

H. P. Seagrim, Capt., 20 April 1942'[10]

He gave another similar certificate to one of his most helpful guides:

'This is to certify that Saw Wnee has been loyal to the British and has helped in the raising of the Karen volunteers. At the risk of his own life he helped me to pass through the Japanese lines near Mawchi.'[11]

Some days after crossing the Mawchi road and entering the Shan states, Seagrim stayed at the house of a Karen sawbwa, where he met up with Lieutenant Ba Thein, the Karen officer who had been charged by Thompson with the demolitions on the Mawchi road a month earlier. On 27 April he finally reached Taunggyi in the Shan states, where he thought it prudent to get word back to Pyagawpu, so he ordered Ba Din and Po Gay to return and help organise the levies. It was an intensely poignant parting. The two Karens burst into tears at the prospect of separating. Deeply moved by their loyalty, Seagrim gave Ba Din one of his two Bibles. 'Only God can help us now,' he said. He also gave him a personal letter and testimonial certificate, which were vital in case the two came across British troops and were treated as deserters. The letter read:

'I wish to thank you very much for following me faithfully for so many miles in search of HQ. It is, I think, better for you to return to Pyagawpu and try to help the volunteers and get the Karens united. Some day the British will return and then the Karens must do great things.

Many thanks and good luck to you.

H. P. Seagrim, Capt.'[12]

For the certificate, Seagrim wrote:

'This is to certify that I have today released from service Sub. Ba Din, 2nd Bn. Burma Rifles and No. 7979 Rfn. Po Gay, 3rd Bn. Burma Rifles. I am sending these men back to Pyagawpu (near Papun), where they will remain and work with the volunteers as long as the volunteers remain in operation.

I wish to state that these two men have shown great loyalty and have followed me for many miles in my search for A.H.Q.

They are NOT deserters, and as long as they remain with the volunteers they are performing the duties of soldiers, and I have on my own responsibility told them that their service with the volunteers will count as Military Service.

H. P. Seagrim

27 April 1942, near Taunggyi'[13]

Unaware that he was embarked on a wild goose chase, and with just Ba Thein and a local guide to navigate through the jungle, Seagrim pressed on in search of the long-vanished British HQ. They weaved stealthily through the dense undergrowth and along lonely dirt tracks. Suddenly they were caught in a deadly ambush. A roaming band of Shan bandits had caught wind of their movements and lay in wait for them. Seemingly from out of nowhere, they were assailed by a blizzard of bullets. Ba Thein was cut down where he stood. As bullets fizzed and whined past him, Seagrim plunged off the path into the forest. He had escaped by the skin of his teeth, but was now alone in the forest and far from his base. Thrown back once more onto his own resources, Seagrim crept through the jungle south towards Pyagawpu. Close to Mawtudo, a local pastor, Thra Kyaw Lay, and Saw David heard a rumour that a white man had returned from the Shan states and was hiding nearby. On learning that it was Seagrim, they went to his aid.

Later, in a newly discovered letter, Thra Kyaw Lay wrote: 'David with his skilfulness and bravery brought back Capt.'[14] They sought refuge in Mawtudo, where for the next six months Seagrim lay low in a remote hut in the forest to find out what was going on before deciding on his next course of action. Acutely conscious that the Japanese were occupying the entire surrounding country, he sent out agents to garner intelligence and bolster morale among the Karens. He was helped by Thra Kyaw Lay and Thra May Sha, the pastor of Mawtudo. Both were graduates from the Baptist seminary at Insein, and both had helped raise the northern levies. In the same letter, Thra Kyaw Lay recalled:

'During Seagrim's six months' stay at Mawtudo, May Sha was always at his side, while David had to go to and fro, collecting news, arranging food, helped by many Karens ... I personally went to Papun as an agent, encouraging every Karen I came across [who was] willing to recapture Burma ... [I] studied the character of the people there and found that the Karens' loyalty to the English was still burning behind the cunning government of the Japs'

Above left: Thra Kyaw Lay and (above right) Thra May Sha, the pastor of Mawtudo, and his wife.

For Seagrim, the outlook was grim. Just two months after his last letters home to his mother and brother Jack, he was cut off in Mawtudo, far from all European contact and his loyal levies to the south. Constantly on the move, and living in a series of makeshift bamboo huts concealed deep in the forest, he was a fugitive far behind Japanese lines surrounded by a ruthless enemy.

★★★

While Seagrim was in Mawchi, back in Pyagawpu the Karens brought in a lone British straggler. He was Private Leslie Cryer of the King's Own Yorkshire Light Infantry, a light anti-tank gunner who had fought his way out of the ring of encircling Japanese forces at Martaban and then fled into the hills near Thaton. Here he hid in the forest, where he lived on leaves and herbs, and even, in his desperation, attempted to eat a scorpion. Fearful of approaching a nearby village, after two weeks he was so desperate with hunger that he decided to take the risk. The villagers were Karens, who were friendly and gave him food and shelter. Somewhat recovered, he then travelled north to Papun. There he was astonished to hear of a mysterious British officer at Pyagawpu, Hugh Seagrim, who now enjoyed the temporary rank of major. He resolved to find him and see if he could serve under him. Cryer wrote to Seagrim. When the runners reached Hugh his hopes were renewed that he might have a useful compatriot who could help him organise an effective intelligence network in the hills. Much heartened, in reply he sent Cryer R125 in currency notes, explained that he intended to return to Pyagawpu, although he was unsure when, and offered friendly words of encouragement.

Meanwhile, Cryer stayed with Saw Marshall Shwin, a well-educated schoolmaster from the Karen School at Shwegyin, who did his best to boost the soldier's morale, while his wife (Ta Roe's sister-in-law) nursed him. Shwin had fled from Shwegyin after being accused of murdering one of the Japanese-trained 'Thirty Comrades'. When Cryer arrived he was thin, weak from hunger and malaria, and dressed only in his stained uniform and an old Karen blanket. Shwin gave him another blanket and got a sweater and uniform from one of the ex-Burma riflemen in the village. He did his best to sustain him and boost his flagging spirits, as he later recalled in a letter: 'He was with us for three weeks and we tried our best to accord him protection, care and hospitality. We gave him cinchona and after a week he was a little bit better and was able to knock about near our bamboo cottage.'[15]

But Seagrim's hopes for a ready-made British recruit and comrade were short-lived. Cryer's morale had collapsed. Shwin wrote:

'He could not gain his strength ... Firstly, we could not give him proper food and he himself could not eat rice and did not find it sustaining. Secondly, being in a foreign country among strange people who were backward and uncivilised, and being in an enemy-occupied area, he naturally felt despondent. The psychological effect was that he was moody and pessimistic. This had everything to do with his definite recovery. I tried to cheer him up and at one time I had a long talk with him, just to deprive him of his defeatist pessimism, telling him that though at present things looked altogether hopeless, surely there would come a time when good would overcome evil, civilisation overcome barbarism, democracy overcome dictatorship, and so on. After that, though he was weak in both body and mind, he looked more cheerful.'[16]

In return Cryer told Shwin about his family, and his sister, Jeanne, whom he loved dearly. Shwin described how they cared for him:

'My wife tried her best to help him get his appetite. As we had no more sugar, milk, butter etc., she gave him coffee with jaggery, or honey with cakes made of rice powder. We had no wheat flour and rice powder did not prove a good substitute. She gave him chicken and rice broth every day. No doubt, he liked tea or coffee mixed with jaggery and egg. My girl servants washed his clothes twice a week and gave him warm water to sponge his body almost daily.'[17]

Eventually, Shwin had to return to Shwegyin to care for his father and family. Although advised to stay put as he did not have the strength to travel, Cryer decided to press on further north to try to find Seagrim.

Shwin arranged for him to stay at Pawmuder village, but en route Cryer was caught in torrential monsoon rains and contracted pneumonia. In his weakened condition, demoralised and despondent, he died shortly after and was buried near Pawmuder, the site marked by simple bamboo poles with a cross on top. His lonely grave still remains in the village, faithfully tended by the local Karens over seventy years later. He was just twenty-seven years old. Cryer's fate was common among left-behind soldiers, many of whom who died in similar circumstances. They could not adapt to the jungle or live off its bounty. All too often it was their despair at the apparent hopelessness of their predicament that killed them. In a melancholy postscript, in 1947 his parents wrote to Shwin to thank him for caring for their son. The letter's understatement is all the more touching for the very evident heartbreak that underlies its restraint: 'The knowledge that he was laid to rest by Christian friends amongst whom he had found refuge, and to know that his jungle grave is still tended by the Karens are thoughts which do much to comfort us in our irreparable loss.'[18]

Shwin wrote a report for Seagrim explaining what had occurred and enumerating the deceased's meagre possessions. To lose such a potential source of help, and a fellow compatriot, was a colossal disappointment for the major, and a setback for his plans. His own prospects seemed bleak, and his chances of operating an effective guerrilla campaign more remote than ever. Deep undercover in the forest at Mawtudo and accessible by just a single secret track, the long days and weeks of monotonous confinement passed slowly. Frustrated by all the inactivity, he helped the local Karens with the clearing, tilling, planting and reaping of their taungyas, the slash-and-burn-clearings they carved out of the jungle. It was unheard of for a British officer to work in such a way alongside the Karens, but Seagrim revelled in the simple, honest repetitive toil – not so different from helping out on the neighbouring farms in far-distant Whissonsett. It made a deep and lasting impression on the Karens. The British were seen as remote colonial officials or traders. For a British officer to work and pray as a friend and equal alongside them, and to read lessons from the Bible, was unprecedented – and it earned Seagrim an affectionate nickname from his allies. The Karens referred to the American Baptist missionaries as their mother, and to the British authorities as their father; the Japanese were 'shortlegs' and the British 'longlegs'. Now, on account of his height, with charming innocence Seagrim was christened Hpu Taw Kaw, or 'Grandfather Longlegs'.

Their affection may have been plentiful, but food was scarce. Rice was the staple dish and often there was little else. Seagrim and his companions were forced to forage in the forests for food. Often, when Thra May Sha could not arrange for chickens, meat or vegetables to be brought up to them, they were reduced to eating wild jungle rats. Sometimes they slit the throats of rhesus monkeys and drank their blood while it was still hot.

Although tigers and snakes were rare, leopards were common. Barking deer, wild pigs, jungle fowl and sambhur (Asian deer) offered an occasional unexpected feast, when they could be trapped.

With the onset of the monsoon rains, the forest swarmed with malarial mosquitoes and leeches. They were a perpetual irritant, sapping the strength of those on whom they gorged, as well as posing a serious risk of infection and jungle sores. Plagued by fever, Seagrim sent runners to Pyagawpu for his medical kit and a small quantity of quinine he had saved. News arrived intermittently from Thra May Sha and the local villagers, much of it uncorroborated local gossip; wild rumours of Japanese activities in the towns and villages of the plains, or recent BIA aggression towards the Karens.

The Karen education officer at Nyaunglebin managed to send various books in English for him to read, including the two seminal works on the Karens, Sir San C. Po's *Burma and the Karens*, and Smeaton's *The Loyal Karens of Burma*, as well as the Collected Works of Shakespeare, and various Baptist tracts. For Seagrim, these were an absolute godsend exercising his mind and increasing his understanding of the Karens. Yet his greatest solace lay in the Bible, which he read in its entirety over a dozen times during his lonely vigil in the hills.

During his time in the wilderness, Seagrim honed his spiritual beliefs into a lasting source of faith and fortitude. As his thoughts turned inwards, through prayer and meditation he became ever more passionate about his belief in the Divine. Quite what drove all this is hard to discern. Clearly his father's simple faith and sense of service to the community were factors, but his four brothers all had a similar upbringing without it triggering such a passionate quest for spiritual enlightenment. There is no doubt that the unquestioning faith of the Karens fed Seagrim's insatiable appetite for deeper truths. Inevitably, long periods of solitude closeted in the jungle in constant danger turned his thoughts towards the more meaningful questions of life. A 2014 study of British troops in Afghanistan revealed just how common it is for soldiers to undergo profound religious experiences while facing death or injury in the front line. [19] There are no atheists in foxholes. At the end of each day Seagrim gathered his small band around the open fire and read to them passages from the Bible, explaining their inner meaning before they recited the Lord's Prayer together. He discussed religious issues with both pastors, often giving them a passage from the Bible to contemplate before debating it with them on their next visit.

Alongside the mystical, Seagrim's humour never left him. Once he amused Thra May Sha by highlighting a passage in the Old Testament that referred to the impending destruction of many captains, laughing that he should be safe as he currently held the temporary rank of major. He was always cheerful, even in the most difficult circumstances. Ta Roe called him 'smiley-faced'. At no stage did he ever say he would try to escape from Burma as his colleagues had done. He was determined to stay with his beloved Karens.

After recovering from recurrent bouts of malaria, once again he began to lay the basis for a covert movement in the hills, ready to be activated when the British returned. While Thra May Sha was charged with maintaining his food supply, Thra Kyaw Lay was given responsibility for gathering news and intelligence. The latter was instructed to contact all the Karen ex-Burma Riflemen he could find, prepare a secret register of them, and let them know that there was 'a friend' nearby, but not to let them know his name. Having thus formed a shadow guerrilla force ready to act when the time came, Seagrim sent Thra Kyaw Lay to Pyagawpu with a bag containing a message for Army headquarters in India explaining the current situation, and to try to find out what was going on. To get the letter picked up, the pastor was told to lay out KV for Karen Volunteers in large white cloth letters whenever a British plane flew over. The bag containing the message was strung on cord between two poles, ready for a flying pick-up, but after three months of waiting not a single British plane passed overhead. While there, the pastor sold three government elephants to raise money to pay the levies.

Determined to move away from Mawtudo, which was insalubrious and malarial, in December 1942 Seagrim wrote to Ta Roe to see whether he could move back to Pyagawpu. Although the operation was risky, the BIA had been expelled from the hills and the Japanese had shown no great inclination to venture further, preferring to consolidate their hold on Burma in Rangoon and the towns and villages of the central plain. After consultation with the village elders, Ta Roe sent two of his own elephants to carry the Englishman down. He was joined for part of the way by Thra Kyaw Lay. En route, Seagrim stayed with Francis Ah Mya, a Karen Anglican priest with whom he spent virtually the entire night in an intense spiritual exchange. Francis was keenly interested in the Oxford Group Movement and explained many of its ideas. For Seagrim, this was a revelation. Suddenly his own personal beliefs were focused in pin-sharp clarity.

Known as Moral Re-armament, the Oxford Group Movement was a religious revolution founded by Dr Frank Buchanan, an American Christian missionary, which enjoyed great popularity and success in the 1930s. Based on the notion of universal Christian fellowship, it offered an alternative Christian vision to militarism, totalitarianism and, in particular, Nazism. International problems, it argued, stemmed from personal selfishness and fear. If the world was to be changed, the only way forward was to change personal lives. It asked: how can you abolish tyranny in the world unless first you abolish it in yourself? At a personal level, it advocated four simple moral standards against which any action or thought should be tested: absolute honesty, absolute purity, absolute unselfishness and absolute love. The Group believed in quiet shared reading of spiritual literature to discover God's perspective on any problem. Sharing allowed one to be healed, and therefore it was a blessing to share. Sharing built trust and mutual respect.

For Hugh, this was a moment of epiphany. Suddenly, here was the creed for which he had been searching, complementing what he had already absorbed from his eclectic forays into Buddhist philosophy with its emphasis on transcending the self and overcoming desire. Before proceeding in the morning, Seagrim received Holy Communion, perhaps as a seal on his newly found coda on how to act in future with greater moral certainty. Emaciated, drawn, barefoot and bearded, but curiously elated and looking more than ever like the ascetic monk described by Stevenson a year previously, before too long he arrived at Chawido, a small village a few miles north-west of Pyagawpu, where Ta Roe was living. Accompanied by three Karens and two Kachins, he was dressed in a Karen tunic, with a tommy gun under one arm, a Bible under the other and a pistol tucked into his belt. He had no spare clothes, no mosquito net and no possessions other than an old blanket.

Ta Roe and his wife were devoted to Seagrim. Both were well-educated Christians. Although Ta Roe's father and two of his brothers were animists, the two religions co-existed seamlessly. Seagrim was welcomed into the family and enjoyed playing with their two young children, Caroline and

Rosalind. However, it was still too dangerous for Seagrim and his men to remain in the village. Although the Japanese tended to avoid coming up directly into the hills, if a BIA informer got wind of their return, they would not hesitate to inform the authorities, or take direct action themselves against the entire village. So, once again, Seagrim was banished to a hut deep in the forest. Here he was kept supplied regularly with food and provisions by Ta Roe and the local villagers. Chawido was a much healthier location than Mawtudo, but after a month Seagrim became increasingly frustrated hiding away. In the end, in spite of the risks, he insisted on returning to Ta Roe's old house in Pyagawpu, where he had spent his early days in the hills. Here, reinforced by a regular diet of fresh vegetables, eggs and chicken, he began to recover his health and put on weight. By means of a stream of letters and runners, he quietly organised the levies in the surrounding areas into a state of readiness.

Each Sunday, Ta Roe met him at the church. Seagrim sat at the front with the village elders. Occasionally the major preached in Burmese, or wrote down his innermost thoughts and shared them with the congregation in the manner of the Oxford Group Movement. Frequently, he discussed the Bible with Ta Roe. Publicly, he pledged his future life to the Karens. 'We must not be downcast, Ta Roe,' he would say. 'We are Christians. After the war, I don't want to go on being a soldier. I want to become a missionary and work among the Karens. I have lived with them now so long that I would like to go on living with them always. I want to devote my life to the Karens.'[20]

After Seagrim had been living openly in Pyagawpu for a while, Father Calmon visited for a day to tell him that some of the levies in the south were getting out of hand and abusing the local villagers. One in particular at Kadaingti was causing problems. Calmon asked Seagrim to rein him in. Seagrim promised to summon the man. He wrote to Saw Willie Saw and the other levy commanders to stress the need for discipline. Calmon was another who was impressed deeply by Seagrim. He thought him a very fine man. Like so many others, he realised that all the Karens loved him, but he was uneasy that Seagrim was living quite so openly in the village. He urged caution and advised that it would be more prudent to retreat to a forest hut known to just a handful of locals and to travel only at night. Calmon was worried that the Karens were like children – too trusting and with no concept of the need for security. Seagrim refused to heed his warning. He simply retorted, 'I trust the Karens.'

When Calmon trekked back to his mission near Papun, he was astonished to find a young British soldier waiting for him. His name was Ras Pagani, a Corporal in the Reconnaissance Regiment, a combative, barrel-chested squaddie with the heart of a lion. He was also a fearless serial escape artist with an amazing story to tell.

Chapter 5

The Master of His Fate

'In the fell clutch of circumstance
I have not winced nor cried aloud
Under the bludgeonings of chance
My head is bloody, but unbowed.

It matters not how strait the gate,
How charged with punishments the scroll.
I am the master of my fate:
I am the captain of my soul.

W. E. HENLEY

When Father Calmon arrived in Papun, the young British soldier was at the mission house. Pagani had arrived shortly before, escorted through the hills by a string of Karen levies into the hands of Father Loizeau, who had entertained him the previous night with a lavish meal of roast peacock, sweet potatoes and green vegetables, all washed down with a bottle of French red wine. They had talked late into the night. Pagani had told Loizeau a tale so incredible that initially the good Father had some difficulty believing it, but gradually he realised that Pagani's story was true. Pagani related how he had escaped from Dunkirk – alone; how he had then escaped from Singapore; how he had just escaped from the Burma railway – alone; and how he was now intending to travel right across Burma to rejoin the Allies in India – alone. The two French priests began to realise that Pagani was a pretty exceptional man.

Roy Anthony Stephen Pagani was born in Fulham on 23 July 1915. His parents were just seventeen years old, his father English and his mother French. At the age of four, in 1919, along with his two-year-old sister, Nina, he was kidnapped by his father and his current girlfriend and taken to France. An inveterate womaniser, his father operated coach tours of the French battlefields in the summer and spent the winter with his mistress on the French Riviera. At the age of seven, the young Roy was left in Cannes with his father's mistress, who promptly eloped with another man and abandoned him. His father never returned, leaving the two children alone and destitute on the harbour front. Quite by chance, they were rescued by a nun, who took them to her convent school in Cannes. Shortly afterwards, Roy was shipped to a boy's convent – the L'Institution de Saint Joseph la Navarre at La Crau, near Toulon, a vast complex with its own farm and vineyards. At the school the emphasis was on making the boys self-reliant and resourceful. 'They were the most wonderful days of my life,' Pagani wrote later.[1]

Alongside conventional lessons and religious instruction, the boys were taught practical things that would stand them in good stead later in life, like mending shoes, sewing, knitting, cooking, farming and country pursuits. At weekends they embarked on expeditions into the surrounding hills to hunt wild boar and deer, forage for mushrooms, fish, and collect flowers and insects for study. In between lessons they played Le Drapeau, a team game in which individuals needed to break through an opposing team to reach a flag at the end of the playground. Pagani was convinced that this game gave him the backbone to survive his future ordeals by forging within him an absolute determination to be the best at whatever he attempted.

In 1927, his mother managed to find him, but as he could speak no English she decided to leave him there to finish his schooling. Two years later he returned to England, uncertain what to do. He started working in

Left: Roy Pagani, aged 17 and (above) his beloved Pip, whom he married in 1939.

various hotels, first as a page boy, and later as a commis-waiter, commis-chef and chef waiter, ending up at the stylish new Park Lane Hotel. On his eighteenth birthday, as he was cycling past the barracks of the East Surrey Regiment in Kingston-upon-Thames, he wondered if he was fit enough to enlist. At just five foot three he was actually an inch below regulation height and had the top of his left thumb missing, but after the carnage of the First World War recruitment was poor. Eager for new men, the recruiting sergeant suggested that his heels were a little heavy on the ground and told him to raise his head slightly, but he was accepted: 'Before I knew it I was 820870 Private Pagani, and told to report back in two weeks. I cycled home, told my mother and she went mad.'[2] After six months' training at Shorncliffe Barracks, in mid-1934 he was posted to Faizabad in India, where he learned signalling. Two years later, he was dispatched to Poona to learn vehicle maintenance and driving. The following year his battalion was shipped to Khartoum, before returning to Colchester in January 1939.

It was here, on 13 March 1939, that Roy met his future wife, Pip, a quiet shy teenager who, like many girls of her age, wanted to be a ballerina. After first going out with her best friend, he asked Pip out and was immediately smitten. 'She was just sixteen years old. We courted for five months and, like all soldiers, I tried "to get my leg over", and eventually decided I would have to marry her. This I always kidded her about, but I really did love her.'[3] Just a week before the outbreak of the war, on 28 August 1939, they married. Shortly after, he was sent to France as part of the British Expeditionary Force (BEF), where, with his fluent French, he was deployed as an interpreter and driver for brigade headquarters.

In May 1940, as the Germans scythed through France, strafed, bombed and machine-gunned, the East Surreys, together with what remained of the BEF, conducted a gallant fighting retreat to Bray Dunes, near Dunkirk. Here, the drivers were told to abandon their vehicles and make their way to Dunkirk itself. With characteristic ingenuity, Pagani booby-trapped his lorry with a hand grenade attached to the filler cap, so that anyone unscrewing it would pull the pin from the grenade and get a nasty surprise as the petrol tank blew up. A loner at heart, and never one to follow the herd, he did not head towards Dunkirk with everyone else. He could see and hear the incessant bombing and shelling, so he turned eastwards alone, looking for a boat. It was a perilous undertaking. Eventually, he found one and sailed to England single-handed. Four days later, he reached the little east-coast village of Shingle Street, got a free ride to Ipswich, then a train to Colchester, and finally walked to the house of his mother-in-law, who promptly fainted when she opened the door.

Seven days later Pagani reported for duty and was sent to Yeovil to join what remained of his regiment. Incensed by what was happening to his beloved France, fed up with out-of-date British tactics and equipment, and loathing the Germans, Pagani was determined to get back into action. He volunteered for the Commandos and then the Parachute Regiment, but, rejected by both, eventually joined the 18th Reconnaissance Battalion, part of the newly formed Reconnaissance Corps. One of a hard core of just a dozen regulars who had seen action, Pagani commanded real respect and was nicknamed 'Ras' by his comrades, after his initials. After two weeks' leave with his new young wife, he was seen off by Pip at Colchester station where, like so many other wartime sweethearts, they said their goodbyes. Ras renewed his promise to return. Neither knew then the hell that he was destined to face, or that it would be five long years before he could hold her in his arms once again, but it was the promise he made then that gave him the strength and fortitude to endure the unendurable.

After leaving England at the end of October 1941, and a circuitous voyage via Nova Scotia, the 18th Division, of which Ras was part, sailed for Egypt, during which time the regulars were made lance corporals, and Ras was elevated to corporal because of his knowledge of weaponry. But with the situation in the Far East deteriorating, they were diverted first to Bombay, where they trained for two months, before embarking on the *Empress of Asia* in a convoy for Singapore. On 4 February 1942, as the ship approached the Banka Strait, some of the Liverpool Irish stokers from the neutral Éire, demanded danger money. When the captain refused, unbelievably they went on strike.[4] The ship then lagged behind the convoy. It was pounced upon by high-flying Japanese planes and bombed – but it stayed afloat. The next morning, as the ship turned into the last ten-mile stretch into Singapore Docks, five enemy dive-bombers swooped out of the sky and scored three direct hits. One bomb plummeted straight down the funnel, exploding amidships in a fountain of yellow flame. At a stroke, all her precious cargo of arms and equipment that might just have tipped the balance against the Japanese was lost.

As fires spread and the ship listed, an Australian destroyer, HMAS *Yarra*, came alongside, guns blazing. Ordered to abandon ship, Pagani ducked below, retrieved his rifle and pack – in which he had photographs of his wife and newborn son – and then leapt onto the deck of the *Yarra*. It seemed like Dunkirk all over again. The destroyer successfully landed the troops on the island, where immediately they were marched to the racecourse to be re-equipped with a handful of Bren guns. On 9 February 1942, they were ordered into the front line, north of Bukit Timah village. After being cut off several times from their main unit and mortared, Ras's men were jittery and fearful. He reassured them, promised to get them through and warned them against taking shelter in the drainage ditches, as the enemy was firing captured Bofors anti-aircraft guns horizontally along the gullies, flensing anyone in the way.

Having made it back to headquarters with his section intact, at 4.15 p.m. on 15 February, Ras, as the senior NCO, was ordered to collect and stack all available weapons pending the British surrender. Having done as he was told, he then approached Major Dutton, his acting commanding officer, told him he was unable to comply with the order to surrender and intended to escape. Dutton wished him luck. As at Dunkirk, Ras set off alone into the inferno of the blazing city. With buildings collapsing around him, and scorched by gusts of intense heat from countless fires, he headed towards the port, which was at the very eye of the firestorm. Close to Raffles Hotel, he found an army truck hit by shellfire; the two men in the front seat were dead and burning like human torches. Corpses lay in the streets, frozen into grotesque postures; soldiers, civilians, women and children alongside the obscene bloated corpses of animals and livestock. Ras put his head down and kept on walking.

At the docks he came across a twenty-foot sampan with a small sail and a rudder. It was filled with fish manure, which stank to high heaven, but it was an ideal unobtrusive craft in which to make his escape – although to quite where he was unsure. Australia lay over 2,000 miles away. Sumatra was the obvious choice, and there were myriad islands in between where he might find sanctuary. While deciding on his next move, he spotted four Europeans on the beach and suggested that they join him and have a pull at the oars: 'We called each other by nicknames, one was "Darkie" and the other "Len".'5 He never knew their surnames. He blessed his convent days for schooling him well in geography, and the army for teaching him navigation by the stars. After grabbing some provisions and water from a nearby Indian Army store, he steered across the harbour. Astern lay the great city, consumed by fires and explosions, groaning and crackling in its death throes, and bathed in a ghastly orange glow. It seemed an utter catastrophe.

Exhausted by days of fighting, the men landed on a small island near the quarantine station of St John's, hid the boat under some overhanging trees and dropped into a deep sleep. Awaking in mid-afternoon, they found a freshwater stream, and slaked their thirst. Then they noticed a launch approaching St John's, full of troops. Initially thinking that they were fellow escapees, Ras soon realised they were Japanese soldiers with fixed bayonets, searching for survivors. The men stayed hidden, praying the Japanese would not head their way next. Fortunately, the soldiers moved off towards the city, but the near miss made Ras realise that they needed to travel at night and lay up wherever possible during the day.

That night, as they sailed towards Sumatra, he took his last view of Singapore: a shoreline of fire, smeared with a colossal column of thick black smoke rising high over the city from the burning oil tanks on the island, which covered everything for miles around in glutinous black smuts. After passing several islands, just before dawn Ras saw some local people waving to them. On approach they seemed friendly, so he landed and was met by a Chinese towkay from whom he bought a sail. Calculating that, as a Chinese, the man was likely to be hostile to the Japanese, Ras trusted him, and was given food and a bed for the day – then was invited to a heavy drinking session. At nightfall Ras was woken from an alcoholic stupor and given food and a can of water, and they were all sent on their way.

After further island-hopping, six days later they pulled into a much larger island called Moro, where they found an impromptu escape organisation manned by British soldiers, who were supplying escapees with five-gallon cans containing tinned food, army biscuits, a bottle of rum, cigarettes and matches. The soldiers pointed them towards Sumatra, which was not yet occupied by the Japanese, and told them to travel eastwards to the mouth of a large river (the Inderagiri), then follow it up to join other stages of the escape route. It was another short hop of about twenty-five miles and the very real prospect of freedom. During that night and the following day, the men made good progress, lying atop the fish manure, which smelt abysmally in the heat – but later that night their luck ran out. On the skyline, looming nearer, towering masses of coal-black cloud – natural clouds this time – lit from within by intense flashes of lightning cast an infernal glow across the rising seas. As the sun died, the tiny boat hit the edge of a massive tropical cyclone, presaged by a continuous barrage of rolling thunder. The first spluttering droplets soon turned into a deluge. Having myself endured a ferocious tropical cyclone on land in the Andaman Islands, it is a fearful experience; but for Ras and his companions, adrift at sea, it must have been truly terrifying.

The wind rose, the sea swelled, and as Ras lowered and secured the sail, the full force of the storm hit them. Continuous lances of rain scarified and goaded every inch of their bodies. The sea broke over them in waves, the wind shrieked mercilessly, and the frail craft was tossed and buffeted in all directions. Ras was forced to stretch himself across the boat, hands on one side and feet on the other, clinging on for dear life. As the fish manure became waterlogged, the boat lost more of its buoyancy. Ras was terrified that it would sink beneath them. For hours – it seemed an eternity – he held on frantically, dazed, soaked and increasingly exhausted. Robert Hamond perhaps best encapsulated Ras's despair in his account of the voyage in *The Flame of Freedom*:

'The wind was now screaming out of the darkness, plucking at him as if to drag him into the sea, and foaming waves broke over the boat so that he was often submerged in the surf, which poured over him. The end must be near, he thought miserably; he found a little strength for prayer but, in his heart, could find no hope of survival.'[6]

Then, just when all hope had gone, as dawn broke, the storm abated as suddenly as it had begun. Drenched and numb with cold, Ras slowly raised the sail. As the sun climbed in the sky, he could see that they were just a mile offshore in the mouth of a wide river. By sheer luck, or providence, they had been swept into the Inderagiri river.

After inching the boat cautiously upriver for several hours, Ras was hailed from the shore. To his relief, he saw that the voices belonged to British soldiers, who formed another link in the improvised escape chain. As he beached the sampan, he had to be helped ashore, rigid with cramp and exhaustion, having braced himself across the boat for so many hours during his nightmare voyage. His four companions staggered away and did not rejoin him. Ras concluded that he had been too severe a disciplinarian conserving food and water while at sea, and that they had had enough of him, but he was not bothered and preferred to travel alone. He was incredibly lucky to have survived.

After being plied with a hot drink and food, he was put on a lorry that took him fifty miles upriver to Rengat, then by train to Padang, where he expected the Royal Navy to transport him and other escapees to safety in India. Arriving at Padang on 1 March 1942, surrounded by his fellow countrymen, and now some distance from the Japanese, Ras felt elated to have escaped from the jaws of death for the second time in less than two years. Convinced that he was free, he threw his boots away, relieved at not having to face incarceration or months of covert trekking through enemy-occupied country – but his joy was short-lived.

At Padang, over 1,000 men of all ranks and services were accommodated in a Malay school. In his own inimitable manner, Ras did not want to be given any responsible jobs, so he stated his rank as private while he waited for a ship to ferry him to Colombo or Trincomalee in Ceylon. Various ships drew in and took off, crammed with men, women and children; several proved to be death traps, sunk en route by Japanese submarines with great loss of life. The last, SS *Palopa*, sailed on 7 March, leaving behind large numbers of British troops still awaiting rescue. A week later, they were told that Japanese troops were approaching the town. In despair at the prospect of becoming a prisoner, Ras joined up with a party of sailors from HMS *Prince of Wales* and hijacked an old steam tug with the intention of heading for Ceylon. Just hours before the Japanese arrival, the tug steamed off, loaded with supplies – only to be turned back at the harbour mouth by shots across the bow, fired by local soldiers. Back on dry land, Ras was forced to watch the Japanese move in, the sun glinting cruelly on their bayonets. Over 1,200 British, Dutch and Australian soldiers were herded back into the school. Despondent and frustrated that all his efforts had come to nought, Ras endured his first taste of captivity.

On 9 May, after the Allies had been left to fend for themselves for a while, the Japanese instructed them to form a labour battalion comprising twenty officers and around 480 men, divided into four companies. Thus came into being the British Sumatra Battalion, an agglomeration of ill-disciplined odds and sods from a variety of different units – including various troublemakers. This assorted group was commanded by a twenty-nine-year-old captain of the Royal Norfolk Regiment, Desmond

Pretyman Apthorp, known as Dudley – and more affectionately by his men as 'Appy'. As a senior British officer, Apthorp rapidly welded this loose group into a coherent military formation known as 'Appy's locusts'. He commanded widespread loyalty and respect, shouldering an immense responsibility for his men over the next three years. One of his officers, Lieutenant Powers, later wrote of him: 'Here truly was the right man in the right place at the right time … a man of courage, moral fibre and integrity with a lovely sense of humour.'[7] Described as looking like a cross between Lawrence of Arabia and the film star Leslie Howard, to most of the men, including Pagani, he was the only 'proper officer': a regular soldier who would appear at tenko or roll call twice a day, properly dressed with regulation cap, a cap badge of Britannia made from a filed-down Australian penny (now in the Imperial War Museum), and a rotting shirt and shorts. To men dressed in little more than loin cloths, he was an inspiration who instilled discipline and leadership over what could so easily have become a disparate rabble. He made a stand against Japanese demands on his emaciated troops, earning himself many vicious beatings that angered the men, but which he took with crushing dignity. Eric Burgoyne, his sergeant major, thought he 'led by example – the true tradition of an "English" officer and gentleman. He was without doubt the most obstinate man I have ever had the pleasure of knowing.'[8]

Under Appy's watchful eye, over the next three days Ras and his fellow prisoners were moved 100 miles to Fort de Kok in north Sumatra, and then on in stages via Kotanopan and Taroetoeng to Uni Kampong, where Dutch internees shared their food and clothing with them. On 15 May they were marched to the port of Belawan Deli, where they were embarked for Burma on a small steamer rather ironically called the *England Maru*, which had been built in Selby in 1898. Battened down in the sweltering and foetid hold, conditions were appalling: there was little room to lie down and dysentery was rife. Periodically, rancid food in the form of a thin vegetable soup was lowered down to them in buckets. After disembarking some Australians off Victoria Point, the convoy sailed on to Mergui, where it arrived on 25 May and the men were then marched through torrential monsoon rains to the high school. They were then deployed building an extension to the aerodrome. Refusing to help the Japanese overtly, Ras volunteered for the camp hospital, working under Colonel Sir Albert Ramsey, the eminent medical

officer. It was grim work. Death was an everyday occurrence. Ras recalled:
'I remember vividly a young sailor, only about eighteen I think, who was dying, named Weaver. I stayed with him all night and he died the following morning. Then, regretfully, a job I had to do several times later: that was with a hosepipe wash the dead body, plug the holes in the body i.e. mouth and anus … so that no fluids from the body leaked onto the two bearers, [then] after, the corpse was sewn into a rucksack which was slung between two poles, carried by two men coolie fashion to the burial site.'[9]

On 11 August they were embarked once again for Tavoy on the *Tatu Maru*, marching down to the docks to the sound of an impromptu Australian band playing 'Good Old Sussex by the Sea', accompanied by the massed rattling of old tin cans and other utensils. Ahead lay another appalling voyage through rough seas, with over 700 men crammed into a ship with space for only 200. Food consisted of a small net of loaves the size of buns, all green with mould. Mercifully, the voyage was short. On arrival in Tavoy, they were accommodated in the Anne Heseltine Home, a large English-style colonial building, where they were deployed on the construction of an aerodrome – but were lucky to receive regular supplies of food covertly from the local pro-British resistance. Here, with astonishing audacity, while ostensibly repairing a high-powered transmitter that the Japanese had discovered in a civilian house, Sergeant Les Bullock RAF purloined enough spares to build a camp radio, which was powered by a lorry battery. For almost three years the secret was kept. The radio was to provide virtually the sole source of outside news for over 10,000 PoWs working in Burma. It took unbelievable courage. When two makeshift radios were discovered subsequently at another camp, the operator, CO and senior NCO were tortured by the kempeitai, the Japanese secret police, who systematically broke every bone in their bodies before executing them.

For some time during that summer of 1942 and into the autumn, Ras had been refining his plans to escape. He realised that for any European to have a chance of escaping successfully, they would need to blend in with the surrounding population. He was fortunate in being short and stocky and therefore about the same height as many locals. Unlike so many taller Europeans, he thought he would not be conspicuous. He was tanned and dark-eyed, and having long since discarded his army boots, he had practised walking barefoot for miles to harden his feet. After carefully watching and studying Indians and local people, he was confident that he could adopt their mannerisms, habits, postures and gait.

On 21 October, the soldiers were all issued with new number tags – always the sign of an impending move. In due course, they were bundled into two barges and taken to Moulmein, where they were housed for a night in the town jail: a typical British colonial prison with radiating cell blocks set behind high boundary walls, which remains exactly the same today. The next day, they were taken to the station, crowded into cattle trucks and transported to Thanbyuzayat, the base camp for the construction of the Burma end of the infamous Death Railway. The railway was intended to form a crucial supply line from Bangkok to Moulmein, where it would link up with the rest of the Burmese rail network. If it were completed, the Japanese could pour supplies into Lower Burma overland by rail from Siam, and thus avoid the long and hazardous sea route around Malaya. Construction took place from Siam on one side and Burma on the other, with the aim of meeting up at the Three Pagodas Pass. For every mile of track laid, 393 men died from malnutrition, disease and brutality. The Allied death toll alone was nearly 13,000. The British Sumatra Battalion, much depleted by sickness and death, mustered only 400 officers and men combined. On arrival at the base camp, the men were paraded before the Japanese commandant Lieutenant Colonel Nagatomo, who stood on a table and raged: 'You are the remnants of a decadent white race and fragments of a rabble army. This railway will go through, even if your bodies are to be used as sleepers.'[10]

Starting from Thanbyuzayat, the Japanese had already cut the trace of the line and built camps at roughly five-kilometre intervals – some occupied by Burmese labourers and others by Allied PoWs. The Japanese engineers took no interest in their welfare. Responsibility for organising all the camps on the Burmese side of the line was vested in Nagatomo, a task at which he was extremely inefficient. Increasingly, he relied on PoW officers. The senior Australian officer, Brigadier Varley, virtually took over all the administration and clerical work involving the movements of the PoWs, including working parties, medical care and conditions. Nagatomo's laziness had an unexpected advantage. By being so reliant on Allied support, the threat of non-cooperation was usually sufficient incentive to discourage him from making outlandish demands. As a consequence, the seriously sick were not forced to work, which meant that the death rate was far lower than on the Siamese side.

Pagani was shipped with the rest of his battalion to the 18 kilometre camp, at Hlepauk, where a force of some 500 Australians was already in occupation. On the way, he took a keen interest in his surroundings and the general lie of the land. The camp was in a clearing in a valley with a small stream running through it, close to the railway and road. To one side, a range of hills swathed in dense jungle sloped up 1,000 feet high. The camp followed the usual pattern, with well-built bamboo huts for the Japanese at one end, a large open square parade ground at the centre and crude shelters for PoWs around the other two sides. There was a cookhouse in the corner and a guardroom at the gate. The camp was unenclosed, the Japanese recognising that 800 miles of jungle were a far more effective deterrent than a barbed-wire fence. The day after their arrival, at the end of October 1942, Colonel Nagatomo came up to the camp and, with the aid of an interpreter, made a garbled speech that contained the usual bizarre mixture of friendliness and threats. He emphasised the sheer impossibility of escape and the dire consequences for those that tried:

'You should be contented. If there is a man here who has at least one per cent of a chance of escape, we shall make him face the extreme penalty. If there is one foolish man who is trying to escape, he shall see big jungles towards the east, which are absolutely impossible for communication. Towards the west he shall see boundless ocean, and above all to the points north and south our Nippon Army is staying and guarding. You will easily understand the impossibility of complete escape. A few such cases of ill-omened matters which happened in Singapore shall prove the above and you should not repeat such foolish things although it is a last chance after great embarrassment.'

Finally, he left them with no illusions as to what lay ahead: 'We will build the railroad if we have to build it over the white man's body ... You are merely rabble.'[11]

For the vast majority of people, this would have had a salutary effect and discouraged any glimmering hope of salvation, but for Ras it did the exact opposite. Forced to work on the line day after day, knee-deep in mud, plagued by insects and leeches, and sleeping in damp, leaking bamboo huts, he realised that, as the months passed, he was only likely to get weaker. In addition, after two weeks the Japanese camp guards had all been replaced by Koreans, who had a notorious reputation for sadistic cruelty. If ever he was going to make a break for it, the time had come. It was mid-November 1942.

Mentally, he sketched out a plan – to make a dash for the sea, just ten miles away, and then along the coast or, if that failed, to double back to the line of the Moulmein-Ye railway and follow it north to Moulmein and beyond, which he knew would be crawling with Japanese troops and BIA sympathisers. After Moulmein, he would have to travel at least 600 miles on foot to the Arakan Yomas, across a country of which he knew little, with a price of R250 on his head, before having any prospect of joining up with Allied forces. Other than basic Hindustani, he spoke no native language. His chances of success were minimal and the risks enormous, but with his innate self-reliance and resourcefulness, plus his practical experience of escaping from both Dunkirk and Singapore, he was confident he could do it. Even though he was a loner, to choose to leave the fellowship and support of his comrades in favour of an uncertain future alone in the middle of the jungle, surrounded by hostile forces, almost beggars belief. It is a remarkable testament to the sheer stubbornness and bloody-mindedness of the man that he could even contemplate such an appalling risk. The consequences of failure did not bear thinking of – sadistic torture and summary beheading. No quarter would be given.

He resolved to pose as an Indian, to leave all his possessions and clothing behind and wear only a loincloth and an Indian turban, or pagri. He would carry only a little money and his identity discs, so if caught he could prove he was a soldier and not a native spy. He had devised his exit earlier. In the camp, sick parade took place after breakfast, after which the working party went out up the line. If the Japanese were not satisfied with the numbers, they would scour through the sick, select those they considered fit to work, beat them up a little as malingerers, give them a changkul – a small trenching tool – and send them on, crucially without escort, to join the main party. This gave Pagani the perfect chance.

A couple of days before making the final break for it, he reported sick and was able to leave the camp unescorted. He climbed the hills at the rear of the camp to get a panoramic view of the surrounding country and plan his route. He could see the sea. If all went according to plan, when he left he would not be missed until evening tenko, and then he would have all night, as well as all day, to get clear. Subsequently, Ras maintained he never told anyone else of his plans, for fear of the secret leaking out, or of reprisals against those who knew, but some of his comrades were only too aware of his intentions and remembered the day vividly. A young naval stoker nicknamed 'Spence' Tracey recalled:

'"You'll never make it," we told him. Then he suddenly said, "Well, so long. I'm off," and just walked away into the jungle. He had no gear, maybe that helped, also no waiting for it to get dark, or fences to climb; there was nothing to stop him. We wished him luck, and that was it. It was tenko [before] the Nips knew.'[12]

About 100 yards from the camp gate, after a quick look around to ensure that he was not being watched, Ras melted into the jungle and disappeared. Stanley Saddington, a leading aircraftsman in the RAF, saw him go:

'I saw him leave the camp, ostensibly to join the workforce, but I never saw him again. It was nine or ten o'clock in the morning when he walked out. He was wearing shorts, socks and boots, and he carried a haversack over his shoulder. He was conspicuously European in appearance – short and thick-set, fair-skinned and red-haired. He had a heavy beard and, emblazoned across his chest, a huge tattoo depicting a chariot and horses.'[13]

Saddington's account suggests that Pagani kept his change of gear in his haversack, but the reference to him as appearing 'conspicuously European' is clearly at odds with Ras's own self-image as a man who could pass unchecked as a native.

When the Japanese found out, they did not appear to be at all concerned. They told Tracey and Apthorp to go out and find him, but by then it was 7 p.m. and getting dark: 'The lads were all chockers [tired] to say the least. But Lt Villiers kept calling out, in the hope that Pagani was nearby. One of the best, I thought, was: "Come back Pagani, we know you don't mean it, you haven't got your water bottle!"'[14] For Saddington, the reaction of the Japanese was quite comical. They selected a score of prisoners and told them to search the scrub around the camp, shouting to Pagani that, provided he returned to camp, he would not be shot. Saddington recalled:

'Off went the searchers into the bush, while the rest of us waited on the parade ground in the gathering dusk. For some minutes, all was silence. Then up went the first cry: "Come back, Pagani, they won't shoot you." This caused some tittering, which increased when the same entreaty was heard shouted from the opposite side of the camp. After that, at short intervals, the message to the escapee could be heard being bellowed from all angles, but at a constantly lessening volume as the search area widened. But to no avail. There was no response from Pagani, who, having departed ten hours previously, I would think was well out of earshot. The pantomime continued until well after dark. The searchers were then recalled, counted and the parade dismissed.'[15]

Once more the game was afoot, with Ras playing cat and mouse for his life against a ruthless enemy. Once more he was on his own, and once more he was heading for freedom ... or so, at least, he believed.

Chapter 6

Walking with Destiny

'I … will never leave you!
Never, ever during your trials and testings.
When you saw only one set of footprints
It was then that I carried you.'
MARGARET FISHBACK POWERS

Euphoric at being free once more, Ras plunged westwards through the jungle at high speed, aiming for the coast, but after a while he ran into dense virgin forest, which slowed him down. It took him four hours to reach the sea near Amherst, but the coastline was deserted. There was no prospect of stealing a boat as he had done in his escapes from both Dunkirk and Singapore, so immediately he put Plan B into operation. Backtracking to the railway, which he reached in mid-afternoon, he followed it northwards to Thanbyuzayat, arriving at the outskirts in the late afternoon. Having lost time and distance searching for a boat, and still only fifteen miles from the camp, he knew he could not afford to wait for darkness, so bold as brass he rubbed dirt on his face and legs, wound his pagri around his head and walked straight down the main street, imitating as best he could the gait of an Indian labourer. Immediately several villagers stared at him, whispering 'Nippon' among themselves, thinking he was a Japanese plant spying on the local population, it being not uncommon for the Japanese, in disguise, to pounce on suspects and hang them from the nearest tree. Fortunately, no one challenged him.

Suddenly, and without any warning, he walked straight into a Japanese guard of five soldiers. They marched directly towards him in line abreast. Overwhelmed with fear, his heart thumping, he had sufficient self-control to avert his gaze, walk on a little further, and then casually saunter over to the gateway of a house, where he squatted down in the drainage ditch as if urinating, just like an Indian, with his back to the guard. His nerves were stretched to breaking point; every second seemed an eternity as they marched nearer and nearer and nearer, but puffed up by their own self-importance, to Ras's vast relief they simply strutted past. It was a narrow escape. After a short time collecting himself, and making sure the coast was clear, he continued up the road, searching for a refuge in which to hide, and vowing that in future he would travel only at night.

By this time, the market was closed. Noticing an unobtrusive stall near a wall, he ducked under the curtain at its base. Drained by his journey and shaken by his recent close shave, he fell into a deep sleep. When it was dark, he re-emerged and headed off down the street to pick up the railway north to Moulmein. Hitting the tracks, he moved at a rapid pace, striding barefoot along the wooden sleepers and making good progress across the country. When dawn broke he had covered sixteen miles and was out in open country, in a wide flat stretch of lush green padi fields. Looking around for somewhere to hide, he spotted a small native hut, towards which he headed. It was the home of an Indian family. Using sign language and some rudimentary Hindustani, he made himself understood and was beckoned in. They gave him a meal of dhal, rice and tea and a place to sleep, indicating that they would keep a watch for any Japanese. They woke him in the late afternoon, gave him another meal and, after he had thanked them profusely, he was sent on his way, guided past a nearby small village by one of their young children. Pagani later wrote: 'The moon was very bright and I was able to move fast by stepping from sleeper to sleeper. I felt very confident at this stage, having learned that it was mostly Indians who grew the rice and henceforth would spend my days with this type if at all possible.'[1]

Soon after midnight, he was puzzled to see the bright lights of a town ahead. It was Mudon. Determined to avoid another hair-raising experience like the one at Thanbyuzayat, he made a wide detour, but as the night clouded over he lost his bearings. As he ploughed through the jungle, he stumbled on a Karen's house, where he was welcomed, and then shaved completely from head to foot before being kitted out in the yellow robes of a priest by a native pastor of the Christian Free Church. He was told to go to the fifth milestone from Moulmein and then head west, where he could get a boat to Bilugyun Island and thus avoid the town. After taking his farewell, he eventually recovered the railway and pushed on until dawn. Once again in the early morning light he spotted an isolated hut occupied by an Indian family in the middle of a padi field and begged their hospitality. This time he was more uneasy about his hosts. The family were clearly nervous, and he was apprehensive that, if a reward had been posted for his capture, they might betray him, but his fears were unfounded. He was fed, given a bed for the day and then sent on his way. It was hardly surprising that the family were on tenterhooks: had they been caught harbouring an escaped PoW, they would all have been shot or hanged from the nearest tree.

Guided by the baleful silver light of a waxen moon, he followed the railway again, walking all night to within a few miles of Moulmein, then left the track and went towards another hut. An Indian emerged and introduced himself as Mohammed Esoof, an ex-Indian Army soldier who was staunchly pro-British. He said he would help Ras on his journey, but stressed that Moulmein was infested with Japanese troops and BIA informers, and that it would be far too dangerous to go near the town or cross the mighty Salween river there. Ras's new-found friend said he had a brother who was a fisherman living on the island of Bilugyun in the mouth of the river, and that if Ras waited for a day, he would send his son to fetch this brother and arrange safe passage.

The afternoon knows what the morning never suspects. That night Ras relaxed, safe in the knowledge that Mohammed Esoof was a true friend who could be trusted. As they ate, they talked, as fellow soldiers, of India and army life. The next day, Mohammed Esoof's son returned with his uncle, who agreed to take Ras to his home on the island, and then on the following night to the far bank of the Salween. Ras could hardly believe his luck. At a stroke he could avoid both Moulmein and Martaban, which were teeming with enemy troops, the worry of which had gnawed away at him for days. 'Was it really luck or God's help?' he later mused. Increasingly, Ras felt that God was watching over and guiding him for some particular purpose.

As he left, after they had shared a final meal together, Mohammed Esoof was delighted that Ras gave him a chit stating that he had helped him to continue his journey. Reaching a small fishing boat to which Mohammed Esoof's brother directed him, Ras climbed in and, after an uneventful journey, arrived at the island about an hour later. The following day he ate and slept at the brother's house, renewing his reserves of strength, before being dropped in darkness on the north bank of the Salween. There, he ditched the priest's robes and dressed as a Burman. He was incredibly lucky. The Salween was not just a formidable barrier, but one lined with Japanese troops. Picking up the railway, he pressed on as fast as he could, anxious to put as much distance as possible between himself and Moulmein.

Today, the land across which Ras travelled remains remarkably unchanged. The narrow coastal plain resembles a carpet of emerald green velvet, a chequer-work of padi fields interspersed with plantations of palm. Just a few miles inland to the east, the ground rises up into a continuous line of cloud-capped ramparts of limestone ridges, scored by steep ravines and studded with bell-shaped white stupas and sacred gold pagodas perched on inaccessible crags. Ras was fortunate indeed to be travelling in mid-November, the dry season. During the height of the south-west monsoon, when I retraced his footsteps, torrential rains sweep in off the Andaman Sea, and spectacular tropical storms torment the coast and hills, turning the fields into quagmires.

As the sun turned the sky into a great imperial canopy shot through with shades of orange and gold, Ras saw that he had reached the outskirts of a village surrounded by orderly plantations. Leaving the railway, he moved cautiously forward and lay up, concealed in a fringe of trees about 100 yards from a group of buildings. He lay there watching for several hours. The people in the village were not Burmese. They were fair-skinned, wore red-and-white clothes and seemed prosperous. Reasoning that people who were prosperous under the British were unlikely to favour the Japanese, he took a monumental risk. With his heart in his mouth, he approached a house. In his disguise as a dirty Indian labourer, he chose to use the back door, from which he had seen various servants coming and going throughout the day, and from where, if things went wrong, he would have a better chance of evading capture by moving back into the trees in the event of any ensuing hue and cry.

With his changkul firmly grasped in one hand, he rapped on the door. It was opened by a rather startled servant girl. Ras attempted to make himself understood in Hindustani, and she asked him to wait. After what seemed an eternity, he was steeling himself for her return – her return with whom? – with his nerves on tenterhooks, ready to run for the trees or, if the worst came to the worst, to defend himself at all costs and go down fighting. Nothing could have prepared him for what was to follow. When the door opened again, he was utterly dumbfounded to be greeted by a serenely beautiful and impeccably dressed young girl, who, after looking him up and down, said in perfect English: 'Please come in.'

'I was so flabbergasted,' Pagani later wrote, 'I stood rooted to the spot, totally at a loss for words. She smiled at me, gently took my hand and again said, "Please come in."' He followed her into the house and was led to a comfortable sitting room. A servant was dispatched to tell her father of her 'unusual guest':

'It suddenly struck me that she knew I was English, and I realised that my disguise was not all that good. The room was a replica of a Victorian lounge, so I sat in a comfortable, deep armchair and looked around as she excused herself and left the room, saying she would get tea ... I could have been in England. Plush furnishings, curtains – this was all like a dream. I was sure now that God was with me.'[2]

A little while later, the girl returned and said her father was on his way home. She introduced herself as Paula and chatted to him about her family, explaining that they were Karen Christians, not Burmese, and that the village was called Kyawaing and was situated a few miles south of Thaton.[3] Her father, Saw Po Thin, was a local timber merchant, who was safe from Japanese persecution because he had been contracted to supply sleepers for the new railway. What Ras did not know until later was that her father used his influential position to supply intelligence about Japanese troop movements to Hugh Seagrim and the Karen guerrillas up in the hills and to spread wild rumours and disinformation about their strength to the Japanese.

Paula talked to Ras with great composure, completely confident that they were safe from the Japanese and their BIA informers, and totally unruffled by his dirty clothing and half-naked self. He remembered those surreal moments vividly for the rest of his life: 'The servant brought in a tea tray and set it on the table. I was amazed and stared at it in disbelief, at the bone china tea set, the thin sandwiches and English biscuits. I had to keep a grip on my manners as I had not eaten for over forty-eight hours and was hungry as a horse.'[4] More extraordinary surprises lay ahead. Paula showed Ras to a large, comfortable bedroom, in which there was a four-poster bed draped in a muslin mosquito net and a complete set of clean Karen clothes laid out for him to wear. There was a bathroom next door, where he immersed himself for over an hour, scrubbing himself clean. It was 7 p.m.

when Ras came back to the drawing room, washed and dressed in his new Karen outfit. In the meantime, Saw Po Thin had arrived and been briefed by his daughter about their new guest. Ras was greeted warmly and invited to sit down to an English dinner prepared in his honour, with roast peacock taking the place of chicken or turkey. After so many months of hardship and starvation, suddenly at a stroke his prospects had been transformed. Ras thought he had died and gone to heaven.

After the meal, Ras told his hosts of his adventures: his escape from Singapore, his subsequent capture by the Japanese, the horrendous sea voyages to Burma, and the appalling conditions on the railway. They talked into the early hours. Saw Po Thin invited him to stay for a few days while arrangements were made to help him on his way north. Ras explained that he wanted to reach the British, to explain graphically about the conditions in which the PoWs were living and the dreadful suffering and brutality they were forced to endure day after day on the railway, with the aim of planning a concerted Allied response. Musing silently for a while, Saw Po Thin considered Ras's plan – before dropping a bombshell. He explained that what Ras was proposing was impossible. He said he could probably get him to Bassein, which was among the Delta Karens, although even that would be extremely difficult and dangerous. But, beyond that, he thought it would be impossible to find a guide willing to take Ras through the dense, disease-ridden jungles of the Arakan Yomas, not to mention the subsequent journey through the Japanese frontlines and battlefields to the British.

Ras was crestfallen. After a further protracted silence, deep in thought, Saw Po Thin suddenly turned his head. 'There is an alternative,' he said. 'There is a British officer in the Karen hills commanding the Karen guerrillas.'[5] After that, he suggested they sleep on it. Utterly bemused, and in complete disbelief at his remarkable good fortune, Ras was only too happy to call it a night, already anticipating the pleasure of sleeping in the luxurious four-poster bed. As soon as he put his head on the pillow, he slept.

Unbeknown to Ras, Saw Po Thin had already sent a runner to the mysterious British major seeking his view. After two days, the runner returned with the message that Ras should be sent up to him. The order was not necessarily based on friendly terms: it seemed unlikely that any Englishman could have made such a journey barefoot without any knowledge of the country; and if he proved to be a Japanese plant, Ras would be executed. Ras was reluctant to abandon his ambitious plan to make his way to the British in the Arakan, but after turning the proposal over and over in his mind, he resolved to accept the offer – at least for the time being. If nothing else, joining up with the British officer would be a very eloquent way of demonstrating that, once again, he had made a successful escape.

Years later, Ras Pagani confided that he was certain he could have reached the Arakan with the help of the Karens, but he was also equally convinced that Divine intervention had played a part. It was, he believed, God's will that he should join the officer in the hills on this next stage of his journey. He was not alone in his belief. Hugh Seagrim too had placed his life in the service of the Almighty, and the scene was set for the two to meet in one of the most unlikely episodes of the Second World War. And, for Ras, the journey began by being buried alive.

In the early hours of the next morning, he was taken outside and told to lie on the floor of a bullock cart. A long box resembling a coffin was then placed over him, above which the cart was piled high with stinking rubbish. The stench was awful, but it soon proved its worth when they were stopped at a Japanese checkpoint in Thaton. Ras clearly heard the Japanese joking about the smell – they waved them on quickly without making a thorough inspection. Fortunately, the floor of the cart was made of planks with gaps between, which enabled him to breathe freely. Although they encountered no more enemy checkpoints, he was forced to stay under cover all day. When the cart finally stopped, at last he extricated himself. Abandoning the cart, the brave driver asked Ras if he could swim, to which he readily agreed. The next morning, they pressed ahead on foot. After about five miles, they came to a deep, fast-flowing river about twenty-five yards wide. They swam across, before scurrying through bamboo and scrub jungle to a dirt road. There, another bullock cart waited to receive them, this time driven by a forest ranger, Saw Willie Saw, the district commander of Seagrim's levies. Ras bade his courageous driver farewell, and set off into the hills to Pawota with his new ally.

Ras was astonished at being able to travel so openly in broad daylight. Everywhere, he was met with friendly greetings and beaming smiles. The local people seemed remarkably content and relaxed. The women wore local tribal dress in red-and-white vertical stripes, and the men red body jackets. Saw Willie Saw explained that this was Karen country. There was no need to hide as the Japanese and BIA steered clear of the whole area, fearful of attacks by Karen guerrillas orchestrated by the elusive British major.

At dusk, they arrived at Saw Willie Saw's house in Molopa, where Ras was introduced to his family and friends. That night a party was held in his honour, beginning with a meal of roast pork and peacock, rice and sweetmeats, followed by endless bouts of heavy drinking. As an honoured guest, it would have been impolite not to take part in the drinking ritual, which was intended to find the last man standing. The men sat in a circle with the headman at the centre. He was given the first cup, which was offered to the gods and then thrown to the right-hand side. The cup was then refilled and passed to the right, where it was knocked back in one go. The ritual was repeated again and again throughout the night. Ras did not last long. After passing out, he woke at midday with the mother of all hangovers – only to be greeted by a grinning crowd of Karens, who, like innocent children, delighted in his plight. He staggered into the sunlight, and after some food, he felt better.

He remained with Saw Willie Saw for a couple of days while a young Karen girl with some nursing experience dressed a nasty cut on his instep, which he had incurred on his journey. During this time, he sat around talking and studying the daily routines of his new-found friends. The Karens lived in simple bamboo huts raised on stilts and covered with plantain leaves. At the centre of each hut was a mud fireplace and at the end of the hut a lavatory, consisting of a bamboo platform with a hole in the centre, beneath which the village pigs foraged.

Two days after Ras's arrival, Saw Willie Saw explained that they were moving up to the 'priest's house'. Travel was by elephant. Ras was shown how to mount and then guide the beast, by jiggling his toe behind its right ear to go left and vice versa. To go faster, he jiggled both ears. With just another elephant and oozie, or driver, for company, plus a single armed guard, the train set off northwards along the dirt road through the jungle. It was a wonderfully exotic adventure, imbued with all the romance of the east. Elated, and rejoicing in his good fortune, Ras felt like a potentate as he was greeted at every village by the brightly attired Karens, who waved and smiled at him as he swayed past. At noon, they stopped to feed and rest the elephants at a village called Kadaingti.

Living alongside the Karens were numerous Indians and Gurkhas, who had been trapped following the blowing of the Sittang bridge in February, nine months earlier. Among them was Lance Naik Mura, an ex-Burma Rifles Kachin from Assam. He and Ras formed an immediate bond. Although Mura spoke only Burmese and Hindi, an intuitive understanding developed between the two of them. In another of those curious examples of the selfless love and dedication that existed between the hill tribes and the British, Mura attached himself, unasked, to Ras as a cook, dhobi, orderly and bodyguard, sleeping that night across his doorway in silent protection. Intensely devoted, he even tasted Ras's food if prepared and cooked by another. In the coming months, time and time again he was to prove his unswerving loyalty. In the morning, Mura joined the party and, with Saw Willie Saw and the guide, they continued on their way.

As the jungle engulfed the group on both sides, they stopped for the night at a small village before continuing the next day to a much larger settlement. It was Papun. Ras was taken to the local village shop to meet the Indian owner, and then on to a large brick-built house standing on a hill, where he was introduced to Father Loizeau, the elderly French priest. Ras's French schooling proved a huge advantage from the off. He was able to converse fluently in French and tell of his experiences over the previous nine months since escaping from Singapore. Father Loizeau gave him a room for the night, with Mura stretched protectively across the threshold. Ras remembered:

'I was woken the following morning and asked by Father Loizeau if I would like to attend Mass. I accepted – after all, I too was a Catholic, having been brought up in a convent, but above all to thank God for my safe journey. So far I found the situation incredible: me, an escaped PoW, being with a congregation of Karens in the middle of the jungle in a beautiful church.'[6]

Afterwards, Father Loizeau showed Ras the garden where he grew coffee and vegetables, which enabled him to be entirely self-sufficient. That night, as they sat down to a fine meal in Ras's honour, he felt that he was being guided by providence for some wider purpose, but for what he did not know. The following morning, the good Father asked whether he wished to take Communion with him, but Ras refused, uncomfortable at having to confess his sins to someone he now knew intimately as a friend.

Later that day Father Calmon arrived. He was much younger, and rather taken aback at Ras's fluency in French. In fact, Calmon was impressed in many ways by Pagani. He was 'not only a nice fellow but also a very brave man, always wanting to fight the Burmese and the Japanese'.[7] After some deliberation, the two priests sent a runner to the British major to tell him that Pagani had arrived at Papun and to see whether he should be sent on to him. For the first time Ras heard the other man's name mentioned – Major Seagrim. Five days later, the reply came back that Ras should go up, and arrangements were made to move on northwards to join him.

In the morning, a party of ten men, all armed, and led by Naik Ah Din, set off on the arduous journey through dense jungle by elephant. Ras found this slow and hazardous, moving very carefully to avoid being lacerated by bamboo and overhanging branches. As the terrain became more precipitous, the elephants maintained their ponderous, steady pace. When going downhill, they trailed their back legs behind them, testing the ground ahead with each forefoot as they moved. On the fifth day, after two hours' travelling, the men left the elephants and trekked on foot through streams and deep jungle, careful to leave no tracks that could be followed.

At long last, they reached a circular bamboo shelter. It was occupied by a Kachin, who then led them for a further hour via streams, far away from the paths, on a twisting, turning route through the jungle that eventually led to a more permanent type of hut raised on stilts. Standing on the verandah was a very tall, thin, dark-skinned man in native Karen clothes, his hair bobbed like a Pathan, who Ras assumed was another native. It was Hugh Seagrim.

Above: Private R.A.S. Pagani, East Surrey Regiment, in 1934, aged 19.

Chapter 7

Lords of the Sunset

'I am monarch of all I survey,
My right there is none to dispute,
From the centre all round to the sea,
I am lord of the fowl and the brute.'
WILLIAM COWPER

For Ras Pagani, this epic meeting in the remote jungle wilderness was one of the most memorable moments of his exceedingly eventful life: 'As I looked forward a very tall man came onto the verandah. I took him to be a native, but as we got nearer I realised that he was a white man and very, very tall.' Ah Din whispered to Ras: 'Major.' Ras recalled of that first meeting:

'The major then raised his hand to us, jumped down and said to me, 'Hello, old chap,' as if welcoming me to a country mansion. I was astounded. We shook hands and I said 'OK, sir.' The situation was so astounding that, due to my military training, I almost stood to attention as he addressed me ... The major introduced himself as Hugh Seagrim, grasped my hand and nearly shook my arm off!'[1]

For both men it was a profoundly moving and yet very English experience. Both attempted to suppress their deepest emotions. For Hugh Seagrim, isolated from contact with his fellow countrymen for almost nine months, it was a joy to have a compatriot and ally to join him, poor Leslie Cryer having died in April 1942 before they could meet. For Ras, it seemed an almost miraculous culmination of his desperate journey to freedom. As Ras fought back tears, Seagrim spoke in a voice choked with emotion as he told Ras how glad he was that he had come. For the rest of his life, Ras was utterly convinced that he had been spared and guided to Seagrim by God.

They made an unlikely pair – the tall, gaunt, major and the stocky, pugnacious corporal, alone and far from home in the distant jungles of the Karenni hills. Both were loners and mavericks, but they were drawn together not just by circumstance. For all their obvious differences, in many respects they were quite alike, and perhaps each saw in the other his own inherent qualities reflected back at himself. There was no suggestion of the formal, detached relationship between an officer and his men. The two became firm friends. Seagrim called Ras 'Roy'; and Pagani, with the regular's respect for rank, first called Hugh Major, then Skipper, and finally Skip.

On that first day of meeting, deep in the jungle beneath a canopy of stars, they talked long into the night of Ras's escape from Singapore, and then the railway – Seagrim was horrified by the dreadful conditions there – their conversation interrupted only by the occasional roar of a distant leopard and the relentless chirping of thousands of insects. It was now mid-December 1942. Together, they calculated that Ras had travelled about 250 miles since he left the 18 kilometre camp. Seagrim was deeply impressed by Pagani's foresight and self-awareness: in particular, his readiness to 'go native', to travel barefoot and to ditch any European aids and accoutrements, such as a compass and boots, that might betray him. Ras was clearly a man after his own heart. Seagrim had done much the same in his pre-war forays into the hills, travelling light and dressing and living like a Karen. It had proved the ideal preparation for his current task, and in Pagani Seagrim saw the perfect recruit to help him build a resistance network among the Karens.

Ras was only too aware that, after his escape, there would be a price on his head. Surely notice would have been passed to other Japanese units and the Burmese police. Throughout the past month, he had been extremely careful not to divulge his real name to anyone, not even to Saw Po Thin or the two French priests. Should the Karens know his real name, they might inadvertently give the game away and reveal his survival. The longer there was no news of him after leaving the camp, the more likely it would be that the Japanese would simply believe he had died of disease or starvation in the jungle. Seagrim concurred. He added that there was a further risk: if a Karen were picked up, he might reveal Pagani's name under torture. Should Pagani be recaptured and his real identity be revealed, then without doubt he would be returned to the camp and executed. Both decided that he should be known only as Corporal Ras, which made it far less likely that the Japanese would make any connection. Ras was greatly relieved. He felt much safer now that the matter had been settled. Finally, exhausted by talking, the two Englishmen curled up on either side of the fire and slept for a few hours under a star-studded sky.

For Seagrim, after almost a year as a fugitive hiding in the forest, during which time the intense frustration and loneliness might have driven a lesser man to madness, it was a sleep made sweeter by his new-found companionship. How often in those long months his innermost thoughts turned to England, Whissonsett, his family and home, one can only guess, but Ras's arrival gave him renewed heart.

Over the next few days, Ras began to realise that he was in the presence of someone truly exceptional, a charismatic leader and the very stuff of legend.

'However close was our friendship, I became aware as the days passed that I was serving under a most remarkable man, who had such a love for the Karen people that he was quite prepared to sacrifice his life for them … It was no wonder that Hugh Seagrim came to be regarded by the Karens as their father, and by both myself and the Karens as a saint.'[2]

Having been raised and educated in a Catholic convent, Ras had his own core of beliefs which he rarely shared with others, but Seagrim had no such inhibitions. He would talk with him for hours about the different paths to truth that could be found in all the world's religions, without suggesting in any way he was a religious crank. Ras was fascinated by his learning and insights. It heightened not only his profound respect for him, but also his own faith.

Pagani now found himself on the horns of a dilemma. In agreeing to Saw Po Thin's plan and being taken up into the hills, he had thought that it would give him a safe haven away from the danger of recapture – but also sufficient respite and opportunity to continue, eventually, with his ambitious plan to escape across Burma to the Arakan Yomas. There, he plotted, he could join up with Allied forces and wreak his own personal revenge on the Japanese for the brutality they had meted out to him and his comrades on the railway. But during their long talks during their first ten days together, Seagrim reasoned with him. The chances of success were minimal. It would mean navigating hundreds of miles across open country occupied by Burmans who, unlike the hill tribes, were generally hostile to the Allied cause. He would then have to cross the Irrawaddy, find local Karens willing to risk their lives to guide him north to the

Arakan Yomas, and, most hazardously of all, steer a path covertly through the shifting Japanese lines before reaching safety.

Yet Ras refused to be put off – an indication of the sheer obstinacy and bloody-mindedness of the man. Undaunted, he argued that he had anticipated the dangers of crossing the front lines, and planned to travel through the Arakan Yomas until close to Akyab, where he felt confident a local Karen would find him a boat. By sailing only by night, he thought he had a good chance of outflanking any Japanese coastal patrols and reaching the British front lines. For a long time, the two of them argued as they examined the plan from every perspective, Seagrim insisting that Ras's chances of survival were infinitely better if he chose to remain in the hills to fight with the Karens.

However, finally, and with great reluctance, Seagrim saw that – once Ras had done everything possible to help the Karens, as a thank-you for their assistance so far – nothing would dissuade him from his goal. Seagrim wrote a long report, which, if successful, Pagani could deliver to Army headquarters, but he told the corporal that if there was any danger of him being recaptured, he was to destroy it. Then the two of them concentrated on more immediate matters. Until Ras was ready to embark on his dangerous journey, he agreed to do all he could to help Seagrim train and organise the levies into a coherent and effective resistance force, ready to be deployed at the right moment. Unbeknown to either of them, far away in London in October 1942 Seagrim had been awarded an MBE for remaining behind the Japanese lines, training up the Karen irregulars and resisting the incursions of the pro-Japanese BIA.

In truth, one of the reasons for Seagrim's reluctance to accede to Ras's ambitious escape plan was his recognition that in Pagani he had the ideal reliable subordinate, who could also act on his own initiative. Accordingly, Seagrim entrusted Ras with the delicate task of reining in the southern levies and mediating in petty disputes between Ah Din and Saw Willie Saw and Father Calmon. All were valuable assets. He did not want disagreements between them to undermine their abilities as a fighting force. With his innate common sense and cool head, Ras was the ideal person to act as an intermediary. As the local levy commanders were all corporals, Seagrim promoted Ras to sergeant and gave him written authority of his new status. This would give him the ability to instruct the levies as he saw fit and command their obedience.

The two men spent their last day together discussing the situation and preparing for Ras's journey to Kadaingti, where the out-of-control levies had been causing problems. Seagrim briefed Ras on their handling, which proved invaluable in the months ahead when Ras was to assess the overall situation personally and then return with clear recommendations. Early the next morning, just before Christmas 1942, Ras set off – heading first for Pyagawpu, to collect weapons from a secret cache hidden beneath the Baptist minister's house. For both men, isolated as they were in the jungle, far from home and far from the company of their own kind, the parting was highly charged. Later, Ras recalled: 'As I left the clearing, I looked back. Seagrim was still standing by the hut, watching me go. To me he suddenly seemed a very lonely figure and, at that moment, I almost regretted my enthusiasm for setting out on this new venture, but Seagrim raised his hand in farewell and I turned and continued my journey.'[3] Although neither knew it, they would never see each other again, except just maybe, tantalisingly, for one fleeting moment over eighteen months later, with their hands raised once more in a final farewell.

Ras was escorted on his journey by Seagrim's personal guard of eight men, and his faithful retainer, Lance Naik Mura. Travelling light and fast, they reached Pyagawpu in daylight, and stocked up on weapons from the secret cache. Ras took a tommy gun with a drum containing fifty rounds and three spare box magazines, each of twenty rounds; of the Karens, two chose short-barrelled Japanese rifles, which were well suited to jungle warfare, two opted for 12-bore shotguns, and the others carried traditional hardwood crossbows, with foot-long bolts of sharpened bamboo guided by 'feathers' of plantain leaves. Silent, lethal and capable of passing straight through a man over fifty yards, they were the ideal weapon for guerrilla warfare with a limitless supply of deadly bamboo bolts cut from the surrounding jungle. Before they left, Ras was offered an elephant on which to ride. He declined, determined to gain the respect of his men and show them that 'an Englishman could do as well, if not better than them, in every aspect of life in the jungle'.[4]

Scrambling up jungle-covered hills and slithering down leech-infested gullies through dense steaming undergrowth, the way was hard. At noon, they paused to drink and rest awhile. After a short break to avoid the hottest part of the day, the small party pressed on for a further three hours, before stopping and making camp for the night. For all his expertise and self-reliance, Ras found the Karens taught him a great deal about jungle survival and living off the land. It enabled them to travel swiftly, unencumbered by heavy supplies. Each man carried a small amount of rice in a cloth hung from the waist, and one carried a basket of chickens.

On the march, they adjusted their metabolism to eat only once a day. Water was taken from pure jungle streams: when they stopped to camp, a small hole would be dug on the margins of a stream and the water allowed to drain slowly into the hole, the earth acting as a natural filter just in case the upper reaches of the stream had been contaminated. The method was highly effective. Where there was no water, rice was cooked inside green bamboo shoots with the ends sealed with plantain leaves, over an open fire of dry bamboo. The chickens were then spliced and cooked over the fire on slivers of bamboo. For vegetables, a plantain tree would be stripped down the centre and eaten raw. After their single meal of the day, the travelling party would fall asleep around the fire. With the starlit night sky framed by a canopy of intersecting palm fronds high above them, the men were lulled to sleep by the unremitting sounds of the enveloping jungle.

On arriving at Papun after two days' travel, Ras immediately visited Father Loizeau, who invited him to stay the night. Once again the priest entertained him with the rare treat of a European dinner with red wine. Ras reciprocated with a present of Burmese cheroots. Pagani stayed at Papun for three days, during which time he began his work by presiding over a trial. The case involved an Indian trader charged with profiteering from the sale of salt. Having established the man's guilt, Ras consulted the village elders about a suitable punishment. They recommended twenty lashes with a bamboo cane across the buttocks. Ras ordered the punishment to be carried out in public by one of the levies, and then fixed the price of salt and jaggery (a coarse form of sugar from sugar cane), both staple commodities, to avoid any repetition of the offence.

Having settled the case successfully, he pushed on for Kadaingti to fulfil Seagrim's orders and resolve the local tensions there. Over the next week most of the levy commanders came in to report to him, including Saw Willie Saw, who had escorted Ras on his journey northward just a few weeks earlier. He was delighted that Ras had been given command of the district – but when Saw Willie Saw produced a map of his new domain, Ras soon realised just what a formidable task Seagrim had set him. It covered hundreds of square miles. much of which was untamed virgin forest rolling eastwards across jagged hills to the tempestuous Salween and the Siamese border. Incredibly, Ras was lord of all he surveyed, with his own private army. He studied the map. Twelve miles west of the Salween was the Yunzalin river, running from north to south and dividing his area of responsibility into two halves. West of that lay the dense forests through which he had travelled on his way up to meet Seagrim. Other than the road up from Bilin to Papun, there were no roads and few passable tracks.

Each day the sun rose like a furnace on the distant eastern horizon, which shimmered in the haze over the steaming immensity of the jungle. Yet for Ras and the levies, this very remoteness was a real blessing. It meant that both the BIA and their Japanese masters steered well clear of the hills, the former having been given a bloody nose during the civil unrest the previous spring. In addition, Seagrim had deliberately circulated misinformation that there were at least two entire battalions of British troops operating in the hills. These rumours soon became magnified in the telling, each levy embellishing the story until artillery and even aircraft were mentioned. For the time being, this discouraged the Japanese from making any incursions into the hills.

During Pagani's time at Kadaingti, Saw Po Thin came up to see him. A long drinking session ensued, during which Ras learned a great deal more about his enigmatic benefactor. Gradually, it began to dawn on him that Saw Po Thin was the *éminence grise* behind Karen resistance in the hills and beyond. He was perfectly placed. As a trusted contractor of the Japanese, he was able to move freely throughout the area gathering intelligence, as well as providing money and even arms to the resistance. A wealthy man, educated in England and with a strong sense of social responsibility, he later did a great deal to advance education and learning among the Karens, even paying for Karen girls to train as nurses and sending the brightest and most promising young men to England to train as doctors.

At the end of a week of meeting the levy commanders, by sheer force of personality Ras had stamped his authority on his subordinates. He settled the petty local bickering that had threatened to destabilise the area, then set off to tour his new command, initially to the south and then in a broad arc eastwards towards the Siamese border. In case of emergencies, he left a detailed itinerary of his movements at Kadaingti. His men were handpicked. Alongside his shadow Mura were Naik Ah Din and six

Gurkhas who had been cut off when the Sittang bridge was blown a year earlier. The southern fringes of the forest ran into belts of open land interspersed with thickets of plantain and bamboo, which rendered the local villages much more vulnerable to attack by the BIA. As a result, many villagers had decamped to live in the jungle rather than risk attack by marauding BIA forces. With Ah Din in support, Ras was in his element, staying a day at each camp to meet the local elders and levies, and spending long hours each night drinking with his comrades. He was exhilarated at his new-found freedom and the responsibilities of his own command.

Crossing the Yunzalin river, the party then moved east in a series of exhausting marches through dense jungle, climbing up and down strength-sapping hills over 7,000 feet high, all swathed in exotic trees and impenetrable walls of bamboo. For Ras, it was a time of immense happiness. Liberated at last from the terrors of incarceration in the stinking holds of prison ships and the brutality of life on the railway, and largely freed from the risk of any surprise enemy attack, he began to appreciate the transcendental beauty of the landscape through which he travelled. The jungle has many moods. Alongside its terrors, it can be sublimely beautiful. The memory stayed with Ras for his entire life, as he later wrote:

'Sometimes we walked in the shade, shafts of sunlight occasionally piercing the gloom and lighting up clouds of yellow butterflies which carpeted damp patches on the paths and rose as we approached to drift away among the trees like showers of golden leaves. In the tree canopy above, unseen monkeys crashed through the boughs or sat muttering mournful cries as they peered down at the human invaders of their sanctuary. The nights in the hills were cool, so I and my men lay around a fire after our meal, listening hard to the sounds of the jungle creatures before falling into deep sleep. If there was a moon, the forest took on a ghostly sheen, a background to the flickering fireflies. With the coming of dawn, a damp chill mist arose, heralded by the shrill crying of jungle fowl and followed by the insect chorus as the rising sun warmed the glades.'[5]

The party marched on for another three days before reaching the Yunzalin river and the Siamese border. Here the local levy commander was a disreputable old ruffian with a gang of twenty or so freebooting individuals, who raided both sides of the border selling arms and ammunition to the Karens in exchange for gold and precious gems. Unpopular and unscrupulous, the commander was nevertheless tolerated by the Karens because his father and brother had been killed by the Japanese. For that reason, they thought it unlikely that he would betray the levies or their activities. With Ras's arrival boosting his status among the local community, the old commander laid on a magnificent party for Ras and his men, including a bevy of Siamese dancing girls from across the border. The party was so successful that it took two days for them all to recover.

Provided with guides, they set out once again, hacking their way through wild jungles and precipitous hills, and emerging periodically into small clearings where the jungle had been burned off for rice cultivation. This was the notorious taungya system that the Karens adopted in the hills: a disastrously unsustainable process of slash-and-burn cultivation, which destroyed valuable timber and caused soil erosion. As they approached one village they were assailed by hordes of fleas, which swarmed up their legs from the contaminated ground, forcing them to cross the river into Siam.

Just over the border at Hot was a Karen village full of refugees – and numerous substantial houses. Here Ras was taken to a traveller's rest house, where he breathed a sigh of relief at being able to sleep in a comfortable bed with clean sheets and a mosquito net. Ras's arrival caused a flurry of excitement. In this remote corner of the Golden Triangle, many had never seen a white man before. People flocked in from surrounding villages to catch a glimpse of him. For three days and nights he was feted with banquets, parties and drinking sessions long into the night. For Ras, it seemed like Shangri-La, far from the occupying Japanese forces and untainted then by its later infamy as a haven of drug smuggling: 'By the end of three days, I felt I had shaken the hand of every man and woman within twenty miles.'[6] After re-crossing the border at Dagwin, they travelled for seven long, gruelling days back to Kadaingti slashing their way through the unyielding terrain.

The trip had achieved much. It had clarified the roles and responsibilities of the individual section commanders, who led a dozen or so irregulars each and, by practical training en route, Ras had welded the disparate groups of levies into a more disciplined, co-ordinated force. It had also given him a real insight into the strengths and weaknesses of those under his command, in particular the four main group leaders. The shock-headed Saw Willie Saw, who was responsible for the vital southern fringe commanding the hills overlooking Thaton and Bilin, was thoroughly dependable. Well-educated and trustworthy, he was someone Ras regarded as a true friend, the man who had guided him through the forests to Seagrim two months earlier. Of Ah Din, however, he was much more wary. As one of Seagrim's personal bodyguards, Ah Din adopted an air of superiority over the other levy commanders. He was a prickly character, prone to bitter quarrels with both Saw Darlington and Saw Gyaw Lai, and Ras thought that if left to his own devices he would probably become an armed dacoit. Recklessly brave, he was soon to prove himself in battle.

Perhaps the most swashbuckling of all was the pipe-smoking Saw Darlington, the buccaneering old roué with the pronounced squint, who was such a great hit with the local ladies. Volatile and easy to rouse, he was just as swift to forget any perceived grievance and liked nothing better than to laugh at his own jokes. Although very different in character from the others, he too was aggressive, itching to take on the Japanese. Ras clearly had a soft spot for him: 'I felt a strange affinity with this strange-looking leader, perhaps seeing something of myself in the man's character.'[7]

The last and most inscrutable of the four was Naik Gyaw Lai, a quiet ex-Burma Rifles regular, cool, calm and collected, but with a heart of steel. In addition to his shadow, the steadfast Lance Naik Mura, Ras also developed a close understanding with Saw Po Hla, a highly intelligent young Karen from Papun, who in time was destined to become Seagrim's most valuable agent, gathering information from Thaton and, later, from much further afield.

On returning from his tour, Ras made Kadaingti his headquarters. From here he continued to stamp his authority on his commanders. He reorganised the levies into clearly defined, smaller areas of command, with explicit orders as to their conduct towards civilians, in order to eradicate any potential friction between the different commands and to foster mutual support and trust. Wanting to keep a close eye on Ah Din, he charged him with responsibility for Kadaingti and the surrounding area. Gyaw Lai was sent to the eastern district around the Salween river, while the piratical lothario Saw Darlington was dispatched to Papun. As the most reliable and trustworthy commander, Saw Willie Saw was given the south-west, which included oversight of the key route up from the coastal strip, from where enemy incursions were most likely to occur.

During the tour of his command, the area had remained calm, except for a few border skirmishes with the BIA, but – anticipating that was unlikely to last – Ras now ordered the outlying villagers to withdraw into the hills, where they could be better protected. He was right to do so. Ras Pagani had reorganised the southern levies just in time. It was the calm before the storm.

Chapter 8

Lord of the Far-Flung Battle Line

'God of our fathers, known of old –
Lord of our far-flung battle-line –
Beneath whose awful hand we hold
Dominion over palm and pine –
Lord God of Hosts be with us yet,
Lest we forget – lest we forget!'
RUDYARD KIPLING

R as Pagani's arrival galvanised Seagrim into action. He seized the initiative. While Pagani was away touring his new command area, Seagrim returned to deep cover at the centre of his web of intelligence at his hideout at Chawido. From here, in order to deter the Japanese from entering the hills, he cultivated rumours that there was a large British force operating behind the Japanese lines. Time and again he organised daring hit-and-run raids on Japanese supply routes and troops passing along the roads on the edges of the Karen hills. Lying in ambush, the levies would rake the unsuspecting enemy with a fusillade of small arms fire and crossbow bolts, and then melt away into the jungle before the bemused Japanese could respond. However, unbeknown to Seagrim or his closest circle, the net was closing fast.

In mid-February 1943 news came up from Saw Willie Saw that a small force of the BIA was on the move. They had raided and sacked one of the border villages, murdering the men and raping the women, and they were now heading north towards Pagani's base at Kadaingti. Immediately, Pagani sprang into action. He summoned Ah Din, gathered up their weapons and headed off to intercept the BIA. The next day, they spotted fifteen men with BIA armbands moving up the road. Ras quickly deployed his men and set up an ambush. They waited, silent and motionless, as the BIA came swaggering noisily up the road. At the crucial moment, Ras gave the order to open fire – to devastating effect. The BIA had no idea what had hit them. Ten of the insurgents were mowed down where they stood and the remaining five captured. The outlook for the captives was bleak. On no account could they be allowed to return to the plains to inform the Japanese. A court was convened, at which all five were put on trial for murder and rape, found guilty and sentenced to death. The condemned were forced to dig their own graves before being lined up and executed by a firing squad of volunteers. There was no shortage. After the graves had been filled, their weapons were collected and taken to Saw Willie Saw in Molopa, where they were hidden for future use. Ras also took their armbands, which he thought might be useful for future spying missions outside the hills.

With a palpable sense of achievement, the following day they returned to Kadaingti to clean up and rest. Rather touchingly, Lance Naik Mura suddenly conjured up a civilian solar topee for Ras in the form of a 'Bombay bowler' – once the very symbol of the sahib, but by then more commonly worn by Eurasians, a minority with whom Ras sympathised, given his own mixed Anglo-French parentage. A couple of days later, danger loomed again. This time it was two Burmans under suspicion. They had called on Saw Willie Saw, offering a bullock cart of salt in exchange for 'two white elephants'. To find two Burmans travelling alone through Karen country was odd enough, but their offer of a cartload of salt for such rare, expensive animals was absurd. Wary of their true motives, it slowly dawned on Saw Willie Saw that the reference to 'two white elephants' was coded language for Seagrim and Pagani. Pretending to play along, he invited them to stay and said he could guide them to one 'white elephant' and help them with its capture. Simultaneously, he sent a runner to Ras at Kadaingti to warn him that he intended to bring them up to the village headman the following day.

Not the sharpest tools in the box, the two Burmans were convinced that they had been believed. On arriving at the headman's house, they were taken aback to be confronted by Ras, Lance Naik Mura and two Gurkha corporals. To add to their confusion, Ras shook each man warmly by the hand, at which one of the men bowed low twice, instantly betraying that he was not Burman, but Japanese. To be certain, Ras suddenly bellowed, 'Kiotsuke!' the Japanese command for 'stand to attention'. Startled, the man snapped upright, revealing beyond doubt that he was Japanese –

almost certainly one of the sadistic kempeitai, the Japanese secret police. As they were Japanese spies in civilian clothes, Pagani had no alternative other than to execute them. Had he not done so, the Karens would never have let them leave alive. He ordered Ah Din to take them outside and shoot them. After his own ill treatment at their hands, Ras loathed the Japanese, but as he gave the order to shoot the two spies, his increasing ruthlessness worried him:

'For a fleeting moment I wondered whether I, myself, was fast becoming as ruthless as the Japanese, but after thinking back to the sickening ill treatment meted out by the Japanese to my comrades in the prison camps, I could find no mercy in my heart for these men. This was a savage war against beastlier men than I. My survival depended on being at least as cunning and ruthless as the Japanese, without indulging in their more loathsome practices of torture.'[1]

Following this unsettling incident, trouble continued to mount as the Japanese and their BIA allies began to consolidate their hold. The very next day, Ras heard that a strong force of Japanese and BIA soldiers was travelling up the road from Bilin to Papun, seizing hostages en route – including several Karen elders. Instantly Ras instructed the villages along the line of their route to melt into the jungle with all their food and livestock. Then he sent word to the impulsive Saw Darlington at Papun that on no account should he attack the enemy until ordered to do so. The enemy column was led by a brutal BIA official, Maung Shwe, who had been appointed Deputy Commissioner and District Superintendent of Police at Papun. Fearful of entering the harsh terrain without a strong escort, he used the excuse to the Japanese that there were strong forces of British guerrillas operating there to coax the BIA's allies into providing armed support. The Japanese had already been alerted to rumours of powerful British forces in the hills, deliberately circulated by Seagrim and the Karens to deter enemy encroachment, but the levies' misleading propaganda now backfired.

On 20 February 1943, Maung Shwe had left Bilin with a column of 700 Japanese troops and detachments of Burmese and Karen police. After arriving at Papun, where they heard tell of the levies' attack, the Japanese sent a strong body of troops up to Pyagawpu, seeking retribution. The enemy soldiers attacked and burned Father Calmon's mission to the ground. As the mission house crackled and burned, the priest, having been warned of the impending attack, scrambled into the forest in the nick of time. Just before dawn on the morning of 25 February 1943, Ta Roe was woken to the sound of someone knocking frantically on the door of his hut at his village in Chawido. Standing before him, wide-eyed and breathless, was a young Karen, who had raced up from a village halfway between Papun and Pyagawpu with a message from a friend of Ta Roe: the Japanese, he gasped, were heading north from Papun and would arrive at any minute. Seagrim was in imminent danger. Ta Roe's only thought was: 'I must save Seagrim.'

Throwing on his clothes, he collected one of his elephants and raced towards Pyagawpu. He arrived in the nick of time. Waking Seagrim and his men, they grabbed their meagre possessions and set off hot-foot into the jungle to an old hiding place several miles beyond Chawido, which Ta Roe had first identified when Seagrim had moved down from the north. They had escaped by the skin of their teeth. Just half an hour after they plunged into the jungle at 6.30 a.m., the Japanese arrived, occupied the church and rounded up the villagers. The Karens were forced to sit on the ground beneath the building while they were interrogated. With great courage, Ta Roe stayed behind with the elders to face down the Japanese. They were grilled: 'Where English? Where English?', to which Ta Roe replied, 'No English.' Through an interpreter, the Japanese lieutenant barked: 'Are there any British officers or soldiers hiding in these hills? We have been told that there are more than two thousand of them and that aeroplanes from India are supplying them with arms.' With considerable presence of mind, Ta Roe calmly retorted, 'There are no British officers or soldiers round here. If you do not believe me, you may search the village. If there are two thousand men here, you would be sure to find traces of them in the village.'[2]

The Japanese took up his offer. Fortunately, after an hour of fruitless searching, they found nothing to betray Seagrim's presence. Even more remarkably, in spite of being extremely scared, not a single one of the villagers gave the game away. The lieutenant then insisted that three of the elders should go back with them to Papun. In fear of his life, Ta Roe nonetheless volunteered, along with the village schoolmaster and another of the elders. They were all exceptionally brave, as the Karens had heard awful rumours of Japanese barbarity and torture. Poignantly, they asked their friends and neighbours to pray for them. Before leaving, Ta Roe was able to whisper to a trusted elder that, as soon as they had left, Seagrim should be moved to another place deeper into the forest, in the mountains north-west of the village.

While the Japanese detachment had been heading for Seagrim in Pyagawpu, Ras Pagani and the levies had attacked Papun. With four groups each of a dozen or so men, Pagani had set off on a rapid forced march to cover the thirty-five miles to Papun. He had a plan to ambush the enemy at night, force them to withdraw from the town – and teach them a lesson they would not easily forget. However, when they reached the outskirts at dusk on the following day, Ras found that the Japanese had beaten him to it. They had already taken up positions around the main crossroads. All the next day Ras and his men hid, resting up outside the town while Ras cautiously reconnoitred the enemy positions and prepared his plan of attack. He decided to wait until midnight, when many in the town would be asleep, then launch a surprise attack from two different quarters. This would sow the seeds of confusion in the enemy in as short a time as possible. He could then withdraw to his main position once the initial impact of the shock attack had worn off. He decided that two sections, led by him, would advance along the Bilin–Papun road, while the other two sections, under Saw Darlington and Gyaw Lai, would group around Father Calmon's house and attack at right angles along the Kadaingti–Papun road.

Two hours before midnight, they crept into position overlooking the Japanese encampment, where they waited quietly for the agreed hour. But the best-laid plans can be derailed by the unexpected. Just under an hour later, as Ras was preparing to give the order to attack, a rowdy band of drunken BIA men came sauntering and shouting down the Bilin road. Ras had to make an instant decision. If they passed him, they could attack his rear as soon as the fighting broke out, so he ordered his men not to fire until he did. Seizing the moment, and flanked by Ah Din and Mura, he walked calmly out into the road and shouted for them to halt. Startled by the unexpected challenge, the BIA men momentarily froze. Ras pulled the trigger on his tommy gun – and nothing happened. The gun had jammed. For Ras, these heart-stopping seconds seemed an eternity. His life flashed before him, but with extraordinary sangfroid he slid off the drum magazine, rammed in a box magazine and let rip at the astonished BIA. His actions were soon followed by Ah Din and Mura. Those BIA men who were not cut down in the hail of bullets ran off towards Papun in sheer panic. As soon as the firing erupted, Gyaw Lai's section opened up on the Japanese camp with everything they had.

For a short while mayhem ensued – until the Japanese got the measure of what was happening and started to fight back, lobbing mortar bombs down the road. This caused some consternation among the more raw recruits, who had never before experienced mortar fire, but the hard core of ex-Burma Rifles men held their ground, calmly picking off the enemy. As the fighting intensified, a storm of Japanese machine-gun fire was unleashed on the levies, blindly raking the jungle to suppress the incoming fire. At this point, Ras decided that the hit-and-run raid had achieved its main aim. He broke off the engagement and ordered his troops to fall back and regroup at the main assembly area, where they were joined by Gyaw Lai and his men. All then rapidly dispersed into the jungle to put as much distance between themselves and the Japanese as they could, lying up all the next day and listening to sporadic gunfire from the jittery Japanese in the distance. Not a single man had been lost.

The next day they pressed on, and then lay up for almost a week in a discreet hiding place near Saw Darlington's village. Reports soon filtered back on just how successful the raid had been. Apparently the enemy force was low on food and ammunition, had suffered significant casualties, and was in the process of packing up and returning to Bilin. While they were holed up, Father Calmon, who had been in hiding, appeared in high dudgeon, visibly frightened at the growing Japanese activity in the hills. Thinking only of his flock, he naively urged Ras and his party to give themselves up to the Japanese in exchange for a promise that the Karens would be left in peace. Ras was apoplectic, and gave Father Calmon a piece of his mind. For him it was a simple military decision:

> 'I saw the situation from a soldier's point of view. My country was
> at war with the Japanese. Seagrim had given me orders to fight
> them. This I intended to do to the best of my abilities. Indeed, I
> had escaped at great personal risk for this very purpose. I was at war
> with the Japanese. In war, people were killed if they took part in it.
> It was as simple as that.'[3]

Angrily, Ras insisted that he had had plenty of experience of dealing with the Japanese. He found them to be sadistic bullies to whom any sign of perceived weakness was an invitation to increased brutality. Did the good Father really think that the Japanese would honour any agreement or treaty made with them? Far from leaving the Karens in peace, all surrender would achieve, he argued, was to provide the Japanese with an unrestricted opportunity to torture and massacre the Karens until they were too cowed to resist. Was that really what Father Calmon wanted? And what would it mean for the brave levies and for Seagrim?

It was a strange confrontation between the two Europeans deep in the jungle, both brave men, each with very different concepts of duty: Ras as pugnacious as ever, while Father Calmon looked ever more unhappy and uncomfortable. The priest had great respect for Ras, but he left a disconsolate and disappointed man. Sadly, Ras never saw him again. However, the young priest's fears were justified. It wasn't long before the Japanese began to exact a terrible retribution on the Karens, and on Father Calmon personally. Jean Calmon commanded great respect among the Karens, and in turn he admired them for their simplicity and natural honesty. When the British had retreated, he had persuaded the Karens not to flee north and abandon the hills. 'Stay here, work as usual. It is the surest way to save your lives,' he had argued. 'I won't abandon you.'[4] Mindful of that advice, and the moral responsibility that he felt went with it, Calmon wrestled with his conscience as he hid in the hills, knowing of the poor innocents in jail.

As for Ta Roe and his friends, on arrival in Papun, they were taken to a house on the east bank of the Yunzalin river that had once belonged to the murdered Indian merchant Ram Singh. There they were interrogated in front of the venal Maung Shwe. Ta Roe was right to be afraid. Maung Shwe and the Japanese knew a great deal more about Seagrim, Father Calmon and their activities than they had feared. In early March, in a situation report to the kempeitai in Thaton, the ruthless commissioner had written:

> 'It has been the mentality of the Karen community as a whole and particularly those of Papun to wish and expect the return of the British. This has been strengthened by the presence of a European captain and a Roman Catholic priest in the district who are continuously spoiling the minds of the people against both the Japanese and Burmese governments.'[5]

Feigning innocence, but expecting a gruelling cross-examination and possible torture, the Karens were relieved to face only three questions:

'Is it true there are many British soldiers in your village?' Answer: 'No.'
'Who was responsible for burning down Papun and the surrounding
villages?' To which they replied: 'The BIA.' Finally: 'From now on, do you
promise to co-operate with us in every respect?' Answer: 'Yes.'[6] Rather
astonished at having their bald assertions taken at face value, Ta Roe then
volunteered that he could be held personally responsible for any trouble
around Pyagawpu. After receiving a short lecture from the Japanese officer
on the importance of cooperating with Maung Shwe, overwhelmed with
relief they were then set free to return to their homes.

Arriving back in Pyagawpu three days later, Ta Roe found that his
instructions had been followed to the letter. His trusted fellow elder
had personally moved Seagrim and his men further into the jungle to
Payasedo, twenty-three miles to the west of Pyagawpu. No one else knew
where he was hidden. Safe once again from detection, for the next few
months Seagrim made Payasedo his headquarters. Shortly after his arrival,
Seagrim wrote to Ta Roe and asked him for supplies, which, in order to
minimise the number of people aware of Seagrim's new hideout, Ta Roe
brought to him personally by elephant. Thereafter, he supplied Seagrim
monthly, in strict security, either himself or through a trusted friend. In
response, Seagrim wrote regularly to Ta Roe, exhorting him to keep up
his spirits and have faith. 'Do not be discouraged, Ta Roe, don't worry.
Surely one day the British will come back to us. In the meantime, we
must put our trust in God and have faith in Him.'[7]

Self-serving and corrupt, Maung Shwe proceeded to feather his own
nest. The police were allowed to behave like dacoits, seizing whatever
they wished with impunity. Inured to official corruption and abuse of
power, the Karens bore this with their customary stoicism, but they were
outraged when several senior Karens were arrested and held in custody at
the Japanese police headquarters in Thaton. To add insult to injury, a price
of 500 rupees was also put on Father Calmon's head. The Japanese ordered
that he was to be executed as soon as he was apprehended. When no one
rose to the bait, Maung Shwe arrested some Catholic families, including
wives and children, and threw more than thirty Indian Catholics, who had
sought refuge at the mission, into jail.

While hiding in the jungle, wrestling with his conscience, Father
Calmon knew what he had to do. With no concern for his own life,
and to shield the Karens from further evil, on 17 March 1943 he calmly

walked into Papun and, fully expecting to be shot, openly challenged the BIA and an astonished Maung Shwe. It was a remarkable confrontation between the selfless priest, who was fully prepared to die for his faith, and the selfish, self-serving politician. Immediately, Calmon was ordered to turn in the Europeans hidden in the district and to denounce the Karens. 'Working in the interests of the administration is the only way to save yourself,' he was told. He was then asked for the weapons he was suspected of hiding. Calmon's reply was a masterly *coup de théâtre*. Placing on the table in front of him his walking stick and rosary, he said, 'Here is one and here is the other; these are the only weapons I own.' With nothing to lose and with incredible courage, he then castigated Maung Shwe and told him exactly what he thought of the BIA and their abuse of the Karens:

'Do not think you will obtain the truth by torturing innocent people. The manner in which you treat women, children and Indians you have imprisoned is a gross injustice. Give them back their freedom. As for collaborating with your political work, I cannot do so. As for labours of charity and peace, I am as able, as ever, to give my all. [I] act [only] in an impartial manner. If I have chosen to give myself up, it is because I do not fear death. Beware that your excesses do not provoke the Karens to act in a manner you will regret. You claim to come to establish peace, forgetting the past, yet you wage war on innocents while no sanctions are taken against your guilty friends. If I must die, let it be here in Papun, amongst the Karens that I love. This is the only favour I ask of you.'[8]

Maung Shwe reacted with further threats: 'It would be better for the other missionary [Father Loizeau] to give himself up and to die as well for the Karens,' to which the resolute Calmon coolly replied: 'I will die for both of us! When is the execution?'[8]

The response was not what he expected. On 26 March, escorted by four armed policemen, he was sent down to Thaton, where he was interrogated repeatedly by the kempeitai. Suddenly, just a week later, he was permitted to return to Papun, where he was asked by an affable and smiling police chief to write a report on what was needed to re-establish peace in the hills. Calmon argued that the Karens would never be placated unless they were administered by their own officials. It was a brave assertion because it undermined Maung Shwe's authority, but ultimately it was to save him.

A few weeks later, Maung Shwe reported back from Pyagawpu to the Secretary for Home Affairs in Rangoon. Chillingly, he knew exactly who the Europeans were: 'The initial motives of this tour were to promote peace measures, to study the topography of the district, and to get general information about the people, their aspirations, what arms they have, and, last but not least, to investigate the whereabouts of Seagrim, Father Calmon and Ras Pagani and their troops.'[9] Pagani would have been appalled to know that his true identity had been revealed. It would have taken only the most cursory check to identify him as the missing prisoner from the railway.

Months later, Calmon's report reached the Burmese puppet government in Rangoon. Tired of the provocative depredations of the BIA, they sent two eminent Karens to investigate the troubles in and around Papun to try to defuse the situation, one being Shwe Tun Gya, the 'Tiger of the Delta'. The Karens' report was damning. It set out in explicit detail the long litany of abuses inflicted by the BIA on the Karens.

'The BIA burned many Karen villages, resulting in many homeless. They took their properties, gold and silver, even daily utensils. They murdered many Karens, including seventeen leading citizens and elders. Lastly, and most important of all, they took away many of the Karen womenfolk, and twenty young girls were taken to Papun and kept as prostitutes in line for the BIA soldiers.'[10]

On the basis of the Karen mission's report and Father Calmon's unsolicited testimony, the government realised that the lawless behaviour of the BIA and Maung Shwe's uncompromising tactics were counter-productive. All that had been achieved was to reinforce the Karens' natural sympathies for the British. In July 1943, Maung Shwe and his cadre were removed and replaced by two, much more sympathetic Karen policemen: Saw Tommer as Deputy Commissioner and Arthur Ta Bi as Deputy Superintendent of Police. Soon they became Seagrim's firm allies.

For poor Father Calmon, though, his March interrogation was just the beginning of a long and harrowing ordeal at the hands of the Japanese under constant threat of torture and death. Time after time his faith was tested to its limits, but this magnificent Frenchman never once wavered: Time after time he was defiant and refused to incriminate anyone. 'I may suffer, but I will not be the cause of others' suffering.'[11] Because of his refusal to incriminate anyone, many, many Karens owed their lives to this courageous man, who was quite prepared to be martyred on their behalf.

★★★

After the attack on Papun, rather than return to his base at Kadaingti, Ras Pagani thought he ought to travel up to Pyagawpu to brief Seagrim on his activities and explain the deteriorating security condition in the south. En route, he advised all the elders in the villages through which he passed of the impending Japanese threat, urging them to retreat into the jungle with their food and animals. The levies were ordered to return to Kadaingti while Ras, Mura and his faithful Gurkhas headed north to Pyagawpu. Passing through Papun – which, following his successful attack was now in ruins and devoid of the enemy – he enjoyed a brief word with Father Loizeau, who was in hiding. This time there were no lavish meals or celebrations. Ras quickly pressed on for Pyagawpu, which he reached ten days later. Here, he received bad news from the local Baptist minister: strong enemy forces had advanced along the Mawchi road to the north. Just a week earlier, a company of over seventy Japanese troops had arrived from Papun, searching for English soldiers. Seagrim had been forced into hiding. The minister had no idea where he could be; it was a secret entrusted only to one or two Karens on a strictly need-to-know basis.

Ras was in a quandary. He coolly reviewed his position. He could return to Kadaingti but, having organised the levies, he believed that they could get on well enough without him, and with his need to be hidden and fed, he would be more of a liability than an asset. Alternatively, he could remain in hiding indefinitely at Papun, in the hope of being reunited with Seagrim, but his mentor's return looked unlikely given the strength of Japanese forces in the area. Also, by now Ras had realised something further:

> 'The Japanese soldiers and Burmen whom I had executed at Kadaingti proved that the enemy knew that I and Seagrim were in the Karen hills... I felt they might eventually catch me and return me to 18th Kilo Camp to be shot. There seemed to me to be no future hiding here, where my presence would not further any operations, and might even endanger the lives of the local Karens ...'[12]

After carefully weighing up his options, Ras reverted to his original plan.

He resolved to head across Burma to the Allied lines, a perilous journey of over 600 miles, to tell them what was happening to the PoWs on the railway, deliver Seagrim's report to Army headquarters, and explain the situation in the Karen states. It was an agonising decision to make: to leave his friend behind in Burma:

'I remembered only too well the lonely figure of Hugh Seagrim as I had last seen him... in December. I loved and admired the man who had given me so much friendship and inspiration, and, although convinced I was doing the right thing, I hated the thought of going away without seeing him or even being able to get a message to him.'[13]

Having made his fateful decision, Ras prepared for the journey. Convinced that God had led him to Seagrim and protected him thus far, he little knew that his luck was about to run out, or that his impending journey would lead him into the most desperate danger.

Chapter 9

Perilous Journey

'Give me liberty or give me death!'
PATRICK HENRY

Haunted by his decision to leave, Ras travelled north for three days, moving surreptitiously from village to village. He moved only at night and rested by day in friendly Karen settlements – the same routine that had stood him in such good stead when escaping from the railway. He was not alone. Accompanied by the devoted Mura and a motley group of Gurkhas, the small party steered well clear of Mawchi, which was swarming with enemy troops. They headed north-west. Eventually, after several night marches, they slithered down the jungle-clad foothills east of the Sittang river, beyond which lay a broad plain of flat, dry padi fields. Keeping a low profile and avoiding all the local settlements, including Toungoo, they slipped across the plain to the Sittang, where their guide arranged to ferry them over. A few miles further on, and still in darkness, they hit the main road and railway from Rangoon to Toungoo. With their nerves stretched to breaking point, they crept across, keeping a careful lookout for Japanese patrols.

As the sun rose they left the baked padi fields and entered the heavily forested hill country of the Pegu Yomas. Here, on the high ground amid dense undergrowth of teak, bamboo and plantain, they felt safe at last. After a short while, they came to a Karen village, where they lay up during the day, ate and slept. From here, a succession of Karen guides led them from village to village, until in a couple of days they reached the western edges of the hills. Ahead lay the most challenging and dangerous part of the journey. It was fraught with the risk of being spotted and captured. Ras and his party had arrived at the vast central plains of Burma: a shimmering horizon of flat fields, which seemed to evaporate in the far distance. There was scant cover, save for a few small villages set among groves of plantain, mango and bamboo, and these were inhabited by Burmese, who were likely to be hostile. They would have little compunction in attacking Ras's party or turning them over to the Japanese.

Ras realised that there was little prospect of a large party covertly negotiating such an open landscape across hostile country with success. Alone he might just stand a chance. After some deliberation, he decided to send the Gurkhas and guides back to the hills, but the faithful Mura insisted on staying with him. Given the risk that when the Gurkhas eventually rejoined Allied forces – whenever that might be – they might be deemed deserters, Ras provided a chit for each, explaining that they had been cut off behind enemy lines, but had helped him to continue the fight against the Japanese.

After bidding the Gurkhas farewell and good luck, Ras and Mura moved off. They carried rations of dried meat and rice – enough to avoid the need to venture near any Burmese settlements for three days, but after that they would need to travel a further six nights to cross the Irrawaddy and reach the Arakan Yomas, where once again, they could rely on friendly Karen support. At that stage in their journey, Ras would have preferred simply to go hungry rather than risk approaching Burmese villages, but with the young Mura now in tow, he had to consider the other man's needs. As Mura was a Kachin, he was far less likely to attract attention than Ras, so they resolved to approach one village en route to get enough food to last them through to the river.

After a while, they came to a likely looking settlement. They agreed a simple secret code. If Mura returned carrying his hat, it would be safe for Ras to join him. If he came with his hat on his head and a party of locals, it would indicate that he had been captured. If that happened, Mura would suddenly dive to the ground and Ras would open up with his tommy gun. In the ensuing melee, both would make a break for it. If just a party of villagers came, then the chances would be it was a trap and Ras should be on his guard.

Ras remained concealed outside the village for a while, his heart pounding, while Mura went in to buy food. It was an anxious time, fraught with danger. The minutes ticked by. Still no Mura. Then, some time later, a group of villagers came to find Ras. They called out to encourage him to join Mura and eat with them. With considerable apprehension, Ras reluctantly agreed. He emerged cautiously from the trees and indicated that the party should lead the way into the village, with Ras bringing up the rear, his tommy gun cocked and ready to fire. His nerves were stretched to breaking point. His sharp eyes noticed that the man ahead of him was carrying a rifle on his shoulder with the muzzle pointed backwards at him, so he gradually slowed his pace. This saved his life. Suddenly, without warning, the Burmese pulled the trigger, but the shot lifted the muzzle and the bullet whistled past Ras's head. Had he not hung back, he would have been shot dead.

It was the signal for an ambush. Three or four other Burmese leapt out of the bushes armed with shotguns and fired, hitting Ras in the buttocks as he turned and ran. He emptied his entire magazine at them, killing the man with the rifle and several others, before the remaining assailants fled back to the village in confusion. Wounded, and having roused the entire neighbourhood, Ras was convinced that it would be suicidal to try to rescue Mura. Both had agreed that should such a situation arise, it was each man for himself. Now alone and in hostile enemy country, Ras knew that to survive he had to keep his wits about him. He calculated that all the local villages to the north and west would be on alert. Having killed several Burmese in the ambush, he could expect little mercy. As night fell, he reversed course and headed south to hide up and recover from his flesh wounds until the hue and cry died down.

As the sun rose, Ras found a dense thicket where he hid all the following day in the flaming heat. In March the central plains are a veritable furnace. The heat shimmered in a miasmatic haze over the scorched fields. Tough as he was, he was tormented all that long day by a raging thirst. When night fell, he crawled from his hiding place, found some water and drank, and drank, and drank to assuage his parched throat. Rehydrated, he then marched west with the night, before hiding up again at dawn near a small temple. Later that afternoon, he was spotted by a pongyi, or Buddhist monk, who invited him into the temple for a meal. Assuming he was safe within the sacred precincts of the temple, Ras ate his fill, but increasingly he became uneasy as, one by one, the monks left the temple. Fearing treachery, he thanked the monk for his food, cocked his tommy gun and stepped warily outside – only to be confronted with a howling mob of Burmese armed with dahs and crossbows charging towards him.

He ran for his life. A Burmese caught up with him and tried to grapple his tommy gun from his hands. A swift upper-cut floored the assailant. Ras then dived headlong into the surrounding undergrowth and sprinted northwards, pursued by a band of screaming villagers, but, fearful of his tommy gun, they began to lag behind. After gaining some distance, gasping for breath, parched and exhausted, he dived into a dense thicket of thorn bushes, ignoring his lacerated flesh, and lay motionless as the howling mob swept past him, their cries fading into the distance. For Ras it was terrifying – an outcast in an alien land, far from home or any prospect of safety, and being hotly pursued by a blood-crazed mob with the sole intention of ripping him to pieces. It was yet another narrow escape, his second in so many days, and it proved how incredibly dangerous the entire central plain was likely to be for him. Both Seagrim and Saw Po Thin had been right: it was a reckless venture.

As dusk fell, he broke cover. Caked in a crust of salt and sweat, wracked by thirst and gagging for water, he searched for a local well, but to his dismay found that the water was brackish. Undeterred, he drank some to replenish the salts he had lost in the pursuit. Still searching, he found another well with a simple, rickety bamboo ladder. Overwhelmed with thirst, he climbed down and found to his utter joy that the water was fresh. He drank and drank as much as he could and wallowed in the water: 'It was such bliss. I could have stayed in the water all night.'[1] As the night ebbed away, he climbed out and found a small bamboo hut, where he sat and catnapped all that day, and the following night. Guessing that it was probably used only seasonally, he remained alert, ready to leap into action at the slightest sound. For the outlaw and the hunted, the peace before sunrise is a time of hope that somehow the new day might offer a brief respite from pursuit and persecution. So it was for Ras.

The following morning, the dawn exploded on the eastern horizon: a brilliant turquoise sky shot through with a dazzling display of crimson and ochre; the harbinger of another day of scorching heat. As the blue-grey shadows across the fields melted away, slowly Ras realised that he was marooned in the middle of a vast open plain stretching as far as the eye could see, with little or no cover at all. Far in the distance, rippling in the haze, he spotted a steep hill topped by a glistening gold pagoda rising out of an immense purple plain. It seemed to hover and swirl like a mirage, swimming in the currents of hot air that wavered and darted on the western horizon. Exposed and vulnerable on the plain, he resolved to press on in daylight until he reached the hill and could hide up again. It was a risk, but one worth taking. Although he did not bear close scrutiny, from a distance and to a casual observer he could pass for an Indian labourer: he was barefoot and wore thin green, silky trousers, a loose shirt and a turban. With feet toughened by over a year of travelling like a native, he marched through the heat of the day – but the heat haze played tricks. The distance to the pagoda was deceptive.

After walking all day, by nightfall he had reached only the bottom of the hill. He decided that, to conserve his strength, he would lie up and rest all night and the following day. He crawled into the bushes at the foot of the hill. Tired and exhausted, his skin covered in a rime of dirt and salt crystals from his exertions, he fell into a deep sleep. In the morning, he kept watch on the monks moving around the pagoda and noticed that it was isolated. No one came near. After another night in the bushes, and with some trepidation after his earlier experience, as dawn rose he climbed the hill. Outside the pagoda, he was greeted by one of the monks, who seemed friendly and spoke some English. Ras was invited to eat and sleep, reassured by the monk that the Burmese and Japanese never came close to the temple. At noon, he was suddenly woken by the pulsating throb of aircraft engines as a squadron of Allied bombers flew overhead, on a mission to bomb Prome. Watching the planes as they flew over was a reassuring sight. He was not entirely alone: up there were his comrades. There was hope that his plan might yet be successful.

The sight of the planes also served as inspiration regarding his perennial concern about his identity, should he ever be captured. He was right to worry; Maung Shwe's report to Rangoon had clearly indicated that the Japanese knew his name, and that he had been operating with Seagrim in Karenni. Watching the planes, Ras decided that, if apprehended, he would pretend to be an American Air Force lieutenant shot down on a bombing mission, similar to the one he was witnessing. He reasoned that if he posed as an American officer, the Japanese would be less likely to associate him with a British NCO and escapee from the railway. He believed – wrongly as it happened – that there were few Americans in Burma, and that the Japanese might treat him as a curiosity. After thinking of various options for his assumed identity, he took for his spurious new persona the Christian names of his baby son, Terry Ashton Melvyn. He was unlikely to forget these, even under torture. It was yet another fateful decision that would soon save his life.

Once the raid had passed, from their vantage point high up on the temple mount the monks pointed out the places where the Japanese troops were usually positioned, as well as the snaking line of the Irrawaddy river and – in the heat haze beyond, where he could see the tantalising sight of the Arakan Yomas – friendly Karen country. Safety. Ras surveyed the scene with joy: the river was just a night's march away. He was ecstatic and even more convinced that he was being guided by a higher power.

Extremely wary after his earlier ambushes, Ras remained alert throughout his stay at the temple and kept a close watch on the monks to check whether any slipped away quietly to inform on him, but they did not. They were friendly and helpful. They genuinely appeared to like him and to sympathise with his position. Before leaving, Ras wrote another of his chits for the head monk, to the effect that they had provided him with valuable help and assistance. Ras explained that when the British returned the monk should show it to them, but in the meantime he should take every precaution to avoid letting it fall into Japanese hands.

As the sun melted into the western sky, Ras descended the hill, rested and buoyed with hope. He headed for the great serpentine loops of the Irrawaddy: the last major obstacle between him and the relative safety of the Arakan Yomas. On his way, he heard Allied aircraft heading for another heavy raid on Prome. He reached the river at Nyaungzaye, midway between Paungde and Prome, and just before dawn found a cave, well screened by bushes, that offered an excellent hiding place. Here he could rest up, plan his crossing and allow his body to recover from his wounds. The musky smell of a big cat assailed his nostrils – perhaps a leopard or a tiger – but, reasoning that it would be more afraid of him that he was of it, he slept for a while. Later that morning, he reconnoitred the river banks, unobtrusively looking for a boat, but found nothing. Uneasy at moving too far away from the cave in daylight, he soon realised that he would have to swim across the half-mile-wide channel, but he was a strong swimmer and the prospect didn't daunt him. There were shifting sandbanks in the river, which might offer some intermediate refuge should he need it.

Before starting across, he transformed himself into his new persona of Lieutenant Terry Ashton Melvyn USAAF, tearing into tiny pieces Seagrim's long letter to Army HQ and his letter of promotion to sergeant. To have been caught with either was a death sentence. He buried the pieces with his old dog tags in the floor of the cave. It was a surreal moment for him: 'I felt a great sense of relief, although I realised that if I was killed under this name no one would ever know what had happened to me. It would probably be assumed that I had died in the jungle from disease or starvation.'[2]

In its lower reaches, interspersed with sandbanks and shallows, the Irrawaddy meanders peacefully across a flat alluvial plain – but it is dangerously deceptive and subject to fierce, unexpected currents. As a gibbous moon rose, the river was transformed into a silver ribbon of light winding across the countryside. Ras waded into the water and started to swim. For about 150 yards he made steady progress. Then, suddenly, he was seized and buffeted by two powerful currents. A strong undertow dragged him under. Weighed down by his tommy gun, grenades and spare magazines, he realised that, if he was not to drown, he had to jettison them, however much he might need them on the other side. Offloading his burdens, he bobbed back to the surface. Fearful, he decided to float downriver rather than try to fight against the terrible currents, in the hope that one of the great curves of the river would fling him within striking distance of the far bank.

But it was not to be. After floating more than five miles downstream, and with his strength all but gone, he ended up once again back on the south bank. Exhausted, he managed to crawl ashore. As he lay gasping for breath in the glutinous mud of the foreshore, he saw three Burmese fishermen coming over to him. Realising they had a small boat, he sensed salvation and indicated that he wished to go across the river. Apparently agreeing to this, they began to push off. Ras's hopes rose once more, but soon it became clear that they were dawdling. Suddenly, a shout went up from the riverbank and an ugly-looking crowd of Burmese appeared, armed with shotguns and dahs. The fishermen were ordered back. As the boat came ashore, Ras was seized and tied, but he had the wits to keep his arms away from his body so that the rope remained loose. They led him like a dog on a lead pulling and pushing him along. Having survived so many close shaves, Ras was bitterly disappointed that he had been captured on the very verge of success – so near, yet so far: 'I was once more a prisoner … the Arakan Yomas had seemed so close as I gazed across the river. There I would have found friends to guide me on my way north, but now they were as unattainable as if they had been on another planet.'[3]

After a short distance, he slipped the rope and made a break for it, running full tilt towards some bushes along the riverbank, but he tripped in a crack in the baked mud and fell headfirst. As he was leaping to his feet, one of the Burmese jumped on top of him. Ras responded with a terrific punch, which knocked his assailant senseless. As he turned and darted off once more, he heard a loud explosion and felt a dreadful pain in his side. He collapsed. In seconds, the mob set upon him, slashing him with dahs and beating him with clubs. Some time later, barely conscious, Ras became dimly aware that they had stopped and were standing around him. Then he heard, close by, what he assumed was a snarling dog. As he slowly turned his head, there was nothing there; but when he coughed, he felt an agonising pain in his right side. He takes up the tale:

'I coughed again and put a hand to my side to try and ease the pain. My hand came away wet and sticky, and I saw dimly that I was holding a thick clot of blood large enough to fill my hand. The snarling continued and then I realised that it was not a dog but air bubbling through the hole in my side every time I breathed. My back and head also were agony where the Burmese had slashed me deeply with their dahs …

I was barely conscious, just alive enough to realise that this was the end for me. I was going to die. My promise to my wife and small son to return would not now be kept and they would never know what had become of me. I was going to die alone without identity in this distant land among hostile people.'[4]

Chapter 10

Undercover in the Jungle

'And I said to the man who stood at the gate of the year:
"Give me a light that I may tread safely into the unknown."
And he replied:
"Go out into the darkness and put your hand into the Hand of God.
That shall be to you better than light, and safer than a known way."
'So I went forth, and finding the Hand of God, trod gladly into the night.
And he led me towards the hills and the breaking of the day in
the lone East.'

MINNIE LOUISE HASKINS

While Ras Pagani was attempting his epic escape towards the Allied lines in the Arakan, deep undercover in his hiding place at Payasedo Hugh Seagrim was busy laying the foundations of an intelligence operation that would make a major contribution to Allied victory. Seagrim did not know what had happened to Pagani. Whether or not word ever came back to him of Ras's journey via the Gurkhas and guides whom he had sent back, we shall never know. Deprived of his erstwhile right-hand man, Seagrim turned increasingly to Saw Po Hla, the resourceful and intelligent young Karen who had worked with Ras. The son of a prosperous Baptist landowner, Po Hla had graduated from Rangoon University with honours in religion and philosophy in 1939 before joining the Irrawaddy Flotilla Company. He became the first non-European to be appointed as a provincial assistant, and in January 1941 he had enlisted in the 11th Battalion Burma Rifles. He was quickly commissioned.

When the British retreated, Po Hla and his men had been ordered to scatter as the Japanese started to hunt down and take reprisals against former soldiers. As an ex-officer, he was particularly vulnerable. After escaping by river to Mandalay, where he lay up for two months recovering from illness, he headed home to Myaungmya in the Delta. There he was betrayed and only just escaped by the skin of his teeth. With the kempeitai hot on his tail, he was forced to flee first to Shwegyin, and then to Kyaukkyi. There the local levy commander passed on a message to Seagrim, who sent two Karens to bring him up to the camp. It was an inspired move. Saw Po Hla was destined to become Seagrim's right-hand man and his most effective agent in the field.

Fluent in English, and with his degree in religion and philosophy, Po Hla was the ideal companion for Seagrim. He delighted in his company. The solitary British officer and the learned Karen became firm friends. At their first meeting they spent nearly the whole night in earnest conversation, Seagrim enquiring as an Anglican how Baptists interpreted some of the passages in the Bible. Initially, Seagrim used Po Hla as a trusted liaison officer between himself and his section commanders. It was in this capacity that Ras had met him and been impressed by his daring and initiative. Ras having vanished, Po Hla took over his functions.

When rumours emerged in the early summer of 1943 that the Japanese were planning to establish permanent kempeitai posts in the hills, Po Hla was dispatched to the plains to find out more. He travelled openly, but cautiously, to Pegu and the towns on the main Mandalay-to-Rangoon highway. After making discreet enquiries, he established that the rumours were false: the Japanese had no plans to move up to either Kyaukkyi or Papun. Both men were much relieved. It meant that they did not have to relocate their headquarters further north – a risky operation fraught with the threat of exposure, capture and death. The local Karens were also less vulnerable to kempeitai brutality.

Next, in July 1943, Po Hla was dispatched to Papun to make discreet contact with the new district commissioner, Saw Tommer, who had taken over from Maung Shwe, and the new township officer, Arthur Ta Bi. With the welfare of the Karens uppermost in his mind, and knowing the new officials – being Karens themselves – were inclined to be supportive of his cause, Seagrim sent a message to both. He explained how pleased he was that the Karens now had local officials and pledged the levies' support in maintaining law and order across the hills. Po Hla then toured Ras Pagani's old command area in the south, ordering the levies to give Saw Tommer and Arthur Ta Bi their unequivocal support.

Po Hla recalled that Seagrim wrestled perpetually with the conundrum of suffering. Why, with a loving God, should man have to endure suffering? What was the significance of the Cross? And what of miracles? Once

Seagrim asked Po Hla whether he believed in them. Po Hla replied that he did but could not explain them, to which Seagrim responded that while he had once discounted them, now he was a firm believer. He explained why. While hiding up at Mawtudo eighteen months earlier in the middle of the rainy season, when the air was thick and sluggish and the jungle a sodden quagmire, they completely ran out of food. Author Ian Morrison wrote: 'One of the Kachins said to him: "Thakin [Master], there are no more rations. What are we going to do?" to which Seagrim replied, "Don't worry. When the time comes, God will send us some rations," and he told his Kachin companion the story of Elijah and the ravens.'[1]

That same morning, after drinking just hot water for breakfast, they all prayed together. Later that day, a pack of hunting dogs rooting in the forest encountered a barking deer, which was a great local delicacy. As they gave chase, bizarrely the deer ran not into the forest and safety as it would normally, but straight into the village, where the grateful Karens killed it with a spear. Immediately thinking of Seagrim, they took the carcass and some vegetables up to him, and skinned and cooked the deer, refusing any for themselves. Whereas before the war Seagrim would have regarded this as a fortunate coincidence, now, somewhat fancifully perhaps, he considered it was the answer to his prayers.

Po Hla's recollections of these spiritual exchanges – which took place almost every time the men met – provide a rare glimpse of Seagrim's

Above left: Lieutenant Ba Gyaw and (above right) the intrepid
Lieutenant Saw Po Hla, Seagrim's most trusted agent.

growing belief that suffering has a purpose; that if one is to achieve enlightenment, life is a pilgrimage beset with challenges and suffering. These must be endured and overcome. 'No cross, no crown,' he would often say. It is no coincidence that when Po Hla went down to the plains, Seagrim asked him to see if he could find a copy of Bunyan's great allegorical work *The Pilgrim's Progress*, the words of which have acted as guidance for so many oppressed souls in an uncomprehending world. Over sixty years later, the same book provided solace and inspiration to Aung San Suu Kyi during her years of confinement.

Surrounded by Theravada Buddhism, which teaches the principle of karma and the perpetual cycle of existence and rebirth, Seagrim was aware of the unity of belief that underlies all major religions. Each offered its own path to the same source. Herein lay the seeds of his subsequent actions: an explicit recognition of karma, that what we do in life echoes through eternity, and influences our future cycles of existence.

Seagrim urged Po Hla to read Ralph Waldo Emerson's *Essays* and often repeated Emerson's credo that 'to think is to act'. Po Hla was unable to find a copy of *The Pilgrim's Progress*, but he did return from Papun with a biography of Dr Adoniram Judson, the Baptist missionary, who had converted the Karens. The congruence between ancient Karen beliefs and Christianity made a deep impression on Seagrim, confirming to him that all spiritual paths lead to the same end. For Seagrim, these exchanges with Po Hla were not just an intellectual exercise in abstract philosophy, but a powerful guiding force which increasingly directed his own moral choices and actions: self-observation of his own behaviour, his ability to put the needs of others above his own, and his willingness to be corrected by others. All were facets of his innate humility.

Self-abnegation became a feature of his daily behaviour. When young villagers brought him food, he would refuse to touch it until the boys returned to share it with him. Often he would cook the rice himself and have it waiting for them on their return – unheard of behaviour for a British officer. He lived off the fruits of the forest and the food that the Karens ate, such as bamboo shoots, nga pi (fish paste), buffalo, deer and even jungle rats and frogs. His humility won the hearts of his many followers. Whatever he had, he ensured that it was shared equally with his boys and any guests who came to his camp. Alongside his humility was an inner calm that never failed to impress. On one occasion a Karen volunteer was handling a gun when it went off accidentally, narrowly missing Seagrim. Instead of getting angry and asking who was responsible, he simply sat smiling and said, 'It is a fearful thing if guns go off accidentally.'[2]

When his army boots wore out, the villagers made him leather sandals but, like Pagani, he insisted on going barefoot to prove he was as tough as them. Unlike Pagani, who drank copious quantities of alcohol with the Karens, Seagrim drank little; the villagers were surprised that he was so abstemious, for the small quantity he imbibed he drank only on special occasions, and then only to please them.

In one exchange with Po Hla, Seagrim complained of the actions of a local Karen pastor, who traded in opium to supplement his meagre living. 'Po Hla, I cannot understand a Christian pastor who carries on a trade like that,' he said, to which Po Hla replied: 'These people are simple uneducated folk. This Karen does not realise that he is doing wrong. He has been told that stealing, adultery and drinking are wrong. He won't do these things. It is for you and me to teach this Karen and others like him that to trade in opium is wrong.' Seagrim replied: 'You are quite right, Po Hla. I misjudged that fellow.'[3]

In another instance, Seagrim arbitrated between some Karens over a trivial local dispute. Afterwards, in sheer exasperation, he turned to Po Hla and said: 'Next time I am going to tell these Karens what I really think about these petty squabbles of theirs.' With wisdom well beyond his years, Po Hla replied: 'These hill Karens are children. If you were not here, they would take these disputes to the elders and the elders would settle them. But they regard you as their Father and that is why they bring them to you. Would you blame your children if they quarrelled among themselves?'[4] For a man who seemed to have transcended his ego, it was a chastening moment for Hugh to realise quite how much he was revered. Like so many others, Po Hla years later recalled that the Karens 'not only loved and trusted him, they almost worshipped him'.[5] The older Karens called him Pu Day Wa, meaning 'young white brother', in reference to the Golden Book: to them he was the white saviour from over the seas who had come to save the Karens in their hour of need.

★★★

Unbeknown to Seagrim, throughout late 1942 detailed plans were being hatched in India to try to re-establish contact with him in the hills. No one knew for certain whether he was alive or dead, but there was a strong presumption that, being among the intensely loyal Karens, he was likely to have survived. If contact could be made, a reliable stream of intelligence could be secured from deep within Burma where the British were operating virtually blind. A plan, codenamed 'Operation Harlington', was conceived with four stages.

Stage One was to drop four lightly equipped Karen parachutists into the Karen hills to carry out a quick reconnaissance, initially without a wireless transmitter. The officer selected to lead this phase was the dependable Ba Gyaw, now a second lieutenant, a quiet, reliable man of great character, who had provided sterling service during the legendary trek out of Burma a year earlier with Captain Arthur Bell Thompson. After an initial evaluation of the scene, he was to decide whether it was safe to drop a transmitter and the rest of their kit. Under Stage Two, an RAF Hudson would fly over the dropping zone and, if signalled all-clear by Ba Gyaw from the ground, would drop a radio transmitter and supplies. Once communication was established with India, Ba Gyaw would carry out a wider recce, and under Stage Three advise on dropping in a British officer, Major Jimmy Nimmo, and a team of Karen wireless operators, who could work with Seagrim to build up a reliable intelligence network. The final stage would follow on. If the local situation looked favourable, and Nimmo signalled that it was safe, another British officer, Captain Eric McCrindle, would be dropped in to join them.

Both Jimmy Nimmo[6] and Eric McCrindle[7] were old Burma hands. Both had already made spectacular escapes from Burma during the great exodus of spring 1942. Nimmo was the driving force behind Captain Thompson's party, who, with Ba Gyaw and Kan Choke, had made the epic 900-mile, four-month trek north to Fort Hertz a year earlier. McCrindle had been part of the same group, but later joined Ritchie Gardiner, Noel Boyt and other Force 136 officers on their harrowing ordeal through the remote Chaukkan Pass to India. Tough and self-reliant, both were former employees of the Scottish timber company Macgregor and Co., which owned vast tracts of forest running from the Pegu Yomas deep into the Karen hills. Civilians at the outbreak of war, they were thoroughly at home in the forest. They were among the first to be commissioned by Noel Stevenson, the man who had pioneered the creation of locally raised levies among the hill tribes. Both were resourceful and immensely brave.

Jimmy was 'a quiet solid person, very determined, fond of his golf and his dogs, not perhaps a fluent talker but very good company'.[8] Thompson, who developed a strong friendship with him during their epic journey, described him in similar terms as 'a quiet young Scot'. He believed that during those months of unimaginable physical deprivation and acute mental strain 'he was responsible for our eventual survival'.[9] Eric McCrindle (Mac) was an accomplished linguist, who arrived in Burma just two months after Jimmy Nimmo in 1934. As contemporaries, the two new arrivals soon became friends and shared a house together with Nimmo's dog, Tuppence. Mac, the only forestry assistant under six feet tall, was renowned for his charming smile, his passion for debate and an exceptional ability to focus single-mindedly on any issue. Having endured enough suffering and hardship during their escapes from Burma to make lesser men wilt, neither had any compunction about stepping forward once again and volunteering for special operations. Both were experienced enough to know that this was extremely hazardous, with very little chance of survival, but neither they nor the Karens who had escaped to India thought twice.

On 18 February 1943 Stage One of Operation Harlington was put into action. Under the cover of a synchronised bombing raid on Toungoo, Ba Gyaw and three Karen companions were dropped successfully into the hills in a bravura display of flying by Jimmy King, a fearless, red-haired flying officer from Paisley, and one of the most daring of the special breed of airmen working with Force 136. The pilots charged with covert missions to drop agents into Burma were the unsung heroes of the Burma campaign. They suffered appalling casualty rates. It was immensely dangerous. From Jessore alone, where Jimmy King was based, the aircrew suffered forty times greater loss of life than the agents they dropped. Only five parachutists were lost in Burma for the cost of over 200 air crew.

For the agents, their moment of greatest danger was actually in transit in the air. Bouncing and sliding through the turbulence over dark jungle-clad ridges, even the most experienced pilot battled with stomach-churning dread. It was common for aircraft to be caught in a downdraft and hurled without warning to oblivion in the impenetrable green morass below. One recalled turning to his navigator, who 'had his hands held up close to his face, his fists were clenched and he was beating them violently against his cheeks … It was clear that he was terrified. He would not, or could not, answer.' As the aircraft was flung around the night sky, and the pilot struggled to keep the control column aligned, he noticed that the navigator 'was holding my right arm, reaching across and clutching it with both hands and whimpering with fright'.[10]

King was a brilliant pilot with the luck of the devil and a very cool head. The drop zone for Harlington involved flying up a narrow valley flanked by hills rising 1,500 feet above him, then, after a couple of miles, performing a sharp right-angle turn, followed by a further three quarters of a mile of flying to the drop zone, before immediately banking up over a precipitous hill, 3,000 feet high, set dead ahead. The slightest miscalculation would have been fatal, but for Jimmy King it was a piece of cake. Time and again when asked to do similar drops, he never demurred or asked any questions, but just got on with it. The phlegmatic King ended the war as a squadron leader with a DSO and DFC.[11]

With Ba Gyaw safely delivered, and his recce proving that it was indeed safe to proceed to Stage Two, it was now time to deliver the transmitter but, exasperatingly, time after time circumstances conspired to frustrate things. Over the next eight months, no fewer than twenty separate attempts were made, but each proved abortive. Given the hazardous nature of navigating at low level through the hills, drops could only be made at full moon. Even worse, after midnight for most of the year the valleys usually filled with thick mist, rendering it impossible to see the ground, let alone drop material in the right place. Other than at the height of the monsoon in July, every month for eight months from February to October 1943 three separate attempts were made to drop the transmitter, usually by the fearless Jimmy King with Jimmy Nimmo on board. In the ageing Hudsons, all too often it was engine failure or simply poor visibility that doomed the flights. On one occasion a bee jammed the airspeed indicator. Sabotage was suspected but never proved. It was immensely frustrating for all concerned, not least the diligent Ba Gyaw on the ground, who was forced to wait at the appointed spot each full moon, in danger of being caught red-handed. Time and time again he heard the Hudson droning overhead, only to have his hopes dashed.

As frustrations mounted, in late March 1943 tantalising news arrived back in India to suggest that Seagrim might well still be alive. A small party of Chindits returning from the first Wingate expedition had encountered a group of Karens and their elephants near the Chindwin river. One had been in Pyagawpu in November 1942. Although he had not seen

Seagrim, he reported that there were two Europeans alive in the hills, one a British officer and the other a missionary. With senior officers now apoplectic at the endless delays, by late August 1943 various alternative plans were mooted to contact Seagrim. Colonel Edgar Peacock, who was later to lead Otter force into the Karen hills in the closing stages of the war as part of Operation Character, was invited to plan an overland route to find Seagrim and ramp up the resistance movement in readiness for the coming British offensive.

Jimmy Nimmo pressed for further attempts to be made by air. He recommended that at the September full moon, despite the lack of success with Stage Two, they should move straight to Stage Three, and he and his party of wireless operators be dropped in the flat country south of Kyaukkyi with only what little they could carry. From there they would make their way up into the hills and prepare two alternative drop zones, from which they could be supplied the following month when there was a gap in the climate. It was an exceptionally risky undertaking. Nevertheless, High Command agreed – but on two occasions around the September full moon they were forced to abort yet again due to bad weather.

Finally, on 12 October 1943, after eight months of perpetual frustration, Nimmo and his five Karen companions set off once more. As he was poised for his blind drop into the night far behind enemy lines, he turned to bid farewell to the indefatigable Jimmy King with a cheerful wave and a quick word of thanks. The self-possessed King was awestruck at Nimmo's courage and spoke of it frequently afterwards. When King looked again, Nimmo had vanished with his companions into the great black void. No one knew whether he would ever be able to find Seagrim in the fearful dark wilderness below, let alone re-establish contact with India; whether he might fall into the hands of the dreaded kempeitai, or, like so many others, just disappear without trace. Operation Harlington was balanced on a knife edge.

Chapter 11

Dark Night of the Soul

'I remained, lost in oblivion.
My face I reclined on the Beloved.'
ST. JOHN OF THE CROSS

E merging from a coma in great pain on the banks of the Irrawaddy,
Ras Pagani was only dimly aware that the Burmese were carrying
him to a boat. He was laid face downwards and poled upstream
to a nearby Japanese patrol boat. Here a Japanese doctor stitched the
most hideous wound in his back – six inches long and very deep – in
an agonising process without anaesthetic using a peculiar instrument
that sewed up the wound automatically. As Ras came round and feeling
returned to his limbs, the wounds inflicted by the Burmese dahs stiffened,
generating electrifying paroxysms of pain.

Ras stuck to his cover story. In agony, he explained haltingly that he
was an American flying officer who had been shot down during the raid
on Prome the previous night. The Japanese, to whom his captors had
passed him, treated him with some care as they were rather curious, being
part of a section that had no experience of action against the Allies. He
was taken by ambulance to the General Hospital in Prome and wheeled
straight into the operating theatre, where he was attended by a Japanese
doctor, who took great delight in causing him as much pain as possible.
First his stitches were removed, and then the doctor probed the wound,
ignoring Ras's groans of pain. When the Englishman asked why he did
not use anaesthetic, the doctor replied haughtily that Japanese troops did
not need anaesthetics. He was certainly not going to waste any on an
'American' enemy. Determined to show his true mettle, Ras retorted
that Americans could stand pain as well as any Japanese soldier. After a
while he passed through the pain barrier and 'the agony itself became
an anaesthetic'.

For over four interminable hours the doctor probed the cavity of
the open wound before stitching him up again, leaving four broken ribs.

Crushed by his failure to escape across the river and exhausted by his wounds, Ras was put on a trolley, wheeled through the wards and into the grounds, where he was placed in a small hut resembling a summerhouse. Beneath was a deep pit. Here, tormented by the agony from his wounds and in despair, he decided to take his own life. Thus began his long dark night of the soul.

> 'That night was the worst of my life. My wounds were so excruciatingly painful that I eventually decided it would be better to die than endure such agony any longer. I said my prayers, placed a blood-stained towel over my face and tried to suffocate myself. Then, as my body struggled against my mind, I suddenly remembered my promise to my young wife that I would return to her. I threw the towel on the floor and, gritting my teeth, forced myself to bear the pain and live out that long, lonely night.'[1]

Over forty years later, he wrote in large bold letters in his own personal manuscript a heart-rending declaration of love to his wife: 'There, you see – this is where Pip actually saved my life due to my promise to her.'[2]

In the morning, he was barely alive. When the Japanese came to change his dressing, he was only semi-conscious. After several more nights of torment, slowly, very slowly, he began to recover and felt that maybe, just maybe, he would not die. When he had recovered enough, Army intelligence officers came to interrogate him. By sticking to his assumed identity of Lieutenant Terry Ashton Melvyn, and using the very plausible cover story of the recent raid on Prome, he seemed to satisfy the Japanese enough not to grill him any further. He explained that his uniform had been burned in the crash and that he had obtained local clothes from a Burman. Amazingly, they never queried his lack of an American accent or pressed him for more details of the raid, the planes involved or potential future operations.

Prome was a regular target for Allied bombers striking back at the Japanese. While Ras was recuperating, a heavy daytime raid set much of the city ablaze. Wave after wave of Allied bombers roared overhead, raining sticks of bombs on the railway and the Japanese positions below. Guided by their fins, lines of bombs marched inexorably towards Ras and the flimsy summerhouse, the ear-shattering explosions generating waves of blast that shook the ground and numbed the mind. At night, the planes returned to complete the devastation. Lying prone on his stretcher in the wooden hut, Ras was convinced that he would be killed by friendly fire, but took grim satisfaction in the terror shown by the Japanese:

'As soon as the air-raid sirens sounded, several of them came running to my hut and jumped down into the pit below it, hissing and chattering with fear. As I lay above them I mocked them, telling them not to be afraid as I was protecting them with my body. Luckily, they were too frightened by the bombs to avenge their loss of face on me.'[3]

Ras was not just as tough as nails, but was a man imbued with all the guile of a survivor. As he grew stronger, he was regularly questioned. He employed various techniques to stall questions, such as saying that under the terms of the Geneva Convention he was not bound to answer. Soon, he realised that their innate arrogance and conceit was a great weakness – one that gave him a clear advantage. He learned that if he stonewalled long enough, they would answer their own questions, proclaiming smugly 'Is that not so?' to any question they had asked. Ras would then appear to nod and reluctantly agree, to which they would say, 'Ah, so!' and go on to the next question. If cornered, he would groan that his wounds were so painful that he could not remember or pretend to faint. He would then be left alone for another day, by which time his interrogators would have forgotten the thrust of their questions.

Ras stayed at the hospital in Prome for about six weeks, slowly regaining his strength as his back muscles recovered. One morning in July 1943, without prior warning, he was collected by two Japanese soldiers, taken to the railway station and escorted to Rangoon. He felt confident in his new identity, with little fear of being recognised as the renegade British NCO, Corporal Ras Pagani, who had escaped from the 18 kilometre camp so many months before. He anticipated being taken to a prison camp in Rangoon. There, at least, he would be in the company of his compatriots. But he was in for a rude awakening. At Rangoon station he was taken not to the city jail, but to the New Law Courts, the national headquarters of the dreaded kempeitai. His heart fell and his spirits drained at the prospect of what lay ahead.

Evil comes in many guises, but sometimes the greatest evils take place in the most unexpected places. Just a stone's throw from the sybaritic luxury of the famous Strand Hotel lay a place of unspeakable horror. Overlooking the Rangoon river, the New Law Courts on Strand Road is one of the grandest colonial buildings in the city. Yet within this imposing building, with its giant arcade of Ionic columns running full length across the frontage, lay the very heart of darkness. There are two inner courtyards. Until recently, each had a single-storey building at the centre. In the east courtyard was a guardhouse, and in the west, under a corrugated iron roof, was the notorious cellblock known as the 'Rangoon Ritz'. For those unfortunate Allied soldiers and airmen who fell into the hands of the sadistic kempeitai, this elegant building was the gateway to hell.

Shortly before the cellblock was demolished in January 2013, I visited it covertly, slipping into the derelict building and then disappearing discreetly out of a side entrance as the military police arrived. It had remained unchanged for seventy years: a nightmare world of sweltering, foetid cells haunted by the souls of those who had died there, rank with the smell of human excrement and decomposition and reeking of despair. If ever there was a place of pure evil, this was it. Overshadowed by the vertiginous walls of the enveloping building, the prison cells received little natural light or ventilation. There were eleven pig-pen cells, under a high corrugated iron roof, laced with barbed wire and with a brick wall at the back. The partitions between the cells were made from stout planks filled with sawdust to prevent communication between them.

Carved into the walls were poignant inscriptions left by former inmates. Alongside the notches and calendars marking the days were heart-breaking personal records. In their suffering many turned to their own particular god. One in Burmese read:

Don't forget your parents.

Don't forget your god.

Another in Pali, probably written by a Burman, said:

Ye people of Burma who are abiding in the hottest corner of hell, forget not your gods nor your religion nor the other deities whom you worship.

Another, probably written by a British officer, simply stated, 'i arrived in this cell on 29th april 1943' with 'GOD IS LOVE' written in the form of a cross beneath.[4]

Normally there were six to nine men per cell, but all too often over twenty were crammed in at night. On arrival, Ras was pushed into a cell with five other male civilians, all naked. Each cell was about ten feet by eight feet. Three men had to squat on each side of the cell, motionless and in silence, except when using the latrine bucket, which stood in the corner. Talking, sleeping, leaning on the wall or lying prostrate were all strictly forbidden. In each cell there was a notice in English listing the rules, which must be obeyed. Japanese sentries patrolled the passage in front of the cells to enforce silence. All day and night the lights were kept burning.

The front of the cell facing the passage was made of stout wooden three-inch-by-two-inch-thick bars. At the base was a small trap door about two feet square for access, beside which was a small six-inch square, through which bowls of food were shoved each morning and evening in a rusty old jam tin: usually a small amount of rice, over which was poured a watery stew of vegetables or shrimps. Half a jam tin of water had to suffice for twelve men. When it rained, water cascaded through holes in the corrugated iron roof, but in the dry season, when there was no rain, there was no water at all to drink or with which to wash. The sanitary conditions were dreadful. A movable commode was placed in each cell, which was wholly insufficient for the needs of up to twenty men. Every morning piles of excrement and urine flowed over the top and across the floor. Each morning the prisoners were forced to empty the contents into the building's sewers. Not surprisingly, disease was rampant.

Above: The Rangoon Ritz – the notorious cell block at the New Law Courts shortly before its demolition in 2013.
Left: Inside the cell block after liberation in 1945.

At night when at last the inmates were permitted to lie on the floor to sleep, they were assailed by swarms of lice, mosquitoes and blood-sucking bugs, which gorged on their emaciated bodies. As fast as the insects were crushed, others took their place. One airman counted fifty lice swarming across two square inches of his threadbare blanket. By a stroke of luck, Ras was placed next to the bars, which allowed him a little fresh air from the passage outside. Each evening the Japanese sentry came around with a flit gun to spray the bars of the cells to kill mosquitoes and reduce the risk of disease. Nevertheless, within a few days, Ras was covered with lice. He begged the guard to spray his head and crotch each night – which so amused the soldier that he agreed, giving Ras some respite.

Under strict orders, the sentries acted like automatons, devoid of all human sympathy and compassion. Savage beatings, clubbings, slappings and being hung upside down from a beam and whipped were routine ways of softening up prisoners for more refined and sadistic tortures, such as the terrifying Japanese water treatment. Bound hand and foot, the poor unfortunates were forced to lie under a tap, while their nostrils were pinched and water poured down their throats, or sometimes injected through their noses, into their stomachs. When their stomachs were full, the guards would jump up and down on them, causing the water to spout forth. All too often, the stomach would rupture, leading to massive internal haemorrhaging and ultimately death. Another particularly excruciating refinement was electric shock treatment to the genitals, along with the burning of sensitive parts with lighted cigarettes.

With an impending sense of dread, Ras knew the most terrifying ordeal lay ahead. Two guards appeared, dragged out one of his companions and then beat and kicked him to the interrogation room. For the next two hours they heard the pitiful screams of the chosen victim as he was beaten black and blue. When he was dragged, half-conscious, back to the cell, his body was a mess, his nose streaming blood and his fingers and toes swollen. Another of the inmates tried to help him sit up, but was screamed at by the sentry and threatened with the same treatment. The poor man was left lying on the floor of the cell until he came round. Each day, a different prisoner was chosen. Those who remained were forced to endure the terrible, bloodcurdling screams. In desperate trepidation, Ras knew that sooner or later it would be his turn.

Sure enough, a few days later they came for him. He was forced to crawl out of the cell on all fours as the guards kicked and beat him about the head and shoulders with sticks. He managed to stagger to his feet and run to the end of the passage, pursued by the guards, who beat his buttocks and his raw, scarred back, which oozed blood from the gaping wounds he had suffered at the hands of the Burmese on the banks of the Irrawaddy. Yet this was just the softening-up process. The interrogation itself took place in a sequence of three separate rooms. In the first, the room was bare, other than for two chairs, on which sat two Japanese soldiers with canes, between whom Ras was forced to kneel. One from the kempeitai asked him questions in bad English. Whatever he answered, they would scream and rage at him, whipping him with their canes.

After about half an hour, he was taken to the next room, which was identical. Of the two Japanese present, one was an officer. With Ras forced again to kneel between them, the officer drew his sword and kept beating him with the flat of it after each question. Then he put his pistol to Ras's head and, in a heart-stopping moment, cocked his pistol and pulled the trigger. It was empty, although Ras was not to know. Then, as the culmination, the officer practised his sword play, slicing the blade of his sword down on to Ras's neck, checking his blow only when it touched his skin – raw, unadulterated terror intended to break his spirit. Later, Ras learned that 'this unnerving performance had finished several natives who had literally died of fright at this stage, although several were beheaded either intentionally or because the officer had misjudged his swing. These sadists smashed and prodded my newly healed and often tender wounds, so that I often passed out from the pain'.[5]

But the worst still lay ahead – a simple room, like a wash house, with a concrete floor and a drain on one corner. Here, Ras thought he would lose his reason. He was forced to lie on his back with his arms and legs tied to iron rings, which were embedded in the concrete and positioned so that his head was directly beneath a dripping tap. This was another variation of the notorious Japanese water torture calculated to drive a man insane. Each few seconds, a drop of water hit him between the eyes. After a while the repetition became agonising, each drip drumming on to his forehead until he thought his brain would explode. Half an hour later they returned, and started the questioning again. Then, mercifully, he was dragged back half-conscious to his cell to await the next session and a similar ordeal.

What little future there might be looked very bleak indeed. Sometimes, as a sadistic diversion during interrogations, they would drive sharp slivers of bamboo under his finger and toe nails, up his nose or into his genitals and then set them alight. On one occasion, he was tied with thongs and water-boarded until he felt he was drowning. He had long been resigned to the probability that in due course he would be executed, and reasoned that this treatment would kill him anyway if it continued much longer: 'How I survived these tortures I do not know. There were times when I felt that I could stand it no longer, and I would prefer to die by my own hand.'[6] But each time he contemplated suicide

> 'the picture of my wife and baby son would come back to my mind. I promised them that I would return and this strengthened my resolve to hold out against these sadistic torturers, but there was always the fear that when they had become tired of playing with me they would just take me out and execute me. I had witnessed this so often – when the cells were full and new victims arrived, the Japanese would just drag out those who had been there longest and kill them.'[7]

After a month of sustained mental and physical cruelty, many simply lost the will to live. Each day was a battle of endurance against despair and hopelessness. Prisoners forfeited all sense of honour and integrity along with their self-respect, ambitions, hopes and dreams. Some were so degraded or broken in spirit that they were prepared to say or do anything to secure their freedom. The guards took sadistic delight in inflicting gratuitous violence and humiliation. One airman recalled: 'There was that bastard who threw three bananas on the floor. When I tried to pick one up he stamped on my hand. Finally, he forced me to eat them, skin and all, without using my hands.'[8] For those that succumbed, it was common practice for certain guards to visit the cells of the dying men, to jeer and mock them, laughing at their condition so as to drive them insane before they died. Only the toughest and most stoical, like Ras Pagani, survived.

However, even Ras feared that there would come a time when his body might just give up and die even if his spirit remained undaunted, but three things forced him to survive. First was his pledge to his beloved wife that however long it took, and however hard it was, he would return. Secondly, long exposure to intense pain actually numbed his senses. Increasingly, he was able to transcend it and live beyond the pain barrier.

Finally, he was absolutely determined not to let the kempeitai break him. He believed that they were no longer really interested in extracting the truth or any useful information from him, but just took sadistic delight in trying to break his spirit. On the plus side, not once had his new identity been challenged, which was a comfort. Had they been more subtle in their approach, his lack of an American accent was an obvious weakness that they could have probed and queried, but in their sadistic enthusiasm for humiliating him, they had missed the obvious.

After six weeks of unimaginable brutality and torture, in September 1943 Ras was hauled outside into a lorry. Convinced that the end had come and that he was about to be taken to a place of execution, he reflected that it would have been so much better to have died at the hands of the Burmese mob beside the Irrawaddy, avoiding all his subsequent suffering. He began to pray, reflecting on his short life, and to make his peace with his maker. Suddenly, and unexpectedly, as they headed west through the city, the lorry stopped outside Rangoon Central jail. He was kicked out and handed over to the Japanese guards. Through an interpreter, he was told that he would be placed in solitary confinement. He was escorted to the upper floors of one of the cellblocks and pushed into a cell. The barred door was slammed shut, but at last he was able to lie on a plank bed and rest his battered body. After what he had just endured, it was a turn for the better, and he fell into a deep, deep sleep.

Chapter 12

This Long War Beneath the Stars

'So shall I fight, so shall I tread,
In this long war beneath the stars;
So shall a glory wreathe my head,
So shall I faint and show the scars,
Until this case, this clogging mould,
Be smithied all to kingly gold.'
JOHN MASEFIELD

After floating down from the sky in the dead of night, Jimmy Nimmo and his five Karen companions gathered themselves together and checked their equipment, including the precious radio transmitter. After burying their parachutes, they moved stealthily through the jungle to search for Seagrim. At long last their luck had changed. Within two days, on 14 October 1943, Nimmo and his party met up with Seagrim and Ba Gyaw. Seagrim was overwhelmed. He welcomed Nimmo with open arms. It seemed as if Nimmo and his companions had drifted in from another world. Finally, his lonely vigil was at an end. Now he could make a real impact, pass a regular stream of priceless intelligence directly back to India, and prepare the levies to take the initiative. Radio contact was established immediately.

But with Jimmy Nimmo came tragic personal news, which must have devastated Hugh. On 6 April 1943 his brother Derek had died unexpectedly after being severely wounded in Tunisia at the battle of Wadi Akarit. Just over a month later on 10 May he had been awarded a posthumous Victoria Cross for an earlier action leading his men, from the Green Howards, through a hail of fire during a critical phase of an assault on the Mareth Line on 20/21 March 1943. He had personally stormed two machine gun posts and captured twenty German prisoners. The citation read: 'By his personal courage, disregard for his own safety, and outstanding leadership he so inspired his men that the battalion successfully took and held its objective, thereby enabling the attack to proceed.'[1] For a while Hugh's thoughts must have returned to those happy days back in 1936 when he had last been together with all his brothers, and to that fateful farewell to Derek outside the Cumberland Hotel. It was a bitter, bitter blow.

Nimmo found Hugh gaunt, emaciated and wearing Karen dress. He had long ago discarded his khaki tunic in favour of the red-and-white shirt of the Karens and wide, cool Shan trousers. He walked around with a red Karen bag over his shoulder, and a little round Karen box containing tobacco and betel nut, which he chewed like the Karens, staining his teeth and mouth blood red. Despite his appearance, he was in good health both physically and mentally: perpetually cheerful in spite of the grim news about his brother, and much amused by the wild rumours flying about the area which gullible Karens brought in. Once they told him with deadly seriousness that the Japanese had trained a battalion of monkeys to throw hand grenades. On another occasion they swore that they had seen British planes with smaller planes slung beneath them, which could detach themselves to drop bombs and strafe ground targets before recoupling with the host plane – probably a garbled reference to auxiliary fuel tanks.

Shortly after Nimmo's arrival, Seagrim wrote to Ta Roe, who was bringing in the harvest, and asked him to come down to hear some good news. When Ta Roe arrived, he saw another white man dressed in khaki uniform with some Karen soldiers. Seagrim introduced them and explained that they had brought a wireless transmitter/receiver from India. Turning to Nimmo, he introduced Ta Roe as one of his most loyal helpers.

As soon as the party arrived, Seagrim sent Saw Digay, one of his most trusted commanders, down from the hills to see if the Japanese were aware of the recent parachute drop. Digay made discreet enquiries at Kyaukkyi, Nyaunglebin and along the main road to Mandalay. The drone of the planes overhead at night had made the Japanese suspicious, but they appeared to know nothing and had no plans to follow it up. Nevertheless, both Seagrim and Nimmo decided it would be prudent to move again to a more remote location further north. The move was wise. The Japanese had an excellent intelligence network, and the kempeitai's tentacles were everywhere. They kept a close watch on the hills from their base at Toungoo. Back in June 1943 they had sent four Burmese agents up into the hills, ostensibly to buy fifteen buffaloes in Pyagawpu, but as the agents had a combined fund of only eighteen rupees between them, their story had seemed unlikely and the Karens had been deeply suspicious. After interrogation, one of them had confessed their true purpose was to spy for the kempeitai. All were shot. Incidents such as these put the Karens on their guard.

Four months later, just before Nimmo's arrival, a similar situation occurred. The same levies seized a Burman and an Indian, who alleged that they had been parachuted in from India, and wanted to be guided to Seagrim. Seagrim was cautious and advised the levies to ask to see their buried parachutes. If they could not produce them, the local commander should deal with them as he saw fit. The Indian later confessed they that had been promised 30,000 rupees if they brought back details of Seagrim's camp. They too were shot.

For Seagrim, Nimmo's arrival was not entirely unexpected. During their long months of waiting, Ba Gyaw had explained to him the different stages of Operation Harlington, and Hugh had not been idle. In anticipation, he had sent Po Hla down to Rangoon to find out from the Delta Karens exactly what was going on there, so he would have the latest information ready to report when the long-awaited transmitter arrived. For Po Hla, it was an extremely dangerous undertaking. The kempeitai were on the lookout for him, but he did not hesitate. He was to bring back priceless intelligence that was to change the course of the war in Burma.

After contacting the Karen community in Rangoon and confirming their continued loyalty, Po Hla secured a covert channel of communication to the commander of a Karen battalion of the Burma Defence Army – a disaffected Sandhurst-trained officer called Hanson Kya Doe – and his second in command, the influential local Karen leader San Po Thin, who had done much to stem the tide of communal violence and genocide around Myaungmya in the spring of 1942. Seagrim had been in written contact with San Po Thin since late in 1942, when he had been asked by the Karen leader for a supply of weapons. Hugh had written a ten-page reply explaining what he had achieved in the Karen hills, the setting-up of armed levies, the appalling depredations of the BIA, and the importance of not attacking the Japanese until the British were due to return. Seagrim stressed how much he loved the Karens. The whole world knew of the Gurkhas, but no one had heard of the Karens, he averred, but after the war he would look after their interests. Afraid that the note might fall into Japanese hands, San Po Thin burned it, but recalled later that it was a very moving letter full of Biblical references urging the Karens not to lose heart and to help each other.

Kya Doe, San Po Thin and Shwe Tun Gya, the so-called 'Tiger of the Delta', were all double agents who pretended to co-operate with the Japanese while simultaneously harbouring Karen parachutists, and even two English riflemen from the Cameronians who had been cut off in 1942. The two stragglers had been passed from village to village for over eighteen months before being surrendered. Both ended up in Rangoon Central jail and survived the war. Constantly suspected by the kempeitai, San Po Thin repeatedly talked himself out of trouble.

The Burma Defence Army (BDA), now led by Aung San, was a much more disciplined successor to the hated BIA, which had wreaked such havoc in Papun, the Delta and elsewhere a year earlier. To all intents and purposes it was a force of 8,000 pro-Japanese levies. Both Kya Doe and San Po Thin indicated that they had been manipulated into their commands against their will and their own personal loyalties. They reported that the BDA was thoroughly disenchanted with the Japanese and ready to switch sides. As soon as the British were ready, they were planning to throw in their lot with the Allies.

Some time before, while visiting his erstwhile mentor Colonel Suzuki at his house in Rangoon, (now the residence of the British ambassador), it had dawned on Aung San that the Japanese had no intention of assisting his cause for an independent Burma. When Aung San and his comrade in arms Ne Win arrived to present their list of thirty demands on a long scroll, the disdainful Suzuki descended the elegant teak staircase and unsheathed his samurai sword. Without uttering a single word, he skewered the scroll and tossed it over his shoulder before turning on his heel and returning upstairs.[2] Humiliated at being treated so dismissively, Aung San was left in no doubt that he had thrown in his lot with the most brutal and tyrannical of masters. His own aspirations had been treated with ill-concealed contempt.

Po Hla had known San Po Thin before the war. At a secret breakfast with him and Kya Doe, he was briefed on the preparations being made within the BDA to rise against the Japanese. In return, Po Hla took them into his confidence about Seagrim's network in Karenni. Shortly after the meeting the kempeitai became aware of the covert gathering and arrested

San Po Thin. He managed to tip off Po Hla, who fled north, while Aung San tried to persuade the Japanese to release San Po Thin. Returning in mid-November 1943, just a month after Nimmo's arrival, the intelligence that Po Hla brought back to Seagrim, was dynamite. Later that month, Seagrim was able to report to India that Aung San and the BDA were so disillusioned that they were poised to switch sides. The intelligence was such a coup that in his account of the war, *Defeat into Victory*, Field Marshal Viscount Slim acknowledged that it was Seagrim, 'a most gallant officer', who imparted the information. Po Hla received a personal letter of thanks on behalf of the Supreme Allied Commander, South-East Asia, Admiral Lord Louis Mountbatten, highly commending him on the outcome of his dangerous mission.

But this was not all. Po Hla had returned with a veritable mine of information that was transmitted straight to India – details of units and troop movements, general living conditions and, perhaps most importantly of all, potential targets for bombing raids, such as the great railway workshops at Insein, which were promptly put out of action by Allied bombers. He also told them what to avoid, such as the kempeitai headquarters in the New Law Courts, close to the waterfront and port, where so many Allied soldiers and airmen were being incarcerated.

Complementing Seagrim's intelligence on the BDA was material from an entirely separate, albeit untrustworthy source: the Communist Party of Burma, which had argued that there should be no compromise with

Above: Thet Wa, Seagrim's young radio operator, at the rear centre with Hyena group, part of Operation Character, in March 1945.

either side. Back in May 1942, two of the Party's leading lights, Thein Pe and Tin Shwe, had escaped to India. Highly suspicious of their motives and believing that they might have been Japanese spies, the British had initially kept them under close scrutiny, but they were later allowed to help – and ultimately to return to Burma with a mission. Inserted into the Arakan covertly by submarine in December 1943, just a month after Po Hla had delivered his payload of intelligence to Seagrim, Tin Shwe made his way to Rangoon, where he met up with members of the Anti-Fascist Peoples Freedom League (AFPFL) and the local underground resistance. He emerged two months later along with a wife, a recruit sent by Thakin Soe, the Communist Party general secretary, and a rich seam of political and military intelligence that enabled the Allies to plan a coherent campaign of resistance alongside direct action in the field.

With Po Hla's return, and the very real prospect of preparing for a major offensive in the hills, Seagrim was keen to see whether he could be extricated by air so that he could brief Army headquarters more thoroughly about the potential for future offensive operations in the Karen hills. Rather optimistically thinking that it might be possible to be picked up by a flying boat on the Salween and dropped back by air, he dispatched Po Hla to reconnoitre the river for a suitable landing place, but this plan was soon ruled out. Po Hla reported that for long sections the riverbed was too rocky and the current too fast, while the security of areas further north and south was far too exposed to hostile prying eyes.

Among the Karens who parachuted in with Nimmo was a nineteen-year-old wireless operator from Bassein in the Delta called Thet Wa, a quiet, introspective and well-educated young man, who spoke excellent English. Educated at the Sgaw Karen High School and later at the Rangoon Technical Institute, Thet Wa had been evacuated to India with his fellow students in 1942 and subsequently volunteered for the RAF and special operations. After the war, he remembered the hard life they all had led in the forest, the endless deluge of the torrential rains and the swarms of mosquitoes. With no mosquito nets, and only one blanket apiece, they could not protect themselves from the insects. Leeches would fasten themselves to legs and arms and had to be burned off, or dislodged with salt. Each night they would all sit around the campfire for prayers, followed by a reading from the Bible, perhaps a Karen hymn sung by the boys, and often then a short spiritual exposition by Seagrim. Deep in the sweltering jungle, this band of lost souls cried out together for help in the darkness; the exiled Englishmen and the renegade Karens raising their voices to the heavens; the plangent strains of 'Onward, Christian Soldiers' sung in Karen echoing across the dense green wilderness that engulfed them. As the sparks from the fire crackled and snapped, their tired faces were suffused by the ruddy glow of the bonfire, the flickering flames shimmering off the burnished blue gunmetal of their rifles and guns.

Thet Wa remembered one evening vividly. Seagrim spoke of Christ and His sufferings, a recurrent theme, explaining that it was only by suffering that man could find God. Seagrim reiterated that after the war he intended to become a missionary among the Karens. He intended to divide his backdated army pay between his mother in England and them. It was his mother, Seagrim explained, who had told him to read the Bible every day. He confessed that until he came to the hills he could not be bothered to do so, but she had been right. It was the finest literature in the world. Alongside the Bible, Seagrim had acquired other reading matter including Tagore's *Gitanjali* and a long-awaited copy of *The Pilgrim's Progress*, to which he referred over and over again.

Reinforced and reinvigorated, Seagrim now presided over a highly effective intelligence operation deep behind the Japanese lines. A torrent of information – sourced from Seagrim's levies – on troop movements, targets, resistance potential and guerrilla activities – was transmitted back to High Command in India. Each day, the indefatigable Thet Wa would spend up to six hours cranking up the dynamo to charge the transmitter batteries. Each night, often sheltering under a sodden groundsheet after he transmitted, they tuned in to hear the latest news from Delhi, and even London, which was a wonderful boost for morale. The levy commanders and trusted villagers visited regularly with reports of activity in their areas, all of which was transmitted straight back to India. Ba Gyaw and Ta Roe travelled up to the Mawchi mines on a reconnaissance sweep and gleaned much useful information, including firm commitments from many old Burma Riflemen that they were keen to help the British as soon as they came back.

Meanwhile, at Papun, Arthur Ta Bi was in position to pass a regular stream of information to Seagrim. When news came in from an itinerant Chinaman that the Japanese were building a huge new airfield near Chiang Mai in Siam, he obtained full details and sent them straight on to Seagrim, who informed India. A few weeks later, the airfield was hammered by a large force of Allied bombers. Ta Bi also passed on details of the location of Japanese workshops on the Burma–Siam Railway and various petrol dumps on the Toungoo–Thandaug road, as well as copies of all-important papers from the government in Rangoon. Another useful informer was a Karen education officer in Papun, who sent through details of troop movements and the precise location of a large ammunition dump near the lake in Toungoo.

Seagrim's camp was a hive of activity, but they needed to be careful to avoid drawing too much attention to themselves. A regular flow of visitors arrived, bearing news and information. One was the reliable Saw Henry, whom Seagrim had sent westwards to the Pegu Yomas some weeks earlier to see if he could prepare a drop zone there. Henry also provided an update on the state of the demolished Sittang bridge and useful information about ammunition dumps along the main Rangoon–Mandalay road.

For Seagrim, at last everything was slotting into place. This was the moment he had been planning for almost two interminable, solitary years.

Much of the wireless traffic between Seagrim and India has been long since lost, but the messages ranged from the strategic to the domestic. One, in typical Seagrim style, was a shopping list, which read: 'On next dropping sortie please send 3,000 rupees silver. 25 silver rings. Pencils. 2lb of tea. Books by Sundar Singh and Hall-Caine's *Life of Christ*.'[3] Other signals from Seagrim stressed that premature offensive action would result only in reprisals, but that when the Japanese were more fully engaged by the Allies, the Karen levies could be raised rapidly. In the meantime, the priority was intelligence. He reminded those sitting at a comfortable desk in India that the Karens were encircled by enemies. He transmitted: 'We can continue to hold this area against Burmese but not yet against the Japanese without trained units.'[4]

Advised by Nimmo in all good faith that an offensive in late 1943 was a real possibility, he notified India: 'All Burma expects a dry weather offensive. We may lose our influence if this is delayed too long and the Japs enter hills.' In anticipation, Seagrim set out his plans and requirements to Army HQ India in clear detail:

'Can lay seeds of rebellion to cause chaos everywhere in plains and hills … Two months before main Allied offensive begins 8,000 arms should be dropped with British officers in the hills. When offensive begins 12,000 more arms should be dropped in Delta and Pegu Yomas and these hills to arm ex-soldiers. They will be able to cut lines of communication, check the Burmese, cause internal chaos, deny the hills and attack the Japanese.

To get widespread Karen assistance, Allies must first cause initial Japanese collapse. Karen soldiers of BDA intend to desert with their arms when Japs on run.'[5]

On 9 December 1943, Stage Four of Operation Harlington was put into effect. In the early hours of the morning, Captain Eric McCrindle was parachuted into the hills with a wireless set and four Karen companions. Mac brought with him the latest intelligence from India that, for a variety of reasons, no major offensive would take place in the dry season of 1943, and that they should be patient, build up their networks and bide their time pending further orders from India. For all of them itching to take action, it meant another frustrating wait.

Seagrim ordered that McCrindle, Nimmo and Ba Gyaw should each take over a different area and report back to him at the centre. Before the officers departed for their allotted territories, soon after Mac's arrival, Seagrim called a meeting of his most trusted followers, as well as more than fifty elders from all over the Salween district. Mac was introduced to each of them individually, including Ta Roe and some of the elders from Chawido and Pyagawpu. The meeting was followed by a celebratory feast. Seagrim had bought a large pig and they dined off pork, rice, curry and pumpkin, all washed down with copious quantities of tea, sugar and canned milk dropped in from India. The days of starvation rations were over, but all the activity meant that they were becoming much more visible. Afterwards, they stood together in the dappled sunlight as the pastor of Pyagawpu conducted a Christian service and read from the Bible. The message was the familiar one about the purpose of suffering. Ta Roe recalled that the gist of it was that without suffering we cannot come to any profit – 'No cross, no crown.' They sang a Karen hymn, then the Karen national song, after which Po Hla and three of the parachutists sang 'Rock of Ages'. They all then recited the Lord's Prayer.

At the end of the service, Seagrim made a more formal address than usual in Burmese. He welcomed them, saying how happy he was that they were all gathered together in friendship. He explained that Captain

McCrindle had brought messages for them all from India. One was a letter from the Karens who had escaped to India as part of the great exodus in 1942, exhorting their brethren not to lose heart: 'We know that you Karens in Burma are undergoing much suffering. But we are always remembering you in our prayers and we ask you to remember us in your prayers.'[6] Seagrim then produced more than twenty blank certificates, intended for his closest followers, that McCrindle had brought from India; some were signed by General Auchinleck, the Commander-in-Chief, and others by Lieutenant General Pownall, Mountbatten's Chief-of-Staff. Auchinleck's read:

'The loyal attitude of the Karens has been reported to me by my officers. Loyalty through a long time in your difficult and dangerous circumstances is worthy of the highest praise. I know that many of you have borne arms in defence of your country and will bear them again to ensure final victory. In the meantime my officers and I do not forget you and the loyalty of the Karenni.'[7]

Seagrim explained that it would be too dangerous to distribute them. Discovery by the Japanese would mean instant execution, so he would retain them for safekeeping. He said that he would give one to each of them when the British returned, so that they could show them to the British, who would then know that they had been loyal allies. In truth, the certificates were something of a mixed blessing. Not only did they entail a security risk, but they were also invidious, slighting those who were overlooked.

Seagrim finished his address with a further short speech. He thanked the assembled company for all their support and assistance since he had come to the Karen hills almost two years earlier. In response, Ta Roe and the elders from Pyagawpu gave all three British officers simple white tunics with two broad red stripes at the front, which they had woven for them to mark the occasion. Amid much laughing and merriment the three insisted on wearing them immediately, after which they ate again. Later, as the moon rose high amid a panoply of stars, throwing the forest deep into silhouette, the happy party broke up. Each went his own way back to his village convinced that, at last, the tide was truly turning.

The next morning, Jimmy Nimmo headed off with a wireless transmitter to establish his headquarters in Noel Boyt's old command area north of the Mawchi road, along with three of his Karen companions. A fourth was sent on ahead to meet with Thra May Sha, the pastor of Mawtudo, who had sheltered Seagrim almost two years earlier, and to alert local villagers that another British officer was coming to join them. The good pastor consulted his old comrade in arms, Thra Kyaw Lay, who two years before had been a circle leader under Major Cecil Smith. Shrewd and committed, Thra Kyaw Lay was no ordinary pastor. He had played a key role in the retreat from the hills in 1942, initially working with Eric McCrindle and Lieutenant Ba Thein, and then subsequently guiding Captain Thompson through the forest after the fighting on the Mawchi road, following which he had blown up the road from Bawgalingyi to Salauchaung. He now had a force of 102 levies, albeit armed with little more than spears, swords and old handmade flintlocks. Together with Thra May Sha, they built some huts in the forest where Nimmo made his headquarters.

While on the way to Mawtudo, Nimmo stayed with Seagrim's friend Francis Ah Mya, the local Anglican priest. Thra Kyaw Lay arrived to collect him and bring him up to Mawtudo. Travelling secretly in driving rain, and only at night, they reached their destination four days later, wet and exhausted.

As Nimmo settled in, every few days the two pastors brought him supplies. He soon revived Boyt and Smith's old network and re-established contact with some local timber contractors with whom he had done business before the war. To reward outstanding service, and as tangible evidence of their loyal support for the British cause, Nimmo distributed some pure silver rings inscribed with the letter 'K' for Karen, which McCrindle had brought from India. Rapidly, he developed a highly effective intelligence operation, signalling India with details of targets and enemy movements. Every two days he shifted his camp, never staying in one place long enough to be tracked down.

As Seagrim's second Christmas in the hills approached, he asked Po Hla to translate a Christmas message to all his levy commanders and followers. It was inspiring and deeply religious, and it casts another ray of light on his innermost convictions. Po Hla recalled much of what Seagrim said:

'Today is Christmas Day, the day when the greatest hero the world has known was born. We Christians celebrate this day because we are His followers. If I speak to you Karens today of "bravery", you cannot fail to associate this word with those who fought and died in this war. We Christians are soldiers of the Cross, soldiers who are commanded by our heroic leader to be brave in destroying evils.

170

The Cross is a badge worn by every true Christian. It distinguishes him from others. The Cross, as Christ wants us to understand it, signifies suffering. We Christians, His true followers, must suffer if we are to free our fellow-men from the evils of this world. If we wonder why we must suffer, let us remember that Jesus Christ, who was without sin, was nailed to a cross and suffered the most shameful death, which could come to any man. How then can we, who profess to be His followers, who wear a Cross as our badge, expect to be free from suffering? By the way in which he faces suffering does a true Christian show his quality.'[8]

Just before Christmas Seagrim went to Chawido to see whether he could spend the festivities with Ta Roe and his family and attend church on Christmas Day in Pygawpu. Ta Roe advised against it because after the service a sports meeting was to be held for villagers from all over the district: it would not be safe to be seen there. Almost certainly word would get back to the Japanese. Ta Roe suggested that Seagrim should wait at his home, and that he would make Seagrim a Christmas tree and have an evening service there. Seagrim gave Ta Roe 150 rupees as prizes for the sports and awaited his return.

The festivities in Pyagawpu opened with a large feast of four pigs and countless chickens. Deep in the jungle over 300 people flocked in from across the whole district to hear the story of a child Saviour born far away in Bethlehem almost 2,000 years before. Afterwards, a service was conducted by the pastor, with a large pine Christmas tree at one end of the church; later, all the children, both Christian and non-Christian, were brought in and given presents. The elders exchanged simple presents too, mostly home-grown fruits and vegetables, chickens, wild honeycombs, tobacco or betel nut. After this, the sports commenced, with races for young and old and competitions between the villages. It was only as the sun set that Ta Roe, Saw Willie Saw and Arthur Ta Bi, together with the pastor, some elders and a few children from the choir, set off for Chawido.

Alone over Christmas for the past two days, Seagrim's thoughts must have turned to the magical Christmases of his childhood, back home in Whissonsett: surrounded by his brothers and parents, the air alive with the excited chattering of his boisterous brothers. Lost in his memories, no wonder he was delighted when the party of thirty or so arrived.

At seven o'clock that evening, they squatted on the floor to eat their Christmas dinner of chicken soup and roast chicken, Seagrim's favourite, which Ta Roe's wife had prepared. A second Christmas service was laid on especially for him. The room glittered with torches made from pine-wood splinters. In one corner Ta Roe raised a six-foot-high Christmas tree. The pastor gave a lesson in English. The choir and a boys' quartet sang Karen and English carols, and more presents were exchanged. The pastor gave Seagrim another Karen tunic. With nothing of his own to give, Seagrim apologised, but gave his revolver to Saw Willie Saw. When they left at midnight, Seagrim thanked them all for giving him such a fine Christmas. He invited Saw Willie Saw and Arthur Ta Bi to return with him so that he could show them their certificates.

Ta Roe stayed with him. They spoke of his young children, Caroline and Rosalind. Deeply fond of them, Seagrim often passed spare moments playing with them. In turn, they loved him. More than seventy years later, it is perfectly conceivable that both children are still living in Karenni, but with the entire region still isolated by ethnic conflict, it has so far proved impossible to find them. Ta Roe recalled that Seagrim said:

> 'Your children are never afraid of me, Ta Roe. The Karen children
> are different from other children. Your children are neat and clean
> and your wife dresses them well. I think they are clever. After the
> war I will send them to school for you and you won't have to spend
> a single pice on their schooling. And if they are clever enough to
> go to university, I will send them to the university, too.'[9]

But it was not to be. The storm clouds of war were about to break over them all with terrifying consequences. Nothing would ever be the same again.

Above: The teak-built church at Pyagawpu.

Chapter 13

Death in the Forest

'Midway upon the journey of ... life,
I found myself within a forest dark.
What was this forest savage, rough, and stern?
Which in the very thought renews the fear ...
So bitter is it, death is little more.'

DANTE ALIGHIERI

At the dawn of the New Year, matters took a pronounced turn for the worse. While attending the New Year's service in Pyagawpu, Ta Roe was told that two Chinese had arrived from Kyaukkyi, ostensibly to buy elephant tusks. While this was not an uncommon practice, they spent only one night in the village. They then vanished, which seemed highly suspicious. Even more worrying, they had stayed overnight just five miles from Seagrim's own camp. Ta Roe warned Seagrim immediately. Ba Gyaw went in pursuit to find out more about the enigmatic pair, but to no avail.

Just days later, alarm bells rang again. This time the problem stemmed from a chronic lack of coordination in India. News came up from Papun that three Karen parachutists had been dropped too far from the hills in a predominantly Burmese area. One of the agents had come down on a clump of bamboo. His two companions had been forced to ask for help from the local village and then pay hush money to keep the locals' mouths shut. It had not worked. The three agents had headed north, but the story had spread like wildfire. The Japanese were bound to be alerted. Unbeknown to Seagrim, the agents had been dropped by the Interservice Liaison Department, the name by which the SIS was known in the Far East. They operated independently of the SOE, which from 1944 was branded Force 136. Not for the first time, the two organisations were falling over each other in the field. Far from protecting their own security by operating on a need-to-know basis, they risked compromising each other.

In mid-January 1944, things became even more uneasy. En route to Papun to buy some jaggery for his brother's wedding, Ta Roe learned that seventeen Japanese had arrived in Papun, ostensibly as part of a 'Goods Distribution Unit' under Captain Inosuke Kurokata, but in fact trying to glean information about local resistance. Kurokata was from the counter-espionage branch in Rangoon. They had tried to ingratiate themselves by handing out free quinine, and cloth and matches at cut prices, before casually enquiring about British officers and Karen parachutists. Seagrim was kept informed. With the help of Ta Roe, he moved his camp yet again to a much more secure location deeper into the hills in an area of virtually impenetrable bamboo thickets at Komupwado, about ten miles south-west of Pyagawpu. Here he was kept supplied by the local villagers.

At this time, Kurokata made a concerted effort to get a message to Seagrim through three different channels. Whether or not Seagrim ever received it is unclear. The Japanese officer wrote:

'Dear Major Seagrim,

You have been hiding in the hills round Papun for two years and must be undergoing extreme hardships. As a professional soldier like yourself, I admire you. But the Japanese are now forming expeditions against you from Papun, Toungoo, Mawchi and Kyaukkyi. Your chances are slight. If within ten days of receiving this letter you surrender to me, I promise that you will not be killed but will be treated honourably as a prisoner of war.

Signed

Kurokata Inosuke[1]'

Even if Seagrim had received the letter it would have made no difference to his plans. Events were serving only to harden his resolve to defeat the enemy. Shortly after arriving at his new camp, Po Hla brought devastating news from Kyaukkyi. It transpired that, following his meeting in Rangoon with San Po Thin and Kya Doe, the Japanese had seized Po Hla's sweetheart, family and friends. All were threatened with dire consequences if Po Hla did not surrender.

Through their highly efficient network of spies, the kempeitai had heard of Po Hla's meetings in Rangoon three months earlier. They were suspicious of his activities and, with his family now held in custody as leverage, demanded that he report to them without delay. They forced a relative of his – Saw Charlemagne – to track him down to deliver the order. Charlemagne had travelled up to Kyaukkyi and was waiting to talk to him now, Po Hla told Seagrim. The future of Seagrim's entire intelligence network was in real jeopardy along with the life of his most trusted and able agent. Seagrim told Po Hla to meet with Charlemagne to verify the facts and then report back. Only then could they decide what to do.

Charlemagne corroborated the story. Seagrim then sat down with a despairing Po Hla and a calmer Eric McCrindle to discuss the options. McCrindle was all for helping Po Hla escape north over the hills and into China. Seagrim was adamantly against it, but also determined to try to save Po Hla and his family and friends. Reasoning that if Po Hla escaped it would be an admission of guilt and his family and friends would suffer severe reprisals, he urged them all to consider other alternatives, to sleep on it and to pray for guidance. In the morning, they were unanimous: the best solution was for Po Hla to give himself up, but with a plausible cover story that would fool the Japanese.

Surrender posed a huge risk to their entire operation. If the Japanese saw through his story and tortured him, the damage would be incalculable. Before setting off, Po Hla rehearsed his cover. He was to say that he was the spoiled son of wealthy parents, who had not given him enough money for his needs. He had travelled up into the hills to trade in medicines and betel nut to earn extra money. He was to say that he had met Seagrim, but that was over two years ago when the British officer was heading for China. Seagrim had given him a message for his mother, but he had not seen him since. It was a plausible story, and much more convincing than outright denial. Po Hla was encouraged to be friendly to the Japanese – even, if necessary, to pretend to work for them as a double agent, yet somehow keep Seagrim informed.

Before Po Hla left, Seagrim gave him some New Testament verses he had copied from the Gospel of St Matthew. These were to comfort Po Hla on the way to what he believed was his certain torture and death. Seagrim wrote:

'Behold I send you forth as sheep in the midst of wolves;
Be ye therefore wise as serpents and harmless as doves.
But beware of men, for they will deliver you up to the
councils and they will scourge you in their synagogues;
And ye shall be brought before governors and kings

for my sake for a testimony against them and the Gentiles.

But when they deliver you up take no thought how or what ye shall speak, for it shall be given to you in that same hour what ye shall speak.'[2]

Desperately worried for his family and friends, poor Po Hla took a long detour out of the hills along the Mawchi road to Toungoo to reinforce the credibility of his story. En route, he spent a miserable night with Nimmo, who agreed, but only with very great reluctance, that surrender was the least worst option. As Po Hla was a potentially compromised agent facing almost certain torture, many of Nimmo's party flatly disagreed and thought that they should kill him instead. It must also have crossed Po Hla's mind. One of the men argued that if they were to be exposed, Nimmo should press for 1,000 rifles to be dropped to them, so they could all go down fighting. It was a tricky moment for Nimmo, who dealt with it with his customary coolness and presence of mind. 'Remember,' he said, 'Po Hla is one of our old comrades. Even if you kill him, that still won't quieten the suspicions of the Japanese, and much suffering will come to his relatives. If he surrenders, he may be able to play a double game with the Japanese.'[3] Reluctantly convinced by Nimmo's arguments, they allowed Po Hla to continue on his way.

With considerable trepidation, on 23 January 1944 he surrendered to Warrant Officer Nakayama at Nyaunglebin. It says much for Po Hla that, under enormous stress and with his own life in the balance, he calmly convinced the Japanese of his story – so much so that he was well treated and cultivated by them. In Rangoon he was even taken out to dinner by Colonel Suniyoshi, the commander of the city kempeitai, who tried to suborn him into helping the Japanese win the support of the Karens. At terrible personal risk, Po Hla managed to smuggle a letter to Seagrim to explain what was happening. However, it eventually dawned on the Japanese that he was deceiving them. He was arrested immediately and interrogated.

Meanwhile, in the Karen hills, the Japanese were closing in. Just a week after Po Hla's 'surrender', a detachment of the kempeitai, under the command of Captain Motoichi Inoue, descended on Kyaukkyi, demanding information about British officers and Karen parachutists operating in the hills. Another, under Captain Kurokata, descended on Papun. With characteristic cynicism, alongside trying to coax the Karens to co-operate with bribes such as cinema shows and sweets for their children, the Japanese simultaneously tortured some of the menfolk, including an old soldier of the Burma Rifles, Jemadar Maung Wah, who commanded the levies in Kyaukkyi. Maung Wah was strung up with his feet off the ground. For three days he was beaten black and blue and then lashed with whip-like bamboo canes. With amazing fortitude, he refused to confess to anything or provide any information. He was then cut down and ordered to go into the hills. It was made very clear to him that if he did not come back within a week with details of Seagrim's location and lookout posts, his family would bear the consequences. He was expressly forbidden to tell Seagrim what had happened, or even that the Japanese were in Kyaukkyi.

For poor Maung Wah, it was an appalling dilemma, but his loyalty never wavered. On being led to Seagrim at Komupwado, he told him everything and showed him his bruised and battered body. Seagrim was deeply moved. His eyes welled with tears at the thought that others were suffering so much on his behalf. 'This is the price which you Karens are paying for your loyalty,' he said.[4] They discussed what to do. Maung Wah, a typical iron-souled Karen hardened by years of Army service, responded with characteristic stoicism. He asked Seagrim to radio India for an immediate arms drop so that the levies in the area could rise, attack their hated enemy and all go down together fighting for their freedom. After quietly listening, Seagrim agreed to contact India.

Later that evening, the reply came. Unsurprisingly, it was a firm refusal. At this juncture, a premature rising so far behind the enemy lines had no hope of success. It would only generate reprisals and unnecessary suffering. When Seagrim read the message to a disconsolate Maung Wah, the brave old Jemadar begged Seagrim to kill him, but he refused. Seagrim simply said: 'Go back to Kyaukkyi and tell the Japanese everything you know. God will look after you.'[5] He handed him a note warning the elders in Pyagawpu.

Fearful but resolute, the courageous Maung Wah headed back to Kyaukkyi and a very uncertain fate. En route, he heard that in a thorough search of the village, the Japanese had uncovered the levies' cache of arms. It appeared that a young boy had broken under torture and revealed not only the location of the arms cache but also the whereabouts of Seagrim's camp. Maung Wah believed that this catastrophic news had sealed his fate. His initial reaction was to run away and hide in the forest, but he steeled himself and dropped to his knees in prayer. He reasoned: 'I thought that when I prayed God guided me to help my country, my people and my king, so that if I ran away now everyone would get into trouble, therefore I must stay and meet the worst. If I died, my friends would not suffer.'[6] Eventually, he gathered himself together and went into Kyaukkyi, prepared to face the worst. He was received by a brutal Japanese reception committee, who beat the living daylights out of him, insisting that he was the local ringleader of the levies and a liar. Fortunately for him, they had already extracted the key information they were seeking from the poor tortured boy and failed to press home their questions.

The next morning, a large detachment of Japanese infantry arrived. This was part of a tobatsutai, or pacification unit, comprising four companies of Japanese infantry from the 24th Independent Mixed Brigade under the command of a Colonel Ohara, although all matters relating to the Karens were the specific responsibility of the kempeitai. The troops were split into three separate groups, one leaving from Mawchi, one from Kyaukkyi and one from Papun. All three planned to converge on Pyagawpu in mid-February 1944. With some of the captured Karens in tow, the enemy determined once and for all to crush the Karen resistance movement and to capture or kill the elusive British officers.

When the elders received the note from Seagrim via Maung Wah, they gathered together in the church in Pyagawpu, along with Ba Gyaw and Thet Wa, the wireless operator. Seagrim's note set out three possible courses of action; he asked the elders which of the options they thought would be in the Karens' best interests. With characteristic selflessness, his thoughts were what was best for them, not himself. He wrote that he could commit suicide; he could surrender; or he could work his way further north into Karenni. The elders concluded that he should opt for the latter. Ta Roe went with several others to Komupwado to tell him of their decision – but when they arrived the camp was deserted. They were forced to spend the night in two lean-to bamboo shelters before returning to their village the next morning.

Seagrim had decided that things were getting too hot. He informed India that he was shutting down the radio transmitter, but before so doing he was proud to hear that he had been awarded the DSO for his determination, courage and devotion of the highest order. He adopted a peripatetic existence, never staying in one place too long. He kept one transmitter with him and gave the second to Thet Wa and Ba Gyaw for safekeeping, with the clear instruction that if anything happened to Nimmo or to him they should advise India and lie low for a while. The third transmitter was up with Jimmy Nimmo in his lair near the Mawchi road.

On the eve of disappearing, Seagrim received a message from Arthur Ta Bi in Papun telling him that the Japanese were hot on his trail: they were continually asking everyone questions about him and his whereabouts. Arthur Ta Bi made an ingenious suggestion – that Seagrim should signal India to drop a corpse of a tall European, which the Karens could then deliver to the Japanese as proof that Seagrim had died in the forest. It was an inspired idea and an extraordinary coincidence as the British had deployed a similar top-secret ruse – Operation Mincemeat – in Europe just six months earlier to deceive the Germans about the invasion of Sicily. Unfortunately, the idea was mooted just after Seagrim had closed down his transmitter. It just might have worked.

Seagrim believed that if they all kept a very low profile for a while, there was a good chance that the Japanese would conclude that they had escaped and eventually give up. But the kempeitai were nothing if not tenacious. On 13 February, Captain Inoue arrived in Pyagawpu along with several Karens and an entire company of infantry under the command of Captain Yamaguchi. Among them was Po Hla, who had been discredited and exposed for having deceived the Japanese, and hauled up from Rangoon, along with the poor tortured Karen boy from Kyaukkyi. On pain of death, he was ordered to accompany the Japanese in their search for Seagrim along with Maung Wah. Immediately on arriving in Pyagawpu, the local Karens, including Ta Roe, were convinced that Po Hla was responsible for betraying Seagrim and for leading the Japanese to their village. Their suspicions were reinforced when Po Hla was seen wearing five blue stars – the Japanese insignia for a good detective – on his Burma Army uniform. The Japanese occupied the church and arrested several elders, including Ta Roe.

The next morning, they headed for Komupwado and pounced on two Karen boys who regularly took food up to Seagrim. They denied this completely, so with their hands tied behind their backs they were strung up and beaten. After two hours, one, Saw Pulu, confessed to taking up food occasionally, but he also said that when he had last visited the camp was deserted. The Japanese forced the frightened boy to take them there immediately. The camp was surrounded by troops ... but deserted, just as he had said. Frustrated at being so near, yet so far, the Japanese vented their anger on the Karens, slapping and kicking them as they descended the hill. Back in the village, another Karen was seized and tortured, but he revealed nothing. A net was thrown around the wider area, before the detachment headed back to Pyagawpu.

By an unfortunate twist of fate, on their return the party saw four young Karens, who turned and bolted into the forest with the Japanese infantry in hot pursuit. They caught and held Saw Yay, a young man in his twenties, who was carrying some Indian silver rupees, which in itself was suspicious; but, much more damningly, he also had a British .38 revolver. He claimed that as an ex-soldier he had owned the coins and the revolver since 1942. Inoue was completely unconvinced. The Karen was strung up and beaten until he confessed that he was one of Seagrim's scouts who had been charged with keeping watch on the jungle tracks. He promised to guide them to Seagrim's new camp.

After a restless night in Komupwado, the following morning the Japanese force of 300 men split into two groups. Moving in total silence, and nervously fingering the triggers of their rifles, they crept through the forest towards Seagrim's lair, each group approaching from a different direction to surround the camp, which lay swathed in dense bamboo thicket on the side of a dark gully. Determined to capture the elusive major and his troublesome guerrillas, Yamaguchi and his men slowly encircled the camp. Then a twig snapped, cracking like a gunshot in the silence, and at the very last moment, Seagrim heard them coming. 'Scatter!' he yelled. His men leapt to their feet and broke in all directions, running for their lives across the gully as bullets hissed and whined around them. On the far side, Eric McCrindle ran straight into a Japanese corporal. He shot him in the chest with his revolver before being cut down himself by a burst from a tommy gun. McCrindle died where he stood – shot in the head, groin and leg, wearing Karen dress, face to the enemy and defiant to the end. It was a heroic final stand. He was just thirty-one years old.

Whether McCrindle drew Japanese fire from the others, or whether in the ensuing melee he was simply unlucky, no one will never know, but Seagrim and his comrades escaped, sprinting through the jungle with the enemy in hot pursuit. Hearts pounding in their chests, they crashed through the undergrowth. It was every man for himself. The Japanese swarmed into the forest combing the hillside for the fugitives. Firing continued sporadically for another half an hour or so as they searched the camp and shot at shadows. The wireless transmitter was captured along with six Sten guns, three tommy guns, two rifles, some money and revolvers. Symbolically, among the detritus was Seagrim's precious Bible, which Inoue retrieved before burning the camp to the ground.

That evening, the Japanese corporal, whom McCrindle had shot in his last moments, died of his chest wound. This made his infuriated comrades even more determined to track down the fugitives. They remained at Komupwado for over a month, randomly interrogating and torturing the villagers, but they knew nothing that could help them. Patrols were sent off into the surrounding hills in search of Seagrim, but the elusive major had vanished into thin air like a phantom.

McCrindle lay where he fell. The Japanese taunted the Karens with it: 'If they were so loyal to the British, why did they not dare to come and bury his body …?' But the Karens had discovered that two military police officers had staked out the site, ready to shoot anyone who came near. Subsequently, efforts were made to find poor Eric McCrindle. But he has never been found. He lies there still, alone and far from home in one of the lost, forgotten places of the earth for which he gave his life.

With the help of the intelligence gleaned at Komupwado, the day after killing Eric McCrindle, the Japanese went for Jimmy Nimmo at his hideout in the north. Nimmo had just returned from a secret meeting with the chief minister of the state of Kyetbogyi at a prearranged location a couple of days' march to the east. He was pleased at the progress he had been making but, unbeknown to him, he was walking straight into a trap. A large Japanese motorised force was heading along the Mawchi road from Toungoo, led by Captain Morino, the chief of the local kempeitai. Leaving their vehicles on the road, they hiked through the forest straight to Mawtudo. There they tortured and whipped the Karens, until one broke and offered to guide them to Nimmo's camp.

Early on the morning of 15 February 1944, the camp was slowly surrounded. The aim was to catch Jimmy half asleep and unawares. In those quiet, peaceful moments just before dawn, the ambush was sprung. Jimmy, dressed in black Shan pants and a sports shirt, dashed out of his simple bamboo hut brandishing a revolver. A single shot rang out. He was hit in the head and killed instantly. Saw Pe was shot in the arm, Toe Kin and Saw Media slightly wounded, and, along with Saw He Be, they were all captured. The rest scattered in all directions, running for their lives into the forest. Poor Jimmy Nimmo was simply left in the open where he fell. That afternoon, some Karens went up from Mawtudo village and buried him beneath a cairn of stones. A few days later, a Karen pastor read the funeral service over his grave. The quiet Scot, who more than any other person had coaxed and driven Captain Arthur Bell Thompson's party forward on their legendary trek out of Burma to Fort Hertz two years earlier, was gone. Like his friend Eric McCrindle, he too was just thirty-one years old. After the war, his body was exhumed and reinterred at Rangoon War Cemetery.

The similarities between the lives and deaths of the two men are positively uncanny. If ever there were two brothers in arms, these were they. Both were born in 1912. Both went to Cambridge between 1931 and 1934. Both applied to join Macgregor and Co. as assistant foresters. Both arrived in Burma in 1934, where they shared the same rooms. Both were among the handful of British officers who took part in epic treks out of Burma in 1942, for at least part of the way together. Both volunteered to be dropped back into Burma for special operations after escaping successfully to India. Both were dropped with their own Karen teams, within two months of each other, to work with Hugh Seagrim. Both were killed, within one day of each other, in virtually identical circumstances. Both drew their revolvers as a final act of defiance, and both were the only levies to be shot dead in the respective raids.

For Thra Kyaw Lay and the local villagers, it was a dreadful time. In a newly discovered letter, dated 10 September 1945, the Karen wrote to Jimmy Nimmo's brother Bill. In characteristically quaint English, and with some misapprehension of what had led to the attack, he lamented:

'We were full of hope and strength by working with Nimmo, but there came a day when Po Hla and Lu Thien by the skill of the Japs betrayed us, resulting in the fallen [sic] of our leader Nimmo into the enemies' hands, leaving the children who were in tears one by one fallen into the Japs' hands. I was the last one who had the strong determination to resist the Japs; after hiding a month I surrendered for they ill-treated my family and villagers.

The Japs hated me the most because I stood bravely [by] what I had done. They even dropped five bombs on my village but no casualty while I was in Toungoo jail. I thought that my life would be over there but by the help of the British force who recaptured Burma automatically saved me by the Grace of God, made me live again and meet with you Young Nimmo as a dream, when our hope and strength revived.'[7]

As is so often the case in the shadow world of espionage, Po Hla was regarded by some as responsible for the disaster, but this accusation was almost certainly unfounded and a product of the fog of war. The local Karens had not wanted him to surrender to the Japanese, and when later he was outed as a double agent and forced to join the Japanese column into the hills they must have feared the worst. But there is little doubt that he was loyal. Few can withstand protracted torture, and if blame can be laid anywhere, it is at the door of the unfortunate Karen boys who were tortured beyond their powers of endurance, not with the brave Po Hla, who was Seagrim's most effective agent.

Unlike Hugh Seagrim, who was a regular soldier and serving officer, Eric McCrindle and Jimmy Nimmo came out to Burma as civilians, simply seeking outdoor jobs as foresters. Neither expected nor contemplated that they would become soldiers on whom the lives of so many would depend, nor that they were destined to die deep in the jungle far, far from home.

★★★

When the Japanese ambushed Seagrim's camp, it had been every man for himself. Seagrim and his followers scattered into the forest. Two Karens – Ohn Gyaw, an ex-Burma Rifles man, and one of the parachutists from India, called Pa Ah – fled uphill through the forest for most of the day before stopping beside a stream to quench their thirst. As they rested, they heard someone approach. Convinced that the Japanese were hot on their tails, Ohn Gyaw ran off into the jungle, but Pa Ah took cover to assess the situation. After a short while, Seagrim emerged alone. Pa Ah called to him. Together they called to Ohn Gyaw to come back and join them. The three then sat down to review their position. Pa Ah suggested that they head for Mewado village, seven miles north of Papun, and twenty-five miles from their current position. He had a sister living there. He was confident that his family would help to shelter and feed them. The villagers loathed the Japanese and the quisling BIA, who had burned their old village on the banks of the Yunzalin river, after which they had been forced to retreat and rebuild higher in the hills.

Avoiding all tracks and villages, and living off esculent jungle plants and freshwater streams, for five days they glided silently through the forests like wraiths until they reached Mewado, which they skirted. They then lay up in the hills above. While Seagrim and Ohn Gyaw waited, Pa Ah went down into the village. That night, he met up with his brother-in-law and sister. He returned the next morning with the village headman, who knew Seagrim and who spoke a little English. The headman, a retired forest ranger, was keen to help and offered to provide food and build a hut for them. Seagrim welcomed the offer of food but decided that a hut would be too risky. He preferred to sleep out in the open under the trees. While in hiding, Seagrim failed to realise the scale and intensity of the Japanese manhunt. Determined to capture him, they had launched a concerted campaign of terror to frighten the Karens into betraying him. Day and night, entire villages were forced out into the forest to search for him, diverting the people from planting vital crops for the next season. Large contingents of Japanese soldiers were stationed in all the principal villages across the hills. For an eight-mile radius around Papun, all food was destroyed and the villages razed to the ground.

Ta Roe was seized by the Japanese and dispatched to coerce the surrounding villages into helping with the search. He was constantly accused of lying and threatened with a revolver: 'They now said I could go and stay with Capt. Seagrim as we were of the same feather. Then I replied that as I did not know where he was now I could not stay with him. I also added that if you all knew the whereabouts of the captain, why ask me to go to him?'[8] While many Karens thought Seagrim long since dead of disease or starvation, the Japanese refused to believe this until they found his body. Had Arthur Ta Bi's suggestion been taken up and a message sent to Army HQ to drop the cadaver of a tall white man, Seagrim might have been able to fool the Japanese. But the opportunity had passed.

The Japanese were very well informed. They knew a great deal about Seagrim and his associates. They knew that Pa Ah was with Seagrim at the site of the ambush and that he had family in Mewado. On numerous occasions, they arrived in the village to bully the villagers into revealing Pa Ah's whereabouts, and to threaten his brother-in-law and family with arrest. Initially, the villagers resisted, but as the threats and brutality escalated they asked Pa Ah to give himself up while Seagrim and Ohn Gyaw remained in hiding. After discussing it together, Seagrim suggested that it was probably the best option if Pa Ah could deceive the Japanese with a plausible cover story.

Professing that he knew nothing of Seagrim or his followers, Pa Ah moved down to Pyagawpu and turned himself in, insisting that since the ambush he had been hiding in the forest, and that he had seen none of the others. The Japanese, who could be shockingly naïve, swallowed his story and took him down to Kyaukkyi, where many other Karens were being held. Here a party of Japanese military police under Captain Inoue systematically beat and tortured them. Inoue was a tough, experienced Japanese officer from a peasant family inculcated with the bushido code of unquestioning obedience. After enlisting as a regular soldier twelve years earlier, he had been posted to the kempeitai. In December 1942, he had been sent to Burma to help pacify the country in the wake of the Japanese invasion.

Pa Ah suffered terribly, as he recounted in the official testimony he made after the war:

'At Kyaukkyi Captain Inoue and his jackal subordinates exhibited their skill in extorting evidence from the Karens ... they adopted the spiteful Nazi methods of torture. With extreme violence, the Karens were tortured daily from 8 a.m. to 5 p.m. with a short interval at noon. Besides flogging, suffocation almost to the point of death, whipping, pressing, hanging by the heels to dangle in the air for an indefinite time, there were so many cruel methods of torture. Everyone undergoing this ordeal would testify to the fact that the JMP [Japanese Military Police], who were devoid of humanity, acted, in expectation of promotion and higher pay, like machines without conscience, sense of pity, emotion and consideration.'[9]

Although Inoue did not participate directly in the wave of torture and brutality inflicted on the Karens, he ordered and oversaw the whole process. His sadistic subordinates were given free rein to try to break the captives' spirits. He was part of a military machine in which unquestioning obedience was seen as a virtue, and any form of empathy or compassion as a weakness. In that schizophrenic mindset adopted by so many perpetrators of evil, he was capable of ordering unimaginable suffering for men, women and children while simultaneously cherishing the memory of his own small son who waited for him at home.

Torture is a blunt instrument. Over 200 Karens were abused. Many died or were scarred for life by their ordeal. Many simply told the truth, but all too often they were not believed and were severely punished regardless. Under great duress and intense pain, some said anything just to please their examiners, even at the expense of incriminating themselves or other innocents. Far from uncovering the truth, false evidence and a tangled web of lies led many an innocent person to be found guilty. Daily in the dak bungalow and police station, Pa Ah heard their cries and shrieks at the hands of the kempeitai. The groaning, yelling and wailing of these poor innocent souls in torment could be heard in the far distance. For many it was hell on earth. Pa Ah's testimony continued: 'Thus Kyaukkyi was converted into a modern "Rama" for two solid months. O God! when would thou answer the cries and prayers of a suffering people.'[10]

Japanese military trials resembled the Inquisition. No opportunity was accorded to the accused to ask questions, to cross-examine connected witnesses for either corroboration or contradiction, or to plead for mercy. As a rule, whipping provided an overture to every important examination. An accused was softened up with severe blows about the head and joints before leading questions were flung at him, and answers given and recorded. When answers were deemed unsatisfactory, further pain was inflicted. Generally, prisoners were forced to give statements based on the wishes of the examiners rather than on the facts of what actually occurred. For Pa Ah – forced to listen to his innocent fellow Karens enduring day after day of agonising torture, in the full knowledge that he knew the answers that could end their suffering – it was a terrible moral dilemma. Desperate to unburden his conscience and talk to another, he opened up to a fellow Karen. By gross misfortune, the person to whom he spoke was the very same Karen who had revealed Seagrim's camp at Komupwado, and who, to save his own skin, had agreed to act as a Japanese stool pigeon. He promptly went straight to Captain Inoue and told him that Seagrim was now at Mewado.

Inoue headed straight for the village with a force of kempeitai, along with the Karen informer and an appalled Pa Ah. On arrival, he informed the headman that unless he revealed the exact location of Seagrim's hideout, the entire village would be razed to the ground and all the men, women and children arrested. Faced with an impossible position, the headman reluctantly agreed to try to find Seagrim in the morning. Later the poor man said: 'In night-time, I prayed to God. In morning-time, I went to Captain Seagrim with my friend. I asked, "What shall we do?"' [11]

Ohn Gyaw contemplated suicide, but Seagrim admonished him. A Christian could not take his own life. He explained calmly that it was his own personal duty to go down and give himself up to the Japanese. Only by doing this could he put an end to the terrible suffering being inflicted on innocent Karens. He asked Ohn Gyaw to continue to remain in hiding, but he refused. With extraordinary courage and devotion, and in the full knowledge of what awaited him, Ohn Gyaw insisted on surrendering too. Seagrim acted quickly. Expecting the worst, Seagrim handed his watch to the headman before going down to Mewado to surrender. He asked the headman to look after it, and to try to send it back to his mother in England after the war.

At 8 a.m. on the morning of 14 March 1944, Captain Inoue was fast asleep in the hut of Pa Ah's brother-in-law. Suddenly, he heard people arrive and a commotion outside. Towering in the open doorway was the tall, thin wraith of a bearded white man in Karen dress. At last: it was the enigmatic Englishman who had eluded him for so long. Inoue jumped up. Seagrim extended his hand and remarkably the two adversaries shook hands. Seagrim then handed Inoue his revolver and they all sat down on the floor. Inoue offered Seagrim a cigarette, which he accepted, telling Inoue via an interpreter that it was his first in two years. Inoue responded by offering him the packet, which he declined. The Japanese captain then ordered his men to prepare some hot orange juice laced with sugar, which he offered to Seagrim, who drained three large glassfuls. Immediately, through an interpreter, Seagrim then pleaded for the Karens. 'Treat the Karens generously. They are not to blame. I alone am responsible for what has happened in the hills.' [12]

For the Japanese, Seagrim's appearance was a revelation. According to their translated testimony, with his 'shaggy hair, the state of him covering his six feet tall body with the Karen's poor clothes, didn't look like he was the major who had a glory of the British Empire honour'. [13] He was grilled by the Japanese: 'Are you British Major Siglem [sic] for sure?' He replied:

'Yes, I am. I have been releasing Japan's information to Britain as a British spy. I hope to be executed honourably for the sake of Great Britain. I have no regrets. I repeat myself, but please release the Karens who I acted together with. They are blameless. I hate this protracted war between Japan and Britain. I hope this war will end soon and peace will come.'[14]

At this point, the astonished Japanese heard Seagrim quietly crooning the British national anthem. Having apparently not eaten for twenty days, he might well have been delirious. Standing stiffly to attention, he answered all the questions put to him briskly, with tears in his eyes, then 'whether from the relief of being captured, he had to sit down on the ground, as if all his tension up to now had drained out. He was scolded by a military-police officer and tied up with rope.'[15]

With Ohn Gyaw and Inoue, Seagrim had a large lunch of rice and dried fish before setting off down the hill. Seagrim had a badly poisoned foot and limped slowly. Inoue arranged for a stretcher to be made from two bamboo poles and a blanket and Seagrim was carried down to the Yunzalin river by a couple of local Karens. At the river, Inoue tried to obtain a boat to take them to Papun, but to no avail, so they started to walk the seven miles. Hugh insisted on walking the entire distance in great pain. Early in the evening on 14 March, the party arrived in Papun. They slept in Ram Singh's old house on the east bank of the river. Seagrim and Inoue shared a room, with a guard just outside the door.

Left: Seagrim's nemesis: Lieutenant Motoichi Inoue imprisoned in Rangoon jail at the end of the war. Above: The New Law Courts, 1945.

They spent the whole of the next day at Papun in discussion. Time and again Seagrim reiterated his request that they could do whatever they chose to him, but they should treat the Karens with generosity. He explained to Inoue that if he survived the war, he intended to leave the army, become a missionary and live among the Karens. Far from there being any personal hatred or animosity between them, there seems to have been considerable mutual respect. As a gesture, Inoue returned Seagrim's Bible, which he had picked up after the raid on the camp at Komupwado. Inoue thought that Seagrim was 'a gentleman, a man of high character' and deeply respected his persistent pleas on behalf of the Karens.

Seagrim may have been in bad shape, but his spirit remained unbroken and unbowed, as one of his old followers later testified. Saw Lin Gyaw, who had worked with Seagrim since October 1942, caught a glimpse of him as he was led away. 'I last saw Major Seagrim on Kurokata's car with red tapes on his neck and wrist. He gave me a farewell wink just before the car started.'[16] While Inoue stayed at Papun, the following day Seagrim was taken with Ohn Gyaw under armed guard to the railhead at Bilin and thence to the 'Rangoon Ritz', the notorious kempeitai hellhole in the heart of the New Law Courts, where months before Ras Pagani had endured such horrors.

Chapter 14

He Who Would Valiant Be

'He who would valiant be 'gainst all disaster,
Let him in constancy follow the Master.
There's no discouragement shall make him once relent
His first avowed intent to be a pilgrim.'
JOHN BUNYAN

Six months after Ras Pagani had been incarcerated in the New Law Courts, in mid-March 1944 Hugh Seagrim was inducted into the nightmare world of the 'Rangoon Ritz.' Imprisoned along with Seagrim were over forty of his closest followers. These had been rounded up in the hills or, following his example, had surrendered themselves. They had been brought to Rangoon and imprisoned either in the New Law Courts or, given their sheer numbers, in the lock-up of the Barr Street police station. They included Po Hla, who was already in Japanese hands, the devoted Ta Roe, his levy commanders Saw Digay, Saw Darlington and Saw Willie Saw, the two pastors Thra Kyaw Lay and Thra May Sha, the dependable Ba Gyaw, who had first made contact with Seagrim after parachuting in from India, Arthur Ta Bi from Papun, the young wireless operator Thet Wa, Saw Henry, poor Jemadar Maung Wah, Pa Ah, who had been with Seagrim at Mewado, Saw Judson, a schoolboy from Papun, and Saw Po Myin, the police chief from Pyagawpu, who had provided a lot of help to Seagrim.

Hugh was kept apart both from the other Europeans and from the Karens in a cell and usually on his own. Although Saw Darlington saw him with a large black bruise on his face, he appears not to have been singled out for ill treatment. The kempeitai commander tried to induce him to use his great personal influence among the Karens to switch sides. It is a measure of how much they misunderstood both the Karens and Seagrim that they could even have contemplated this, but it brought him some respite. Disease was rampant. The inmates died like flies. Of fifty-seven airmen incarcerated in the first six months of 1944, twenty-three died from disease or beatings. Even the most chronically sick with dysentery, malaria, dengue fever or contagious diseases were not segregated. Soul-destroying headaches, fevers, scabies and beri-beri were commonplace. The sick were refused medicines. The wounded were taken to a Japanese doctor about once a month to have their dressings changed, by which time usually wounds were covered in maggots, or – fatally – gangrene had set in.

The guards were given nicknames, such as the 'Killer', an ignorant brute who did not care what happened to them. Another, 'Snoop', was an insignificant little man who had a propensity to lurk outside windows to try to catch them talking. 'Smiley' was a more compassionate man, who smuggled them little candies, dried fish and even parts of his own meals. To the Allies, the Japanese were unfathomable. They were capable of engaging in friendly personal conversation one minute, only to mete out the most inhuman treatment the next. Prior to November 1943 most aircrew were sent to Rangoon Central jail, but as the bombing offensive over Burma increased, a new edict was issued by the Japanese Burma High Command that all airmen were to be treated as criminal prisoners and given special treatment, which is why such a disproportionate number found themselves held in the 'Rangoon Ritz'.

One of the unfortunate Allied airman incarcerated in the Rangoon Ritz at the same time as Hugh Seagrim in the spring of 1944 was Lieutenant Roy Wentz, a navigator with the 9th Bomb Group of the US 10th Air Force. He had been shot down with his crewmates in a B24 bomber over Rangoon on 1 December 1943. He endured over six months imprisoned in the cells at the New Law Courts. For Wentz and his crew, life inside was the usual mixture of sickness, malnourishment, beatings and mental torture, the long hours of boredom and silence overcome by mind games to maintain a positive mental attitude. Hours were spent devising elaborate menus that they planned to enjoy when they returned home, memorising whole passages from books or the Bible, or covertly making chess sets and even a Monopoly board. As is so clear from the graffiti, intense suffering turned many to look beyond themselves for succour. Wentz had an incomplete copy of the New Testament. In his unpublished memoir of those harrowing months he wrote: 'Never again will I read it with more understanding and hope.'[1]

By February the Americans noticed their feet swelling, a sure sign of beri-beri. Wentz's pilot, Captain Bill Wright, swelled up over his entire body and up to his head. For those deemed hopeless, the Japanese doctor would administer the *coup de grâce* with a hypodermic needle. For many with no hope of salvation, this proved a blessing.

Seagrim's arrival in March galvanised the entire jail. Tall, defiant and refusing to kowtow to the Japanese, his charismatic personality gave renewed heart to all those around him. Soon news of his exploits spread like wildfire. Wentz never forgot it. Later wrote in his memoir:

'Early in March, an English captain was brought into the jail. Through the grapevine we soon learned that he was Capt Seagram [sic], an Army man who had stayed in Burma after the Japs came. He had hidden in the hills with a village of Karens operating a radio transmitter for over two years. They, therefore, threatened to burn the village where he had been unless he gave himself up. He had then walked into Jap hands and had been brought here with many of his followers.

He was a tall, well-built man with a complete knowledge of life in the jungle, beri-beri, and other information, which helped us greatly. When we went out for sun baths we could always see him standing at the bars of his cell holding up his hand in the best Churchill 'V' manner. His spirit gave us all a lift even though we were never allowed to talk to him.'[2]

Shortly after Seagrim's arrival, Wentz's friend and captain, Bill Wright, was caught trying to retrieve a cigar butt left on a windowsill by one of the guards. The unfortunate pilot was forced to sit cross-legged in the centre of the cell while he was beaten systematically over his left shoulder and head by the 'Killer' with a solid hickory club four feet long and one and a half inches in diameter. Wright took his punishment bravely and said that it did not bother him. Two days later, while sitting furtively reading the New Testament, he keeled over unconscious and died within a few minutes. Wentz recalled: 'There was nothing we could do. I could not attempt to describe how we felt but I do know that a great man died that day.'[3] Another who died from malnutrition and beri-beri was left in the cell for twenty-four hours. By the time he was taken away, a rat had chewed away part of one of his feet. Seagrim heard all this in his nearby cell, but was never despondent.

Random, casual brutality was the norm. Shortly afterwards, the jail was affected by a terrible itching skin disease. Men's bodies were reduced to a seething mass of running pustular sores.

At midnight on 5 July 1944, some four months after Seagrim's arrival, there was a desperate escape attempt. In a cell jam-packed with thirteen men, seven broke the chains securing the door of their cell and knocked one of the guards unconscious, but the alarm was given by Burmese prisoners in the adjoining cells. When the seven headed out of the courtyard to the main outer gate, they were confronted with machine guns and gave up. Retribution was swift and merciless. The offenders were stripped of all their clothing and beaten with clubs and whips. For three days they were forced to sit nude, cross-legged in their cells, with nothing to eat. They were then placed on one-third rations. Twice a day, a guard came into the cell and beat each prisoner with a club. One American bombardier lost the use of his limbs and could not eat. He also lost his mind and later died after being transferred to Rangoon jail.

By chance, Ta Roe spent one night in the same cell as Seagrim, along with just two other men – an English airman and a Chinese. For a while they were able to converse in whispers out of earshot of the patrolling sentry, as Ta Roe later recalled in an interview with Ian Morrison.

'Why are you here, Ta Roe?' Seagrim asked.

To which Ta Roe replied, 'I was brought by the Japanese.'

'Did you come alone or with others?'

'I came with others.'

'Who are they?'

Ta Roe listed their names. Seagrim must have been devastated to hear that his entire network had been rolled up, just as they were about to reap the rewards of two long years of hardship, planning and preparation, but he never showed it and remained as resolute as ever. To Ta Roe he said:

'The Japanese are very bad men, Ta Roe. They said that if I surrendered they would stop troubling the Karens. But now they have arrested you and the others. They are not to be trusted. But don't worry, Ta Roe. We are Christians and must have faith in God. Christ came down to earth and suffered on a cross. We must suffer like him.'[4]

Overhearing them, the sentry in the passageway outside screamed and told them to be quiet. Forced into silence, Seagrim took out his Bible and pointed to one of his favourite verses, St Paul's epistle to Timothy: 'For if we be dead with him, we shall also live with him.' After sharing the cell with Seagrim for the night, Ta Roe was moved to another.

The imprisoned Karens suffered terribly over the ensuing months. Run down both physically and mentally, mistreated and abused, starved and beaten, they faced a bleak future. The Japanese systematically used every possible device, both physical and mental, to break their spirits. Prolonged mental torture paralysed a victim's sanity. It took a determined struggle just to stay alive. Some simply chose not to. One by one, the Karens died. Among the first were two young Karens from Mewado, then poor Pa Ah, depressed and distraught at having inadvertently revealed Seagrim's whereabouts to the informer at Kyaukkyi. Wracked by dysentery and tormented by guilt, day by day he weakened until one morning he just never rose from the floor. Ohn Gyaw, who had refused to stay hidden in the jungle at Mewado and instead surrendered with Seagrim, also succumbed to dysentery. Death came in many different guises in this evil place: to two Kachin boys, who had served Seagrim faithfully since 1942; to Tun Shwe, who had parachuted in from India with Ba Gyaw. All of them died in agony from beri-beri. Two of Ah Din's men died of malaria.

But there are other snatches of information about Seagrim at this time. The most remarkable comes from two Germans, Rolf Magener and Heins von Have, who were actually in the New Law Courts in July 1944, having escaped over 1,500 miles across India to Burma in one of the most audacious and little-known escapes of the entire war.[5] The two German traders had been interned as enemy aliens at Dehra Dun in India in 1939, but in April 1944, with five companions, they had made a daring escape. After splitting up, one of them, Heinrich Harrer, travelled alone over the Himalayas to Tibet, where he stayed for several years with the Dalai Lama. Later he achieved global renown with his autobiography *Seven Years in Tibet*. Magener and von Have's adventures were no less astonishing. Posing as British officers, they travelled right across India to the Arakan. With amazing daring, they slipped through the Allied frontlines, where they joined up with their Japanese allies, who had no idea what to do with the pair, treated them with undisguised hostility and assumed they were spies. In early July 1944, they were hauled off to Rangoon and kept under lock and key on the roof of the New Law Courts at the very moment when Seagrim was in the courtyard cells four floors below.

As Magener later wrote in his memoir *Our Chances Were Zero*, gradually the Germans realised that the conditions in which the Allied prisoners were being kept were 'unspeakably horrible … It was clear that we were in the grip of the most dangerous of all Japanese institutions, one that had absolute power of life and death, and could give our case any turn it chose … The headquarters of the Japanese military police, we soon saw, led nowhere beyond itself; no way to freedom led through it. It was a terminus, and those who arrived stayed there or else were destroyed. We saw the rations on which prisoners starved, and were told that Japanese soldiers charged with breaches of discipline – a very rare occurrence – preferred to take their own lives rather than await sentence. Twice we saw a detachment of kempeitai men go off by lorry with spades to bury the corpses of the prisoners.'[6]

One of the reasons that the Japanese treated the two Germans with such suspicion was that the official dealing with them was also dealing with Seagrim. Magener realised that

'the Japanese fear of espionage was not without good cause. They had had some unpleasant experiences … The official who sat opposite to us at our table was dealing with the case of three Englishmen who had been dropped in East Burma and had succeeded in enlisting a small troop from the local tribes for guerrilla warfare. It took a detachment of the kempeitai weeks to put them out of action, and weeks more to capture the Englishmen, or rather their leader, as the two others were shot during the pursuit. The leader was later caught, half-dead, after a wild chase, in which elephants were employed, and was now facing a court-martial.'[7]

Magener went on to describe how some Allied agents who had been turned by the Japanese were also in the building.

'Englishmen were not normally expended on these tasks; it was usually Burmese … equipped with radio apparatus for transmitting their news. Many of them surrendered to the Japanese without delay, but there were some who remained loyal to their British principals. We got to know one of them; in fact, we saw him every day, as he was one of the minor officials … He was a young man, perhaps eighteen years old … he was taught Morse by the British and dropped back in to Burma. The most surprising thing about him was the fact that he was alive, and had not even been punished; we found out that several Burmese with a similar record were employed by the kempeitai as clerks, translators or messengers.'[8]

Quite who these men were it is impossible to say, but it is an indication of the moral ambiguity facing many in this shadow world, who were forced to live their lives under the daily threat of terror.

It was not just the Germans who caught wind of the charismatic English major's presence. Seagrim's irrepressible personality radiated through the entire prison. Several American airmen who survived the horrors of the New Law Courts before being transported to Rangoon city jail testified that Seagrim was a true inspiration. One remarked:

'He never seemed to be sick. He was a very religious man who carried the Bible with him at all times. He would not call the Japanese master. He would not bow to them. He walked tall, and straight, with his head in the air. Always calm and friendly and doing what he could for his fellow men. He loved the Karen people as he loved his own and was dedicated to their freedom.' [9]

But it was a young RAF officer who left the most eloquent testimony of Seagrim's serenity in the face of the institutionalised evil of the kempeitai. Flight-Lieutenant Arthur Sharpe, a Beaufighter pilot from Weybridge, Surrey, was held at the New Law Courts for six months from March to August 1944. He recalled Seagrim's arrival vividly:

'I saw him as he was led in, handcuffed, by a strutting Japanese NCO of above-average stature. I was strangely stirred the moment I saw him, his tall, proud, erect figure, his fine-cut, sun-tanned features, high forehead and deep-set kindly eyes. He had a fine beard, which increased his aristocratic and unassumed appearance of superiority over ordinary men. I knew at once that I had seen an exceptional personality.' [10]

When, months later, Sharpe was transferred to Rangoon jail, he conveyed his impressions of Seagrim to Wing Commander Lionel Hudson, an Australian airman, who later wrote of his wartime experiences in his book *The Rats of Rangoon*, in which he quoted Sharpe's recollections. 'This strange-looking fellow was brought into the cells at the New Law Courts at the end of March 1944,' Sharpe told him. 'He towered over the little Japs. He had long hair, a heavy dark brown beard and was bare-footed. He wore a black longyi with a red, smocked shirt hanging loose. His cheerful face was a joy.' Sharpe continued:

'We were intrigued by this mystery man. He was interrogated continually and guarded all night. He was put into Cell 5 with a Chinese. There was something aristocratic about this man. Even when taking out his latrine box in the morning he walked tall and winked at us as he passed our cell. He refused to call the Japs 'master' and persisted in making cheeky remarks to them. He had us laughing all the time. When the Japs said, 'No talking,' he would ignore them. They would hit him on the head with their clubs and he'd start talking again. He laughed a lot, kept very fit with exercise and was never sick.'[11]

Although held separately from Seagrim, Sharpe managed to exchange some whispered words with him. Seagrim told him his story, how wonderful the Karens had been, and how their operation in the hills had been frustrated by Japanese brutality against innocent Karens. Seagrim also described how, while in hiding in the jungle, he had eaten bush rats and caught rhesus monkeys, slitting their throats and drinking the blood while it was still hot.

One night in mid-June, the roof leaked badly in Cell 3. Sharpe was shifted temporarily into Cell 5 with Seagrim, who confided that the Japanese were trying to get him to organise the Karens to change sides. Seagrim intimated that he was willing to pretend to do this because he knew that he could keep them secretly loyal. He knew the Karens loathed the Japanese because of what they had done to their families, but felt confident that they would go along with the deception. Anything to play for time. There was another reason, too. Seagrim was convinced that the Japanese had no intention of letting anyone out alive, and that, in the event of an invasion, those still in the cells would be killed.

Sharpe told Hudson that Seagrim was an exceptional man and wondered what had happened to him. Subsequently he wrote:

'In case no further evidence comes to light, I would like to conclude with a very inadequate appreciation of Major Seagrim. I believe him to be the finest gentleman I have ever met. He had a complete disregard for his own life and at the same time the greatest concern for the Karen NCOs and men under him.

His men informed me that he was not captured by the Japanese but gave himself up after they had repeatedly taken cruel reprisals against the villagers who were shielding him. He had developed a profound philosophy and a strong religious faith. He was ever cheerful and caused us much subdued laughter in neighbouring cells with his constant witty backchat at the expense of the Japanese guards.

His personality commanded the greatest respect from every Briton and American in the gaol. The Karens, themselves Christians, who came under his influence held him in great reverence. Their regard was such that they expressed a willingness to die for him. I personally saw two of his most faithful followers die in great agony. Major Seagrim's concern for his men was expressed to the British and American prisoners that each of his Karens should be treated as one of themselves. He was very worried about the breakdown of his plans and specially the hardship, which it had brought upon the Karen villagers.'[12]

Sharpe was deeply moved by Seagrim's Christian example. One evening, an officer from Sharpe's squadron died from dysentery and beri-beri. Seagrim was invited to conduct a short ceremony. They all stood together and recited the Lord's Prayer. Seagrim read some lines from the New Testament. After reading the brief passage, he continued with an impromptu prayer of his own, which, to fool the Japanese, he pretended to read from the Bible. Almost certainly they were the words from *Forgiveness* by Giovanni Papini, which Seagrim had copied into his personal anthology years beforehand. Sharpe later wrote:

'I would like to be able to recall that prayer word for word. It moved me very deeply and was an insight into Seagrim's very soul. Nothing could reveal better this man's wonderful character than those words which are now lost. A tribute to the dead, a prayer for the living, and, greatest of all, a word for his cruel captors, for of the Japs he said, in the words of Christ, "Lord, forgive them, for they know not what they do."'[13]

Chapter 15

The Yank from Battersea

'Stone walls do not a prison make,
Nor iron bars a cage.'
RICHARD LOVELACE

While Hugh Seagrim was imprisoned in the New Law Courts, Ras Pagani was being held less than a mile to the west in Rangoon Central jail. It was one of the largest in the British Empire, with space for over 3,000 prisoners. Covering a huge area to the south-west of the downtown city, it had fallen into disuse before the war. By 1942, when it was taken over by the Japanese as the main PoW camp, it was semi-derelict and filthy.

Built to the same classic hub and spoke design as many other colonial prisons, the jail was surrounded by a fifteen-foot-high perimeter wall and approached through a high two-storey gateway, in which were located the commandant's office and guardroom. At the centre was a water tower, around which seven cellblocks radiated like the spokes of a wheel. Each two-storey block was separated from the next by a wall enclosing an inner court, with the first floor accessed by a set of steps at each end. On each floor were five rooms with five long barred windows to each side, open to the elements to allow the air to circulate. In each block two of the upstairs rooms were occupied by officers, who slept twenty-six to a room. The other rooms were occupied by other ranks, who lived forty to forty-four per room. The end room downstairs was used as a hospital.

Outside in the block compounds were a couple of kitchens made from sheets of corrugated iron on a base of brick and mud, where rice was cooked in huge vats. A cement trough about thirty feet long with several taps was used as a crude communal bath. At the opposite end were the latrines and a dug urinal. Filthy beyond description and a breeding ground for all sorts of infections, the latrine tins were insufficient in number; those they did have leaked badly. The floor was always soaked with waste from the tins and gave off an abominable smell, even though it was washed twice a day. The noxious waste was dumped into a huge shell hole, which soon became a breeding ground for millions of flies. To use the latrines during the monsoon rains the prisoners had to walk through squelching mud, water and latrine washings, with nothing to clean their feet when they got back to bed. Their meagre bed coverings in turn became a breeding ground for masses of infectious germs and intestinal diseases. Conditions were infinitely worse than in any of the PoW camps in Europe. The Chief Medical Officer, Colonel K. P. Mackenzie, later wrote: 'I do not believe that it is possible for anybody who was not with us to appreciate fully the conditions under which men were ill or became ill.'[1]

After his arrival in July 1943, assumed to be an enemy airman, Ras was held in solitary confinement for four and a half months in No. 5 block under his new false identity of Lieutenant Terry Ashton Melvyn USAAF. In August 1943, two young American airmen, John Boyd and John Leisure, arrived in the same block. They were appalled by what they saw. Looking through an iron fence into the courtyard around No. 6 block next door, they were astonished to see prisoners wearing only loincloths, and so emaciated that they were walking skeletons. Boyd later wrote of that scene: 'Absolute skin and bones ... I later learned that these "skeletons" were British commandos and had been in prison since 1942.'[2] Boyd and Leisure were placed in a single cell on the ground floor facing the stairway. Save for an ammunition box for use as a latrine and a three-foot-by-six-foot board sitting on four bricks as a bed, it was empty. Each was brought a thin rag as a blanket and a small, handmade mess tin. Unbeknown to

Left: Rangoon Jail: Solitary confinement block where Roy Pagani was held.
Above: Interior of cell block.

Boyd, his had been taken from a previous inmate who had just died of dysentery. Within days, he fell seriously ill with the disease.

As soon as the guards left, the Americans heard an Englishman's voice from the top of the stairway. Boyd wrote:

'It was like music to our ears, but his sound didn't match his story. There was no mistaking the English dialect. But the man said he was Terry Melvin. He claimed to be an American lieutenant and a B-25 pilot who had been shot down near Prome.

I didn't know who this man was, but I was sure he was not an Air Force lieutenant. I later told Leisure, "He doesn't sound like an American to me." He wasn't an Air Force pilot. But he was someone special.'[3]

It was Ras Pagani.

When Ras arrived and realised that he had escaped the clutches of the kempeitai, his spirits had soared. For him, solitary confinement was the best thing that could have happened. He had never felt lonelier than when crammed into the cells at the New Law Courts, cheek by jowl with so many locals, because they were so alien to him. Now he had a plank bed, a view over the courtyard of other European prisoners, and the chance to rest and regain his strength. Each day, he exercised by walking endlessly up and down his cell. At roll call or 'tenko' each morning, he had to carry and empty his latrine. Initially, he could not do this without pausing to rest, for which he was viciously beaten. Eventually, the guards realised that he was incapable and another, more able prisoner was ordered to do it for him.

The guards in the solitary confinement block were among the worst in the jail. Ras was beaten and interrogated daily, but compared with the systematic torture he had endured at the hands of the kempeitai, it was nothing that he could not bear. Others who survived the New Law Courts took a similar view. To those inured to torture, levels of abuse were relative. On being brought to the prison from the 'Rangoon Ritz', most were kept in solitary confinement for up to five months, with many so traumatised by their experiences that they could only move in slow motion or just sit and stare into space. As one man slowly recovered and leaned against a wall, he commented:

'You can't imagine the pleasure I get out of this. In the cells at the Ritz, you know, we had to sit up straight, not allowed to lean against the walls. We were punished if caught talking. Some guards would make you stand for an hour or two with your arms outstretched, others had you place three fingers of each hand on the cell door crossbar while they crashed down on them with a teakwood club.'[4]

As for Ras, when he enquired of his new captors why the Japanese persisted in beating him when they already knew all about him, they said it was to teach him the Japanese way. Eventually, they lost interest and left him alone. But there was one exception: the camp interpreter, Matsuda, who persisted in visiting and asking him questions – ostensibly to improve his English, which was poor. To every answer Ras gave, he replied, 'Ah, so,' leading Ras to christen him 'Arsehole'. Believing he was a bit simple, Ras relaxed his guard. When jokingly he replied that he could only teach him American and not English, Ras received a terrible shock. The interpreter looked slyly at him and then said, 'You no American, you English,' and pointed to the florid tattoos on Ras's arms and chest, one of which was in French. Stunned at having his identity challenged so casually, Ras kept his wits about him. He replied calmly that although he was English by birth, he had taken American nationality several years before the war. Fortunately, the interpreter seemed satisfied. He never raised it again. It was a close shave.

Wisely, Ras thought it prudent to keep on the right side of him. When asked, he agreed to teach him English in exchange for extra fruit, sweetcakes and cigarettes. Each afternoon he was taken to Matsuda's office, which made a pleasant change from the confines of his cell. This regular routine did nothing to allay suspicions among the other inmates about precisely who Ras was, but he reasoned that it could only help if it reduced the scope for misunderstandings between the Japanese and the PoWs. In exchange for teaching Matsuda English, Ras requested a mirror in which to shave. The next morning, he promptly used it to signal messages to the men in the compound below. In response, he gleaned a lot of useful information.

For Ras, life soon settled into a regular routine – heliographing messages in the morning and then in the afternoon teaching his rather slow-witted pupil, who somehow never noticed that Ras still sported his beard. Matsuda, however, seems to have been much shrewder than he appeared. He had good connections with the upper echelons of the Japanese military. In August 1945, he was photographed standing on the deck of the USS *Missouri* at the formal surrender of Japanese forces to General MacArthur in Tokyo Bay.

For Boyd and Leisure in the cells below, Ras was a huge help. He passed on his experience of how to dupe the Japanese by telling them not just to stick to name, rank and serial number, but to concoct a plausible, if spurious, story and then to stay with it. Ras stressed the need to bow to any soldier who passed by. One particular guard, Private Koigotsu Ueno, nicknamed 'Limpy' or 'Tarzan', was exceptionally brutal, with a particular dislike for Americans. If they failed to bow properly, he would motion them to the door of the cell and then take great delight in beating them over the head with his walking stick. Initially, both airmen were highly suspicious of Ras. His cover story seemed so fantastic that neither Boyd nor Leisure could bring themselves to believe it, but gradually they began to trust him.

The Japanese often planted 'stool pigeons' in the cells to glean information. Once, a Dutch colonel and captain arrived in the block with plenty of cigarettes and cigars and started pointedly to question a British fighter pilot who had broken his jaw when crash-landing. They too were suspicious of Ras, so he advised everyone to be careful. A few days later, they disappeared. No one ever saw them again.

One night after the Japanese had left the block, Boyd and Leisure were astonished to see an 'Indian' with a big smile on his face creep past their cell and up the stairs to see Ras. One of the locals had learned to pick the locks with a skeleton key. On the floor above them, Ras was amazed to see his cell door opening. It was the mysterious 'Indian'. Standing in the doorway grinning all over his face was his faithful Mura, who had brought a plate of food that the other occupants of his cell had saved from their evening meal. Ras was overjoyed. He had not seen Mura since they had become separated after being ambushed months before. Overcome by this altruistic gesture of kindness, Ras choked back his tears.

Every night for the next two months the devoted Mura came to his cell, bringing him titbits of food and information. Each night he would go around and open all the cell doors so they could gather together and chat in one cell. Ras explained why he had changed his identity. He stressed that it was imperative that Mura must never acknowledge his previous identity or past to the Japanese. Remarkably, they never discovered these illicit night-time gatherings. Sometimes others, mainly Karens, would join them. They would sit talking and laughing long into the night. For Ras, it was an immense boost to his spirits. He felt both pride and sadness for this simple man, who had dedicated himself to caring for him in the most extreme circumstances. In return, all Ras had done was to put his life and liberty in peril.

One night in September 1943, Mura slipped into Ras's cell and explained that the Japanese no longer saw him as a threat. They were about to release him. He said he planned to make his way back to the Karen hills to rejoin the resistance movement. Ras was delighted for him, but deeply sad to lose the company of his faithful shadow. He never saw Mura again. For the rest of his life he wondered what had become of him and what he had ever done to deserve such selfless dedication and love.

By November 1943, Ras's wounds had healed. He was moved out of solitary confinement into No. 6 block, but suddenly his assumed identity proved unexpectedly problematic. Concerned that he might be perceived as a stool pigeon, at considerable personal risk, he confided in his new commanding officer, an Indian Army major. The man had no compunction about him living under a false identity, nor the reasons that had brought it about, but he insisted that, as a mere sergeant, Ras could not live among the officers. He would have to move in with the other ranks. It was a monumentally stupid suggestion that would have put Ras's life at risk in an instant. Stifling his anger, Ras explained that, if he did so, the Japanese would suddenly find themselves short of an American officer and with an extra British sergeant. They would begin to ask questions, which were highly likely to lead to his arrest and execution at the hands of the kempeitai: Ras challenged him as to whether he was really going to divulge his true identity to the Japanese and thus sign his death warrant. The major snorted that of course he was not, but he insisted that Ras could not remain with the British officers.

As Ras was posing as an American officer, the answer was for him to go and live with the Americans, if they would have him. Following an earlier recent failed escape attempt by a crazed British soldier, the major ordered Ras that on no account should he attempt to escape. Afterwards, Ras worried perpetually that one day the major might inadvertently betray him. If Matsuda had any inkling of deception, then Ras stood to be exposed as a fraud, with fatal consequences.

For both the British and Americans, it was patently obvious that Ras was neither American nor an officer. However, he was warmly welcomed by the Americans and made friends with them all. Lieutenant Donald Humphrey, a fellow free spirit who, like Ras, loved sending up the Japanese, took him under his wing. Despite Ras's discretion, as the months passed, word spread. Many feared he was a spy and were exceptionally wary of him. Few believed he was an American pilot, and those who had heard about his true identity thought it too outlandish to be true. John Reid, an Australian pilot, felt it was common knowledge among the inmates who Ras really was: 'He used to wander around the place at night and whisper his story'.[5]

Years later, Lieutenant Alec Gibson, who had served as a Chindit, remembered him well: 'We used to call him the "Yank from Battersea,"' he said.[6] Gibson also knew him as Lieutenant Melvyn. They chatted a great deal. Gibson was also from the East Surrey's, but Ras was always exceptionally cagey about his own background. He showed great interest in aircraft and had even told the Japanese that, as a fighter pilot, he had refuelled in mid-air. Once he confided to Gibson that during his time in the New Law Courts the American airmen there gave him information on their planes so he could improve his cover story.

Each morning a sick call was held to screen the men for daily working parties. 'Healthy' prisoners were sent off into the city under armed guard to do hard labour, unloading ships and railway wagons, and digging trenches and air-raid shelters. The 'slightly sick' were placed on garden work inside the prison. Alec Gibson and Ras were often on the working party at the docks unloading petrol, ammunition and supplies – a welcome opportunity to venture beyond the claustrophobic confines of the prison, forage for extra food and occasionally sabotage the cargo. Any opportunity was taken to put one over on the Japanese – at considerable personal risk. Fuses were dropped 'accidentally' into the sea. Rice sacks would be ripped open, leaving a trail of rice. They then complained to the Japanese that the sacks were torn. At other times, groups were taken to some of the former European clubs, where Ras would scrounge whatever he could lay his hands on. Although on their return each man was searched, the working parties were able to smuggle food, and even English-language books, back into the compounds. In one case a magnificent set of Dickens novels was recovered, following which an unholy row broke out between the readers and the smokers, who found that the paper made excellent roll-ups.

In a country where maintaining face is so important, it was hugely damaging to British prestige for British officers to be seen to work as coolies. On one memorable occasion, the inhabitants of Rangoon were treated to the unedifying spectacle of British PoWs, dressed in only the briefest of loincloths, pushing cartloads of manure through the streets: 'We amused ourselves by imagining what the reaction of the Poona Club would have been if they could have seen us.'[7]

Between 1942 and 1945 half of the PoWs died from malnutrition, disease and neglect. Death came in many forms – beri-beri, malaria, dysentery, jungle sores, diphtheria, cholera, physical abuse and torture. Mis-targeted Allied bombs were a constant hazard. With its close proximity to the river and the docks, the prison was frequently used as a homing point by Allied bombers. Sometimes they dropped their loads short, causing panic among the Japanese as sticks of bombs 'walked' towards the prison. It was only a matter of time before there was a direct strike. In September 1943, the Americans hit the jail, damaging No. 3 block and killing several Indians and British soldiers, along with three Americans. But for most, the greatest threat was losing the will to live. When that happened, nothing could be done to save them. Nearly always they passed away peacefully, content to go, usually in their sleep; yet despite this morale remained remarkably high, reinforced by a stubborn determination 'not to let the sadistic bastards grind you down'.

Medical conditions were dire. Dysentery was endemic. One British soldier had 254 bowel movements in three days before he died on the morning of the fourth day. Another common condition was scabies, which caused septic or jungle sores. These ate into the flesh, leaving deep pockets of scab-covered infection and pus, some the size of dinner plates. In one extreme case, the infection went right through a man's leg and left a raw, infected hole. Beri-beri, caused by a deficiency of Vitamin B, was the biggest killer. It took two forms: either a wasting disease, which generated chronic diarrhoea and massive weight loss, or causing the body to swell up to an obscene size, starting with the legs. In the penultimate stage, the victims had double vision – a sure sign that the final coma and death were near. One morning, Colonel Mackenzie was doing his regular rounds when one young soldier joked with him, 'Oh sir. I can see two of you.' Mackenzie forced a smile and said, 'That's a pity, surely one of me is bad enough.' The young man smiled, lay back and died.[8]

Mackenzie, a dour, self-opinionated Scot, was as tough as nails, but even this experienced Army medic was heartbroken by some of the pitiful sights he witnessed day after day. Many men, who could have been saved by even the most basic care and medication, died. He was powerless to help. To the Japanese, the lives of the PoWs were worthless, but their quiet, understated heroism was incredibly moving. Mackenzie recalled:

'I often used to watch a man named Bartram moving by with his working party. He was of exceptional physique, over six feet tall and with a magnificent body. I saw him become a walking skeleton before my eyes within a few weeks. He was dying from an inability to absorb the kind of nourishment he was getting. The day he was admitted to hospital, this splendid fellow turned to me and said in a gentle voice, "I am so sorry, sir, I am letting you down."'[9]

John Boyd witnessed similar stoicism among the fatally sick in the hospital. Many were worried about being a nuisance or a burden to their mates. When each man was asked each day how he was, the reply was always 'OK, sir' or 'Mustn't grumble'. Most would answer, 'Not too bad, sir.' 'I never heard a single man complain,' wrote Boyd. 'They just gradually faded away and died silently. Their courage in the face of hopelessness was remarkable.'[10] With only the most rudimentary instruments and few drugs, the medical staff and amateur orderlies performed miracles. On one occasion Mackenzie carried out an amputation on an American airman whose arm had been shattered by a splinter from an ack-ack shell. Using a butcher's saw and some dental anaesthetic, he removed the forearm. Remarkably, the man survived. Another, Corporal Usher, had his lower leg removed.

The most harrowing experience occurred when an American B-24 crew were brought in swathed in bandages, suffering from appalling burns. The men were kept in solitary confinement for five days before Mackenzie was permitted to see them. 'They could not see and were crawling about on the dusty floor blindly, like badly bitten animals. The burns on their necks, heads and faces had been dressed with Vaseline, on top of which sheets of greaseproof paper and layers of gauze had been placed.'[11] Ras and the other prisoners thought that they were being tortured by the Japanese. They could hear the men screaming and pleading with their unseen attackers to 'stop sticking those sticks in my eyes' and 'get those sticks out of my ears'.[12]

But the pain was not coming from sticks. On removing the bandages Mackenzie was horrified to see that the burned areas and cuts on their scalps, ears, eyes and noses were teeming with maggots. 'There were maggots in the nostrils, maggots in the cheek wounds and maggots between the fingers.'[13] Mackenzie and his assistant picked out the larvae one by one with a pair of old Japanese dissecting forceps, but one man had practically nothing left where his face had been. He died during the night. The second lingered on for forty-eight hours. 'He was a brave man, sane and courageous to the end, despite his desperate plight. How he maintained his reason, I just do not know, for both his eyes had been destroyed, eaten away by maggots, which, when we had first seen him, filled the whole of his orbital cavities,' Mackenzie later wrote.[14]

The Japanese allowed the dead to be buried in the cemetery at Kemmendine. Frequently, Ras was on the burial parties. He never got over the grim task of having to stuff the orifices with bandages prior to taking the bodies out for burial. All too often, it was a daily ritual. Bodies were sewn up in rice sacks by a Jewish tailor. All the occupants of a block would fall in to give their final salute to honour their dead comrade, as the body was slow-marched out of the compound. In the later months of captivity, the Japanese even provided rough coffins and a Union Jack. The officers took it in turns to take the funeral service. Homemade wooden crosses were placed to mark the graves.

Incarcerated behind fifteen-foot-high prison walls, the men had few comforts beyond simple comradeship, and no news of the outside world. At night, some would look up at the moon and take simple reassurance from the fact that, however far away they might be, their loved ones could see the same view as them. Lionel Hudson took solace in the stars. 'To look into the remoteness of dark sky for detachment is natural. When I stop making discoveries like that I want to stop living. This is a lovely world. So much in it, which is sweet or pleasant or stirring or worthwhile. There is so much I can get out of life.'[15]

In his personal memoir, Ras says little about his time in the jail, but his sheer resourcefulness and irrepressible spirit made a big impression on the other inmates. Lionel Hudson – the man in whom Seagrim's erstwhile cellmate Sharpe later confided – was an Australian Air Force Wing Commander, captured when his plane was shot down on a low sweep over the Irrawaddy. In whispered conversations, he made casual contact through the compound wall with 'Pinky', a British soldier in the adjacent block, who worked in the food store. Although everyone knew Ras as Lieutenant Melvyn, he was called 'Pinky' because his skin was so pale, and he went red rather than brown in the sun.

Hudson could only ever glimpse the man from the top of the steps into the upstairs cells, but soon a close bond developed between them. Pinky tossed over the wall a tiny thirty-page notebook just three and a quarter by two and a half inches made from a school exercise book, together with an indelible pencil. 'The extraordinary thing about it was that there was no way Pinky could have known it was my birthday. I was twenty-nine. Nobody knew but me. It gave me a funny feeling.' When he told Ras, the response was typically laconic: 'I must have been psychic,' he grunted.[16]

Hudson used the paper, and whatever more Ras could steal, to start a diary, which he stuffed into an empty chutney bottle and buried in the wall of one of the compound foxholes. It offers a rare insight into Ras's life in the jail, and his guile in selflessly helping others. On one occasion, in his characteristic fashion, Ras was in the store, taking great risks to get eggs and onions through to Hudson and his men to help the sick. Four days later, Hudson watched him in action from the balcony of his block. Two coolies had wheeled in a big barrow. As brazen as you like, Ras walked over, lifted the bamboo-strip lid and fish leapt out. He whipped up four live fish and flashed around the corner to hide them, only to be spotted by a Japanese sergeant nicknamed 'Banjo-Eyes', who ordered him to return what he had taken. Pagani returned two fish, and received a dressing down and slapping. It was a dangerous moment, which could have earned him solitary confinement. 'Pinkie stood there perhaps a shade pinker,'[17] while Hudson and his mates prayed. Eventually Ras, who intended to give the fish to the sick, gave them the thumbs-up and carried on as normal. The next day, Pinky was paraded before the Japanese for his misdemeanour in stealing fish. 'They were very nice to me,' he said later to Hudson, 'and told me there was no need to steal. If I wanted anything all I had to do was ask.'[18] No wonder the Japanese seemed incomprehensible.

As well as helping others, Ras was a reliable channel of news between the compounds – Hudson's best source for 'good gen'. Other than a distant view from the block balcony, Hudson had no idea what Ras looked like. In his diary he wrote: 'I really ache to meet him. We all owe so much to him. He has smuggled to me most of the paper on which this diary is written. I asked him to put down something about himself on paper the other day.'[19] In response, over the wall came 'an amazing letter' written on torn-out pages from a book on Catholicism, in which Ras confided his real identity and a brief outline of his remarkable story.[20]

Chapter 16

Into Thy Hands
I Commend My Spirit

'Let me not then die ingloriously and
without a struggle but let me first do some great thing
that shall be told among men hereafter.'

HOMER

While Ras Pagani was ducking and diving to outwit the Japanese inside the city jail, Hugh Seagrim had been incarcerated in the New Law Courts for almost four months. On 8 July 1944, he and his devoted Karens were hauled up before the Japanese for indictment. Seagrim, the parachutists, the ex-Burma Rifles men and some of the most important Karen leaders were transferred, not to Rangoon Central jail, where Ras and most Allied prisoners of war were being held, but to Insein prison, six miles north of Rangoon.

The civilian offenders were taken to a room, lined up, berated and given a lengthy lecture by Detective Chief Isnoayshay, before – miraculously – being released. A post-war report on the Shwegin Karens described the scene: 'They presented a queer spectacle … They were ugly and untidy. With three months' growth of moustache, hair, beard and whiskers, with long nails never clipped in the cells, and with shabby and dirty shirts and longyis, the Karens stood before the military officers to receive the admonition … The whole crowd looked quaint, morbid, grotesque.'[1]

The released civilians were fortunate indeed. They were reminded that they had been found guilty of offences punishable by death or penal servitude, but that the authorities had condescended to be magnanimous and grant them an amnesty, providing they pledged never again to support enemy activities in their villages, and assisted the Japanese and Burmese to prosecute the war to a successful conclusion. Crippled in mind and body, the Karen civilians had no alternative but to agree. Three days later, they were permitted to return to their homes. But for many it was too late. The months of abuse had taken their toll. Two died of beri-beri on their way home. Many took months to recover from their horrifying ordeal. All were tormented by sores, itches, bites and skin diseases, which took over a year to cure. Some hovered between life and death for weeks before turning the corner. All too many were broken in spirit and suffered permanent psychological damage.

Unlike the city jail, which was demolished after the war, Insein prison remains to this day a fearsome place of detention for political prisoners and criminals. Like the city jail, a characteristic British design with radiating cellblocks set behind high walls, it was in 1944 the holding place for people who had been convicted in the Burmese courts under the quisling government of Dr Ba Maw. Seagrim and his military followers – who were not released following the indictment – were kept in the old reformatory building next to the jail, which was used by the kempeitai for those awaiting sentence. Set within its own compound and enclosed by a high wall, it had been used since the outbreak of war for political prisoners. It was run entirely by the Japanese under the command of 'an elderly moustachioed Japanese captain', who lived over the gateway. To the right of the gateway was a two-storey building with cells fronted by stout wooden bars, similar to those in the New Law Courts.

Japanese prisoners convicted of military offences were kept on the ground floor. On the upper storey was a single large room with an iron grille dividing the space into two halves. This was where the Indians, Burmese, Karens and other prisoners were confined together. Beyond this was a long, low block of cells, each about twelve feet square, with a bare cement floor and plaster walls, earmarked for special prisoners who were held in solitary confinement. This was where Seagrim was imprisoned. Adjoining the block were a carpentry shop, a large wooden shed and, further on, the old reformatory schoolroom. Nearby lay the hospital, a small Buddhist shrine, a mortuary and, at the centre of the complex, an octagonal building used as a cookhouse.

Occasionally, from their elevated position in the large communal room on the upper storey, the Karens glimpsed Seagrim in the mornings, emptying his pot. They also picked up news from around the prison. Such was the awe in which Seagrim was held throughout the compound that even the Japanese guards were affected by it. One who spoke with Po Hla referred to Seagrim as 'Big Master – hearto – very good'. Others referred to him as 'Big Master' or 'Seagrim Master'. When one Karen was asked if he would like to see Seagrim, the Japanese NCO pointed out a tall, thin bearded figure and, with some pride in his voice, said, 'There he is. There is Seagrim.'[2] For a Japanese to refer to a British prisoner in this way was an extraordinary inversion of the usual relationship. It was they who expected to be bowed to with great formality and called 'Master'.

Unbeknown to Seagrim, over the preceding months and in quiet desperation, his mother, Amabel, had sought news of him. She had heard nothing for almost three years. He had disappeared completely behind an impenetrable bamboo curtain. No one professed to know where he was, or even whether he was still alive. In fact, for many months Force 136 HQ had known that he was alive. They had received a stream of messages from him once wireless communication had been established following the arrival of Jimmy Nimmo and Eric McCrindle in Burma in October 1943 – but they could not divulge this, or send Amabel his salary, without disclosing more. She was beside herself with anxiety, but it was another whole year before any news emerged that could be passed back to the family.

On 26 August 1944, top-secret information was passed to Ritchie Gardiner, the head of the Burma section of Force 136 in Calcutta: news had come in from four Inter Service Liaison Department (SIS) agents just returned from Burma. They had obtained information from Saw Herbertson, a Moulmein Karen forced to work for the Japanese near Toungoo, that four British wireless sets had been captured at the end of March or beginning of April in the Papun area. Herbertson had reported that two British officers from Macgregor's (Jimmy Nimmo and Eric McCrindle) had been ambushed and killed in the subsequent fighting. The agents also reported that they had heard from a separate source that Seagrim had fled north but, on the threat of reprisals against the Karens of Papun, had given himself up and was being held in the New Law Courts in Rangoon.

Gardiner immediately sought urgent instructions on whether to post Nimmo and McCrindle as 'missing' or 'missing believed killed'. Before they had left for Burma, both men had given orders for certain telegrams to be sent once a month to their relatives. This instruction had been acted on for some time, but increasingly the messages had a hollow ring. They sounded rather peculiar to the two families. By an unfortunate oversight, the previous month the man in charge had been on leave and neglected to send them, which meant that it had been over two months since their relatives had last heard a word. Gardiner also asked whether there was any more information on Seagrim, who had already been posted as 'missing', and whether his mother should be told that he was believed to be a prisoner of war. On 16 September 1944 both Nimmo and McCrindle were posted as 'missing believed killed'. Given the need for the security of future operations in Karenni, a cover story was released to their relatives, implying that they had died in June in the Chin Hills rather than revealing their true activities.

Just three days earlier, Amabel wrote to her son Jack's wife, Camilla, at Abbott Hall, Abbottabad, revealing in her own restrained way her desperate concern for Hugh:

'... and now I have some dreadfully sad news, perhaps you will have heard before this comes, as I had a wire yesterday to say that Bumps was "reported missing in action". It was a dreadful blow, you never get used to them, but after reading J's letter I expect it was bound to happen. You can't go on taking great risks and not get done in, in the end. If he was killed it would be easier to bear, but he may be a prisoner with those devils, or lost, [and] not knowing anything about him, no word from him for so long, makes it harder to bear I think, dear B. Anyway he lived up to his high ideals and gave no thought to himself and has left a fine memory which he says is what matters for the future generation. I have written to J. I am afraid he will be very upset. They were such friends. What a cruel war it is ... Bye, dear C. I am afraid this is a doleful letter. It's very difficult to be brave when all the ones you live for are in such danger ... I wish B. was known.

Love,

Mrs S.'[3]

Jack Seagrim made official enquiries about his younger brother from a certain Lieutenant Colonel Ambler. He explained that another brother had been killed in action, and that his mother was desperately worried about Hugh, from whom she had heard nothing in almost three years. Jack had already told her that most probably Hugh had been killed, believing it kinder than reporting his possible capture by the dreaded Japanese. Jack pressed hard for all possible details, including the reasons for Hugh's award of a DSO earlier in January 1944 – a clear indication that he was still alive at that time. Ambler told him the barest details of Hugh's work with the Karens and of his voluntary surrender. He intimated that they had no reason to disbelieve it as the Japanese had announced his capture on their radio back in March. Jack was instructed that on no account should he reveal to anyone what he had been told. Jack assured him that he would keep the story strictly to himself and merely tell his mother that he had 'good reason' to believe that his brother was a PoW in Japanese hands. At the end of his report, Ambler freely admitted his indiscretion: 'I have, as you will see, committed a breach of security with my eyes open, but hope you may agree that in the circumstances it is pardonable.'[4]

Meanwhile, on 1 September 1944 at Insein jail, Seagrim and the remaining Karens were informed that the next day five Japanese officers would arrive to sentence them. Around seven o'clock in the morning of 2 September, two staff cars drove into the compound. Their occupants went to the superintendent's office, after which a Japanese guard went to the Karens and read out the names of seventeen, who were summoned for court-martial and sentencing. A table had been installed in the old schoolroom, behind which were seated five officers and two interpreters, the President of the Court Major Shunji Koga with two judges, Lieutenant Tanenori Fukuchi and Lieutenant Akira Hanawa, plus an Observer Inspector, Captain Shinpei Hoshino. The Japanese military command structure was inherently rigid. At every stage of the process, reference was made up the line to ensure that the correct procedure was followed. Prior to the court-martial, the case of Seagrim and the Karens was referred right up to Field Marshal Count Terauchi, the supreme commander of all Japanese forces in the south, and also to the War Office in Tokyo.

The Karens were organised into two lines, following which Seagrim was brought in and told to stand at the end of the line on the right. He towered above the diminutive Karens and his Japanese accusers. Barefoot, bearded, bedraggled and still wearing Karen dress, he stood gaunt and erect, his arms and legs riddled with scabies, but calm and composed, smiling serenely at his devoted Karen friends. Through an interpreter, Major Koga asked Seagrim. 'Do you agree that we should pass sentence on you?' to which Seagrim replied: 'I am a prisoner in your hands. I can have no objection.'

Major Koga then passed sentence, which was translated into English and Karen. Major Seagrim, Lieutenant Ba Gyaw, Saw He Be, Saw Tun Lin,

Saw Sunny, Saw Pe, Saw Peter and Saw Ah Din were all condemned to death. The remainder — Saw Po Hla, Saw Ta Roe, Saw Digay, Thra May Sha, Thra Kyaw Lay, Saw Rupert, Saw Henry, Saw Po Myin, Saw Tha Say and Saw Yay — were sentenced to eight years' imprisonment. The verdicts were curious. Virtually all of Seagrim's closest followers — such as Ta Roe and Po Hla, who had deceived the Japanese and might have expected the death sentence — received eight years' imprisonment, while, other than Ba Gyaw and Ah Din, those condemned to death were more peripheral figures. Quite how the Japanese allocated levels of guilt remains a mystery.

There are various surviving statements of what then precisely transpired. Seagrim acted with utter selflessness. He took a step forward and said:

'First, you said that I would be treated honourably as a prisoner of war. Now, you sentence me to death. I do not mind what you do to me. But I do ask you, if you are going to punish anyone, punish only me. Do not punish these Karens. It is only because of me that all these Karens have got into trouble. This war is between the Japanese and the British, not between the Japanese and the Karens. I beg you to release all these Karens here.'[5]

In the Japanese accounts, although the detail differs, the spirit remains the same. His words and actions commanded their immense respect. Colonel Sunyoshi, the commander of the Rangoon kempeitai, later told some Karens how after his arrest Hugh had been prepared to bear any punishment if only the Karens were released. In a remarkable tribute to his enemy, he said: 'I have never come across a finer gentleman.'[6] According to another, Seagrim said: 'The war between Japan and Britain is truly unfortunate. As an honourable British officer, I was just fulfilling my duty obeying supreme orders from my country. I have no objection to being taken prisoner and executed. However, these Karens here who were captured with me, they only worked obeying my orders. Please find them not guilty.'[7] On receiving the death sentence, not only did Seagrim say that he deserved to be condemned to death for his activities as a secret agent — but he wished to have the punishment executed immediately.

After Seagrim had spoken, Major Koga declared the proceedings at an end. All the prisoners were taken to the cookhouse and offered a last meal of rice and hot tea, but kept in silence. No one wished to eat. Shortly afterwards, those Karens sentenced to eight years' penal servitude were put in chains. Seagrim and his seven Karen companions had their hands tied behind their backs and were taken to a waiting truck for their last journey. Po Hla later testified:

'There was no shadow of fear nor regret on his face as I watched him led on to the truck with both hands bound at his back ... a radiant smile of triumph on his face which seemed to say, "This is Thy way, Lord – I have lived to save my country and king and humanity – may Thy name be praised."'[8]

As the Japanese threw a few picks and shovels into the truck, climbed up and drove off through the gate, Seagrim called out to his beloved Karens. 'Goodbye to you all!' Moved to tears, Po Hla, shouted back, 'Goodbye' ... and was slapped around the face for his impudence. Ta Roe's last glimpse of his friend was of Seagrim sitting composed, apparently unconcerned and 'smiley-faced'.

Kemmendine is an outlying district of Rangoon about four miles south of Insein prison, but only just over one mile north of the main PoW camp at the city jail. As Seagrim embarked on his final journey to his own personal calvary, it seems, intriguingly, that he may have said a fleeting farewell to his old comrade in arms Ras Pagani. For, of all Pagani's extraordinary experiences, one particular episode remains a tantalising conundrum. Ras had long wondered what had befallen Seagrim in the months since they had waved their farewells and he had left him alone once more in the remote forests of the Karen hills. Although others now in the jail with Ras, like Arthur Sharpe and the American John Boyd, had seen and even talked with Seagrim during their time in the New Law Courts, Ras seems to have been unaware of this and makes no reference to it in his memoir.

Immediately inside the prison gatehouse of the city jail were two low lines of buildings. To the left were the Japanese guards, and to the right a block of cells thought to contain Burmese prisoners and petty local criminals. Adjacent to these cells was a compound used for storage. Occasionally, Ras would be on a working party carrying sacks of rice from that compound to the cookhouse. One day, he was told that one of the cells was occupied by a British officer, but he gave it little thought. And then, one morning in early September, he was in the same working party when he noticed a truck standing outside the block. When he returned with another load, the truck was just moving out of the gate, loaded with natives and a bearded man, whom Ras took for an Indian.

The man waved to him and he waved back. But Ras was 'puzzled by the incident':

'I knew no one in that part of the jail, let alone an Indian. It played on my mind for some days, then slowly it dawned on me that it had been Seagrim who had waved at me … I did not know until much later that the truck was carrying Seagrim and several Karens, including my old friend Ah Din, to their execution at the kempeitai cemetery.'[9]

One needs to pass through Kemmendine en route from Insein, but it is just conceivable that Seagrim and the prisoners were taken there via the city jail, perhaps to collect other prisoners awaiting execution, or corpses awaiting burial, which is when Ras may have seen them. The timing – early September – is uncannily accurate and the description of the truck loaded with locals and Japanese guards is consistent with Ta Roe's last sighting of them as they left Insein.

Ras, of course, could have been mistaken. It was only later that he surmised that it was Seagrim. The man could have been an Indian acquaintance who recognised him. But whether or not it was Seagrim, the memory of that poignant, fleeting moment – two brave men with their arms raised to each other in final salutation – haunted Ras for the rest of his life.

***

A short dirt track off the Prome (Pyay) Road leads to a large open space. After the war, it was laid out by the Commonwealth War Graves Commission as Rangoon War Cemetery. Today it is a serene and beautiful place, dominated by the simple Portland stone and bronze cross of sacrifice common to so many memorials across the world. Before the war, it was a multi-faith cemetery with different sections devoted to Christians, Buddhists, Hindus and Muslims. In 1944, however, it was a forgotten and melancholy place, rank with rampant vegetation and overgrown bushes, the once proudly tended gardens allowed to run riot. Along the dirt road outside were small shelters where crude coffins were knocked together and then, all too often, salvaged at night to be recycled and reused. This was the Japanese execution ground, in a corner of which was a row of brick ovens for cremating the Japanese dead.

Executions were carried out in a far corner of the cemetery, which was screened by tall grass and bushes. They took place in great secrecy.

Local residents were instructed to stay indoors. Traffic was halted on the main road, and sentries posted around the perimeter to keep people away. It was here that Seagrim and the other prisoners were taken on the morning of 2 September. Contrary to some later reports, they were not beheaded, but faced a firing squad. First, they were lined up and told to dig their own graves, at which the Karens, who had already endured so much, began to quail. But, quietly unfazed, Seagrim picked up a spade and said with a smile, 'Come on boys! Let's do it!'[10] Before their execution, they asked to be allowed to sing the hymn they had been accustomed to sing whenever any of their comrades were going to their deaths: 'The Solid Rock'.

'My hope is built on nothing less
Than Jesus' blood and righteousness;
I dare not trust the sweetest frame,
But wholly lean on Jesus' name.'

As their voices rang out plaintively across the overgrown burial ground, each was blindfolded. Quite what passed through their minds in those last minutes one can only conjecture. Perhaps, for Hugh Seagrim, his final thoughts were for his beloved Karens, some of whom stood alongside him as they faced their final journey together into the unknown. Just maybe, too, he thought of his family and happy upbringing far away and long ago in the peaceful surroundings of Whissonsett-with-Horningtoft.

According to Japanese sources, in those last moments of life his final thoughts turned to higher things. A year later, on 9 November 1945, Major General Shiokawa wrote a short report on Seagrim's trial and execution. He recorded his last moments at Kemmendine and wrote in fractured English: '[Seagrim] prayed his last prayer at the execution ground and died with composure, which was really solemn attitude.'[11] Another source wrote:

'Just like Japanese soldiers were educated with the Field Service Code, he, without committing suicide, faced his trial and was executed in a dignified manner. This fact must be rated highly. The major who sacrificed his young life for his country in the name of espionage, might have been declared a hero in his own country. You could say that his death was another tragic casualty of war. Also his constant appeals to free his subordinates, the Karens, were utterly praiseworthy.'

Even he who fought for his country
Suffers a penalty
And dies pitifully on the scaffold.'[12]
And so, sometime on the morning of 2 September 1944, died a gallant English gentleman and a very great man.

So he passed over, and all the Trumpets sounded for him on the other side.[13]

Above: 'Prisoner of Conscience' by Horace Knowles

AFTERMATH

Seagrim's Legacy

Chapter 17

Reaping the Whirlwind

'This I beheld, or dreamed in a dream:
There spread a cloud of dust along a plain;
And underneath the cloud, or in it, raged
A furious battle, and men yelled, and swords
Shocked upon swords and shields.'
EDWARD ROWLAND SILL

While Hugh Seagrim was imprisoned between March and July 1944, the tide of the war in Burma and South-East Asia turned decisively in the Allies' favour. By trial and error the British had got the measure of the Japanese. On the very borders of India, the two leviathans had been locked in a life-or-death struggle in the two epic battles of the Far East War – Imphal and Kohima. Kohima was the British Thermopylae. Outnumbered ten to one, a scratch force of just 1,500 battle-weary British and Indian troops withstood waves of frenzied assaults by an entire Japanese division. Months of trench warfare and hand-to-hand fighting led to conditions that resembled a First World War battlefield. Kohima was a charnel house, with dismembered body parts strewn across the shattered hillsides.

For the Japanese, the defeats at Imphal and Kohima were catastrophic – the greatest ever suffered in the entire history of the Imperial Japanese Army. They shattered Japanese morale and left the way open for a lightning advance by the battle-hardened British Indian Army into the central plains of Burma. The Allies entered into a race for Rangoon and its vital port before the monsoon broke. It was now that Seagrim's legacy came into its own with fatal consequences for the Japanese.

The British Indian 14th Army swept across Burma from April 1945 in one of the most successful British campaigns of the Second World War: a great multi-national Imperial Army united in a single noble purpose. Men from the shires of England fought alongside Gurkhas from Nepal. Soldiers from the valleys of South Wales stood shoulder to shoulder with Rajputs, Dogras and Jats from India. Scots stood and died beside fierce Baluchs, proud Punjabis and Assamese. Men from distant Nigeria, Gambia, Sierra Leone and the Gold Coast formed an entire division fighting their way across Burma. There were Australians, Canadians, New Zealanders and Burmese, plus contingents from the hill tribes of Burma, from head-hunting Nagas and Kachins to Seagrim's beloved Karens. This was the last romantic gasp of Empire as peoples from across the globe came together, locked in common cause to defeat a monstrous tyranny.

It was a magnificent sight, which moved many at the time. John Masters wrote:

> 'Twenty races, a dozen religions, a score of languages passed in those trucks and tanks ... The dust thickened under the trees, lining the road until the column was motoring into a thunderous yellow tunnel, first the tanks, infantry all over them. Then trucks filled with men, then more tanks, going fast, nose to tail, guns, more trucks, more guns ... This was the old Indian Army going down to the attack, for the last time in history, exactly 250 years after the Honourable East India Company had enlisted its first ten sepoys on the Coromandel Coast ...'[1]

In Rangoon, Field Marshal Terauchi had ordered his troops to fall back on the city and defend it to the death. As the British swept all before them, the iron-souled Japanese were thrown into panic. Their commander General Kimura cut and ran to safety in Moulmein, flying out in a small three-seater scout plane. It was the first time in the history of the Japanese Imperial Army that a high-ranking officer had so blatantly disobeyed an order from his commander. The official Japanese war history draws a discreet veil over the incident.

Such was the panic and confusion that the man charged with defending the city, Major General Matsui Hideji, was never even told that his commanding officer and staff had gone. It was an ignominious end to Japanese dreams of Empire. Ashamed, Tamura Masataro, who had been Third Secretary at the Japanese embassy in Rangoon, later wrote in disgust: 'People always talk of the Battle of Imphal, when we were defeated on the verge of invading India, as being the great tragedy of the Burma campaign. This is not so. The damage to the Japanese army caused by the panic retreat from Rangoon was three times more than we suffered at Imphal.'[2] As the victorious British Imperial Army thundered southwards, strafing and harassing the retreating Japanese, Seagrim's Karen guerrillas played a decisive role in hampering the Japanese withdrawal.

On the fringes of the Karen hills, Toungoo was critical in the race for the capital. Mountbatten insisted that it absolutely had to be taken by 25 April to coordinate with Operation Dracula, a seaborne invasion of Rangoon from the Delta. As two Japanese divisions retreated south from Mandalay, they headed for Toungoo. There they could form an impenetrable defensive line, and check the entire Allied advance until the monsoon broke. This would deny the Allies the use of Rangoon and force the British to rely on a tenuous 500-mile supply line across mountainous muddy tracks from India. The stakes could not have been higher. For the Japanese, the road to Toungoo lay along a 200-mile narrow salient of the Sittang valley, snaking in great serpentine loops down jungle-clad slopes and across narrow ridges and deep valleys right through the heart of Karen country. There were three enemy divisions in the Shan states. If just a fraction of this force reached Toungoo before Slim's 14th Army, then the whole advance on Rangoon would be imperilled.

Mountbatten was so exercised that he instructed Slim that he would take personal responsibility for getting up to 3,000 men killed in an attempt to speed up the advance. Slim was doubtful it could be done, but as he contemplated the formidable task ahead of him, he realised that the foundations laid by Hugh Seagrim over the previous three years might tip the balance. The Karen levies might just prove decisive. Slim concluded that he

'still had a shot in the locker for them … Over a long period in preparation for this day we had organised a secret force, the Karen guerrillas, based on ex-soldiers of the Burma Army, for whom British officers and arms had been parachuted into the hills. It was not difficult to get the Karens to rise against the hated Japanese; the problem was to restrain them from rising too soon. But now the time had come, and I gave the word, "Up the Karens!"'[3]

The British Indian Army had twelve days to win the race for Toungoo, and with the Japanese reinforcements already fifty miles closer, it was going to be a close-run thing.

★★★

By 1945, Burma was no longer starved of equipment and men, the lack of which had so bedevilled earlier operations. With the war in Europe entering its apocalyptic end, vast resources were switched to the Far East. Burma was the springboard for the re-conquest of Malaya and Borneo, and it began to benefit from a huge influx of personnel and equipment. Some officers came straight out of fighting with resistance forces in Europe to be dropped behind enemy lines in Burma. Unlike in the early days, when Seagrim had to cope with obsolete Italian rifles and Karen crossbows, Special Operations was now flush with the latest arms, explosives, aircraft and equipment.

After the rolling up of Seagrim's guerrilla operations in the hills and his execution in September 1944, those Karens who had been released had returned to their homes despondent and demoralised. When news finally reached India of the loss of Nimmo and McCrindle, and then of Seagrim's arrest and execution, it was clear that any future operations in Karenni would need to be co-ordinated much more closely with 14th Army operations. Thus was born Operation Character. Originally conceived as an intelligence operation, its aims were to establish and organise radio communications with India, partisan bands for sabotage operations against road and rail targets, and political warfare aimed at stimulating a Karen rising. Those in charge had been warned in no uncertain terms not to exceed their remit or start offensive operations.

Fortunately for Slim, the three buccaneering characters who led the separate sections on the ground soon transmuted the whole set-up into a fully fledged guerrilla force, built on the foundations so painstakingly laid by Seagrim. Many were ex-Chindits, or part of Orde Wingate's circle. Wingate, who was half mad and had a disconcerting habit of wandering about stark naked with an alarm clock hanging round his neck, had liked to surround himself with adventurers, mavericks and eccentrics.

The first into the hills was Major Guy Turrall, a short, spare, hard-looking man in his fifties, a former geophysicist, who sported an over-large bush hat pushed down over his ears. Turrall had won an MC in the First World War and had worked with Wingate in Abyssinia, where he had been wounded by an Italian hand grenade, which left a splinter in his skull and may have accounted for his fearless behaviour. With the Chindits he acquired a reputation for extraordinary bravery, disappearing for days into the jungle with a small unit of men to wreak mayhem and leave false trails intended to make the enemy believe that an entire Chindit column was in the area. Turrall, then aged fifty-four, landed at Pyagawpu on 20 February 1945 in command of a force codenamed Hyena. Unsurprisingly, after all they had suffered, he found the Karens less than enthusiastic at the prospect of another bout of fighting with the Japanese. However, their attitude changed when on 23 and 24 February two Dakotas full of British and Karen parachutists arrived under Lieutenant Colonel Edgar Peacock, the second of the triumvirate.

Peacock, a sturdy, no-nonsense, forty-four-year-old Rhodesian farmer with a military moustache, was an old Burma hand. He had spent sixteen years in the Burma Forestry Service, and was an acknowledged authority on Burmese game. Under his hair was a long pallid scar from a blow by a Burmese dah, which had almost killed him during a Burmese uprising years earlier. Highly regarded, he was loaned to the Indian Army and Force 136 in March 1943, where he displayed a real aptitude for guerrilla activities, leading deep penetration forays in the Chindwin and Manipur campaigns. Peacock's force, codenamed 'Otter', had been intended to drop at the same time as Turrall, but when flying over the drop zone they became suspicious of activity on the ground and fortunately aborted the drop. They escaped disaster by the skin of their teeth. The designated zone was an enemy camp bristling with Japanese troops. Otter operated north of the Mawchi road in Noel Boyt's old area. With Peacock was Jimmy Nimmo's brother, Bill. Within a week of their arrival, Peacock had mobilised over 600 levies, and Turrall a similar number.

The third, and by far the most eccentric, of the three commanders was Lieutenant Colonel Cromarty 'Pop' Tulloch, the perfect music-hall caricature of a blimpish British army officer, complete with waxed moustache and a monocle attached to the top button of his bush jacket by a black silk cord, a useful prop and delaying tactic which he deployed in either eye, depending on how awkward a question was. Well into his fifties, he was a dapper little man and a thorough-going rogue, who cultivated such fanciful stories about himself that no one could ever quite decide what was fact and what was fiction. Rescued from regimental disgrace in England over an unpaid cheque by Ritchie Gardiner with the promise of operations in far-off Burma, Tulloch was promoted to lieutenant colonel and given command of 'Walrus' force. Among his many alleged exploits were flying with the famous Canadian fighter ace Billy Bishop in the First World War; driving the first tank into battle on the Somme in 1916; spending eight years in Africa as a big game hunter … and a year under cover in wartime Germany, disguised as an Arab carpet-seller. When he tried to persuade his chief parachute instructor, Bob Thornton, that he was experienced, even to the point of wearing wings on his uniform, he was rumbled by the canny teacher. 'Never done a jump in his life,' Thornton said later; 'Biggest bull-shitter I've ever met.'[4] Yet this did not deter Tulloch one iota. When flying into the Karen hills with Walrus, the stories continued unabated. He told his pilot Terence O'Brien that he had once broken his back on a jump in Arizona and had to ride on a donkey twenty miles to hospital, where they put a metal joint in his spine. When O'Brien wryly asked if it had a hinge to allow him to bend, he promptly ignored the question, talked about prospecting in Alaska, 'gave his monocle a twirl and went back to the fuselage for a nap'.[5] This was definitely 'Carry On Up the Jungle'.

The first wave of Walrus flew in from Jessore on 24 March. By early April 1945 all three parties – Hyena, Otter and Walrus –were in position, well equipped with arms, explosives and radio transmitters, recruiting static and mobile levies ready for action when the call came. The groups were fairly fluid. Walrus operated in the north between Bawlake and Loikaw, Otter straddled both sides of the Mawchi road and absorbed a separate force, Ferret. Hyena homed in on Seagrim's old haunts around Pyagawpu. Further south a fourth team, Mongoose, formed by splitting Hyena, was commanded by Lieutenant Colonel Ronald Critchley, who also had served with Wingate in Abyssinia and later with the Chindits. By mid-April 1945 there were around 6,700 armed levies and troops in the Karen hills.

Among the Karens who were dropped in to join Tulloch was Kan Choke, the old Karen warrior, who had trekked out of Burma in 1942 with Thompson, Jimmy Nimmo and Ba Gyaw. He had formed close friendships with all of them and, as the centre-forward of the 1st Burma Rifles football team, knew Seagrim well as a fellow team mate. Awarded the Burma Gallantry Medal for his courage in 1942, this inspirational man had served for over twenty-eight years in the Burma Rifles, holding the honorary rank of lieutenant. Although he had not been dropped to Seagrim in 1943, on no fewer than nine separate occasions Kan Choke had flown out on abortive missions with Jimmy Nimmo to try to drop a wireless transmitter to their friend Ba Gyaw. And so, despite being well over fifty years old and with only one eye, when Tulloch was due to fly in, he begged to be allowed to go along to avenge Jimmy Nimmo's death. A staff officer recalled: 'He was so importunate, however, that I finally acquiesced. To say his face lit up is to put it mildly. He went in to Tulloch and did extremely well. He was a most lovable character, with the very highest sense of duty.'[6]

Following exactly the same surprise tactics that Seagrim had preached over three years earlier, Otter sprang a series of ambushes and blown bridges under Peacock, harassing the enemy at every opportunity. Crucially, it delayed the Japanese retreat by seven days, by which time the 14th Army had arrived at Toungoo, blocking the enemy's exit from the hills. Slim later wrote:

> 'The Japanese, driving hard through the night down jungle roads for Toungoo, ran into ambush after ambush; bridges were blown ahead of them, their foraging parties massacred, their sentries stalked, their staff cars shot up. The galled Japanese fought their way slowly forward, losing men and vehicles, until about Mawchi, fifty miles east of Toungoo, they were held up for several days by road blocks, demolitions and ambuscades.'[7]

Otter's relentless hit-and-run tactics using Seagrim's Karen levies were instrumental in the British winning the race for Toungoo. The road to Rangoon now lay open. Slim was delighted. On 3 May, he sent a signal of appreciation to all stations in the field: 'Am more than pleased with the splendid work all parties in the field have already done in killing Japs and passing [on] Intelligence. I call on you for one last all-out effort to hit the Jap hard while you still have [the] chance in this final Burma phase. Good luck to you all.'[8]

After succeeding in their primary objective of facilitating the capture of Toungoo, Otter and Walrus found themselves hard put to beat off the enemy. The Japanese had recovered from their initial surprise and hit back hard with the large forces available to them around Mawchi. Hyena and Mongoose were relatively quiet. One of the earliest actions involved Seagrim's former wireless operator Thet Wa, who had been rounded up at the time of the major's arrest and held at the New Law Courts along with many of the other Karens. As the Burmese became ever more unreliable, the Japanese sought to cultivate the Karens as potential allies. With little choice, Thet Wa became an interpreter for them. Early in 1945, he was sent as an interpreter to a kempeitai unit and then, under duress, dispatched with them to the hills. When news came of British parachutists landing in the hills as part of Operation Character, Thet Wa and his kempeitai unit were sent to investigate. At the first Karen village they reached, Thet

Wa realised that the headman spoke English and the Japanese did not, so he interspersed his questions with English messages. The Japanese knew the name of the village where the landings had taken place. Thet Wa told the headman to arrange an ambush and planned to escape beforehand. Unfortunately, he was unable to do so, the suspicious Japanese having placed him in the centre of the unit. About five miles from the target village the villagers opened fire and cut down the unit – with the miraculous exception of Thet Wa, who dived for cover and shouted his name from behind a tree. Thet Wa later went on to join another operation, codenamed Nation, in the Pegu Yomas.

On 15 April, Turrall led a direct assault on the kempeitai headquarters at Kyaukkyi, killing over forty Japanese and releasing some Karen prisoners and himself being slightly wounded, but open action of this sort was rare. The guerrillas favoured stealth and ambush to open confrontation. Three weeks earlier on 26 March, Aung San and the BNA had finally risen up against the Japanese, killing some officers and sowing the seeds of confusion among the enemy. Slim had been aware of their disaffection since Po Hla's covert foray into Rangoon in early 1943, and which Seagrim had passed on to Army headquarters, but Slim had bided his time before acting.

On 21 April, agents of Force 136 offered Aung San safe conduct to 14th Army headquarters with Slim's specific assurance that, irrespective of the outcome of their discussions, he would be returned unharmed. After some hesitation, on 15 May Aung San responded. He was flown to Meiktila. Dressed in the uniform of a Japanese major general, his sudden appearance startled some British staff officers, but he behaved with the utmost courtesy. Slim recalled 'a short, well-built, active man in early middle age, neat and soldierly in appearance, with regular Burmese features in a face that could be an impassive mask or light up with intelligence and humour'.[9] It was a fascinating meeting.

Initially, Aung San took a rather high hand, arguing that he was a representative of the Provisional Government of Burma, only to be deflated by Slim, who pointed out that 'there was only one Government of Burma and that was His Majesty's, now acting through the Supreme Commander, South-East Asia'. Slim maintained that he was doing quite nicely, thank you, destroying the Japanese forces without their help – and didn't need him. Indeed, there were many on the British side keen to press charges against Aung San for murder. Slim told him so, and enquired if he wasn't taking a serious risk in coming and adopting such a high-handed attitude, to which Aung San coolly replied, 'No, because you are a British officer.' Slim laughed and the meeting continued in good humour.[10] Slim liked him. 'He was not the ambitious unscrupulous guerrilla leader I had expected,' he recalled in his memoirs.[11] Slim insisted that the BNA would be subordinate to local British commanders. Aung San agreed.

By the end of May 1945, rather disconcertingly, groups of the BNA dressed in Japanese uniforms suddenly marched into the British front lines and joined the Allies. This caused some confusion for the British. Behind the Japanese lines, Force 136 readily recruited them, whereas in liberated areas all too often Civil Affairs officers sought to have them arrested as collaborators.

As the British swept towards Rangoon, the Japanese still had about 20,000 troops on the west bank of the Sittang and over 50,000 in the Karen hills, mostly strung out in a long line from Toungoo to Mawchi. To escape the British onslaught, they were impelled to move east and south. The seeds of resistance and guerrilla activity cultivated for so long by Hugh Seagrim now reaped a deadly harvest as his levies went into action once again. All four Operation Character sections proceeded to wreak havoc on the retreating Japanese, picking them off at every opportunity in hit-and-run raids and ambushes. One particularly effective tactic was the controlled explosive trap – a long line of cordtex over 200 yards, laced with charges and grenades at ten-yard intervals. With the tug of a string, a colossal booby-trap could be detonated as an enemy convoy or troops were passing. The co-ordinated impact of more than twenty grenades exploding simultaneously was shattering. The entire track and anything on it was shredded. Hidden in the jungle at each side of the track were punjis, lines of sharpened bamboo stakes in hidden pits, designed to impale any who leapt off the track to escape.

Trapped on the west bank of the Sittang, the Japanese made widespread, but uncoordinated, attempts to cross the river that was becoming ever more engorged each day by the monsoon rains. Both Hyena and Mongoose went into action, the latter under pressure from enemy troops to the south. With the monsoon hampering air support, the most serious problem was tiredness and sickness among the eighty British officers and thirty NCOs, exacerbated by intense strain and the debilitating climate. At the end of July, the stranded Japanese 28th Army made a concerted effort to cross the Sittang and break through to Moulmein. Before they even reached the hills, they suffered heavy casualties from both regular and guerrilla forces. Those that made it to the river split into smaller groups. Using bamboo rafts, and anything that would float, these defeated remnants of the much-vaunted Imperial Army were cut to ribbons by British and Karen partisans. No quarter was asked or given as the Karens sought revenge for years of abuse, torture and suffering.

At the Shwegyin river, the area commander lined up thirty Bren-gun crews supported by mortars along twenty miles of riverbank. Despite the appalling weather, waves of RAF Mosquitoes, Spitfires and Thunderbolts strafed the retreating Japanese relentlessly. The chattering of massed machine guns, interlaced with the crackle of rifle fire, turned the jungle-clad riverbanks into a symphony of death. In one week of August alone, the levies inflicted at least 900 casualties. Seagrim's training methods paid off with deadly effect. The impact of such intense and sustained guerrilla activity devastated Japanese morale. Colonel Tsukada, the commander of the Japanese 215th Infantry Regiment, said later:

'The guerrillas spread alarming reports, which caused great uneasiness to our men, and their morale was badly depressed. The non-fighting troops in the rear felt terror with the sense of hopeless battle … The sabotage troops had been so well trained over a considerable period of time and their activities were so skilful that we were unable to obtain successful results. Our lines of communication were cut, and, as their activities increased, we had to keep strong guards posted day and night which gave the men no time to rest.'[12]

Operation Character was a triumph. Hugh Seagrim had laid the basis for the most successful guerrilla operation of the entire war. The delay imposed on the Japanese 15th Division in the race for Toungoo had a vital impact on the outcome of the entire Burma campaign, and for less than a fraction of the lives Mountbatten was prepared to sacrifice. So successful was the operation that Lieutenant General Sir Montagu Stopford, commanding the British Indian 33 Corps, remarked that in the previous month Force 136 and Karen forces had inflicted more casualties on the Japanese than the entire regular army. The Karen levies killed more than 12,500 Japanese, over twice the number killed on the battlefield at Kohima. They were almost certainly responsible for dispatching several thousands more by directing air attacks on to the retreating Japanese columns. The Karen levies lost just over 100 men. For the British, the human cost was remarkably light – just six British officers and men.

Initially, the British had banked on raising between 3,000 and 5,000 Karen levies. In the event, they armed over 12,000 from a cowed and demoralised people, who had suffered years of brutal oppression. That so many flocked to join the rising after all they had endured over the previous three years was due to the inspirational legacy of Hugh Seagrim, who lit a lasting flame of freedom that could not be extinguished. The Karens may have fought for their liberty, but they also fought for the memory of the man who had found his own personal salvation by sacrificing himself for their sake. It was savage reckoning. At the time of his death, with his organisation broken up by the Japanese and his closest associates scattered or dead, Seagrim could not have dreamed that his long, lonely years of hard work and suffering would deliver such spectacular results.

In his report on Otter, Edgar Peacock paid tribute to Seagrim and the inspiration he gave to the Karens, and also to the memory he had promised his mother that he wanted to leave behind:

'I have left to the last all mention of Major Seagrim who, although not directly concerned in this operation, was, at its inception, the focal point of all attempts to start a resistance movement in Karenni. This is not the place to tell his story; of how he "stayed put" in Burma and gave his life to save the Karens from persecution on his behalf. But he was very definitely an inspiration to the Karens and to us all, and I like to think his valorous spirit, and those of Major Nimmo and Captain McCrindle who were dropped to him and died in Karenni, were more than a little responsible for the loyalty and gallantry shown by these hill men throughout the campaign.'[13]

It was an astonishing victory.

★★★

While the fighting was raging in the Karen hills, and the 14th Army raced against the clock to beat the impending monsoon, the atmosphere in Rangoon jail by April 1945 was one of intense excitement. Increasingly Ras Pagani and the PoWs in the jail realised that the Japanese were losing the war. It was a dangerous moment, with the risk of either summary execution by a nervous, demoralised enemy or devastation from a concentrated Allied bombardment.

There were reports of riots and looting in the city. At night, shots could be heard outside the gates. The Japanese began to behave as though something was up. On 24 April, they started burning piles of documents and papers, and carrying heavy kit outside the main gate. The guards discarded their old clothes, put on new uniforms and looked as if they were about to evacuate the city. After over two years in prison, Ras Pagani's antennae were on full alert as he bided his time waiting for another opportunity to escape. Over the compound wall a whispered voice told him that the Japanese were planning to take away 200 fit prisoners, but for what purpose was unclear. Lionel Hudson gathered the men together to mark all those who could walk with a red tick. Those doubtful were left unticked.

Ras Pagani was determined to join the column. He thought it would offer an excellent chance for yet another escape and the possibility to return to his friends in the Karen hills. For others, it was an agonising choice. To go or not to go, that was the question. Hudson was determined to go, but he was pushed aside at the last minute – 'You trouble-maker,' hissed a guard known as the 'Human Ape' – but all the other senior officers, including the elderly Brigadier Hobson and the medic Colonel Mackenzie, were selected. Finally, 76 American and 365 British PoWs were lined up in groups. After a final prayer meeting, at about 4 p.m. they set off in the sweltering heat, the rain falling in torrents drenching everyone to the skin. Hudson watched from the balcony: 'We had sad hearts when they moved out, surprisingly cheery, and facing the unknown like that takes guts. They were gallant men.'[14] Led by the towering figure of Brigadier Hobson walking proud and erect, Ras and the column marched out of the gates in good order. It was an inspiring sight tinged with great sadness for those left behind. They too faced an equally uncertain fate.

For Ras, and the men in the column, it soon became clear that this was a forced march. Many who had declared themselves fit suddenly found it was turning into a harrowing ordeal. Weakened by disease and malnutrition, and unused to exercise, it became a battle for survival as men began to fall behind, only to be subjected to brutal treatment by the guards. Shots were heard as the Japanese killed the stragglers where they fell. Those who had been in solitary confinement for months were among the weakest. They suffered dreadfully. Soon it became a walking nightmare. Ras had no other thought than to put one foot painfully in front of the other – or face a bullet in the head.

For many in those last, desperate days, fate was both random and cruel. Some took the chance to melt away into the jungle. Others finally gave up and fell by the wayside. Ras tried to help a dark-haired soldier, who was becoming exhausted. At last the man could go no further and he sank to the ground: 'A guard approached us, shot the soldier through the head and then screamed at me to get moving, threatening me with his rifle. I needed no further bidding as I saw that the guard was working himself up into a fury which was so characteristic of Japanese guards before they went berserk.'[15] The road was strewn with broken glass, which cut to ribbons the feet of those walking barefoot. Throughout there was the constant nagging fear of being strafed by Allied planes. As they were dressed like their captors, the unsuspecting Allied pilots would have no way of distinguishing them from the retreating Japanese.

At the junction of the Prome and Pegu roads at Taukkyan, where the huge Commonwealth War Graves Cemetery now stands, they branched to the right towards Pegu. At this point, the men were convinced that they were hostages being taken across the Sittang to south Burma, well behind the Japanese lines. On the night of 27 April 1945, a large force of Liberators flew overhead towards Rangoon, followed by a squadron of fighters. Ras suggested to his American friends, Major Lutz and Captain Humphries, that they should make a break for it and head for the Karen hills, where they would be safe, but the two Americans advised against it until they were closer to the Sittang river. Ras bided his time, champing at the bit to be the master of his own fate rather than continuing to march on passively, eroding his reserves of strength.

After two days, Colonel Mackenzie, who had done so much to save so many people in the prison, was close to collapse. He was placed on one of the few handcarts and had little recollection of the third day. Every twenty minutes or so, Allied fighter bombers flew over as they sheltered in the jungle by the road. In the evening, as they prepared to move on again, he drew upon all his reserves of strength and determination and took his place in the line of march. After moving beyond Pegu, following the line of the railway, Mackenzie could go no further. He asked to be left behind: 'When the order to move again was given, I just lay still, relieved to think that it was now all over and that I should not have to renew the struggle.'[16] But it was not to be. As the column began to move off, Squadron Leader Duckenfield and Captain Brown came up, silently laced their arms around his shoulders and bore his inert body between them. As they too faltered, exhausted, other equally exhausted men came forward to drag him along and speak words of comfort and encouragement. For the last two hours, the burden was taken by Sergeant Handsell and Sergeant Martin. They too had had no food themselves for forty-eight hours. They were on the brink of collapse, but refused to show it. Ras too was plumbing his deepest reserves of strength and endurance.

At about seven o'clock in the evening, when they stopped at a small village on the Pegu–Waw road, Mackenzie asked one of the guards to allow him to see the Japanese commandant:

> 'I am finished. I cannot march any further. My legs and feet are useless and I am impeding the progress of my friends. I have disposed of my kit and, before we leave here tonight, I want the Commandant to do me a personal favour. I want him to put a bullet through my heart. I will mark the place on my shirt with a piece of paper or mark my chest with a coloured pencil, so that there will be no mistake. I cannot face being left behind and murdered. The sooner the better please, so that I may be buried before the column moves off again.'[17]

Stunned, the Japanese went into a hasty discussion. As they conferred, Mackenzie was carried to lie beneath the rambling branches of a banyan tree to await his fate.

As daylight broke on the morning of 29 April, Brigadier Hobson strode into the glade. In a loud and clear voice, he called out something they had all dreamed of for years. The Japanese had abandoned the march, and the prisoners. They were all free men. While Mackenzie was awaiting the *coup de grâce*, the commandant had sent for the brigadier and told him that he was going to release them. He had given Hobson a note to show to any Japanese troops they encountered, saying that they had been officially liberated. The Japanese guards then scarpered like 'bats out of hell'. Mackenzie was so weak he could not speak. He held out his hands feebly and was surrounded by thirty or forty NCOs all shouting 'You've made it, sir,' and 'Well done, Colonel, well done.' It was the proudest moment of his life.

As the news sank in, Ras, too, was euphoric. He had made it. Maybe, just maybe, after all he had endured, he would be able to keep his promise and return to his beloved Pip and young son.

The freed men spent that day foraging for food from the surrounding villages, while the RAF boys began to make a huge Union Jack from pieces of cloth scrounged from nearby villages and the long white pants issued to them by the Japanese, so that Allied planes might be able to identify them. They were overjoyed at being free and so close to rescue. Unfortunately, fate still had another tragic surprise in store. Despite the homemade flag, the entire party was in grave danger of friendly fire from Allied planes. Hobson took over a bamboo hut in the village. Mackenzie had just been placed with him there when there were shouts that Allied aircraft were overhead. Hobson rushed to his side and said: 'What are you going to do, Mac?' He pulled Mackenzie down to the floor and lay beside him on his side, with his hand and forearm laid protectively across the colonel's thigh.

A 43-pound bomb exploded just behind the hut, showering it with fizzing, red-hot splinters. Miraculously, neither man was hurt. 'My God, that was a near one,' Mackenzie heard Hobson say, before the aircraft turned again to rake the village with machine-gun fire. The first bullet from the left-hand gun hit Hobson in the kidney and inflicted a deep wound; the force it generated was felt by Mackenzie lying beside him. The first bullet from the right-hand gun whistled past the colonel's ear … and lodged itself in the junction of the wall and floor. Had he been leaning on his elbow, as he usually did, rather than lying flat on the ground, he would have been killed instantly. When he looked around, Hobson was dead, blood pouring from his wound. 'Poor Hobson! Could anything be more poignant? He was destroyed by our own side, after the years he had suffered at the hands of the enemy,' Mackenzie mourned afterwards.[18] After three long years of captivity, hardship and abuse, Hobson had been killed in the very moment of his triumph. For the elderly civilian soldier, it was his finest hour.

Left: Allied prisoners outside Pegu holding the Union Jack which they used to signal to Allied aircraft on 29 April 1945.

Bullets are capricious things. For those who survived, God did indeed move in mysterious ways. Mackenzie, who had been resigned to death and pleading for a bullet to relieve his suffering, survived. Hobson, who had led them all for years through thick and thin, and who just moments before had announced their freedom, died lying next to him, his arm placed protectively over his friend. Had the aircraft come over just a few minutes later, the Union Jack, which Duckenfield and his men were preparing, might have averted this final tragedy. Hobson was buried by a large tree adjoining the railway line as, moments after the raid, Duckenfield finally spread out his message across the fields: FOUR HUNDRED BRITISH PRISONERS HERE. NO FOOD. SOS. At each corner, and at considerable personal risk, stood four men, including Ras, with pieces of mirror to signal to the Allied pilots. They were soon spotted by a Spitfire pilot, who informed brigade headquarters.

As dusk approached, once again Ras tried to persuade Lutz and Humphries to make a break for it. In the distance, they saw artillery fire and an aircraft dropping supplies. Volunteers were called to try to contact the nearby British 14th Army. Eventually Lutz, a short stout man, was selected to go as he had the remains of what passed for a uniform. He had no desire to dress like a Burmese for fear of being shot by mistake either by the Japanese or the British. Soon Lutz and Lucas, a British sergeant, had made contact with a Chinese boy and a Burmese, who had been sent out by the British troops to locate them. Lutz and the two messengers set off to establish contact with the relief column. The remainder of the party lay up under cover. The area was still crawling with Japanese troops in complete disarray.

Right: Allied PoWs elated after their rescue on 29 April 1945.

Late in the afternoon of 29 April 1945, a convoy of trucks drew up on the road next to the copse. Initially apprehensive, the men slowly realised they were Allied lorries. An almighty cheer went up. The entire column surged out of the trees to meet their rescuers, a detachment of Indian infantry. Half an hour after swarming on board the trucks, they were being greeted warmly by officers and men from a battalion of the West Yorkshire regiment. Short on rations, they clubbed together and at great cost to themselves gave Ras and his companions the best meal they had enjoyed in years. The following day, stragglers hiding in the outlying villages were brought in safely.

Three days later, the entire area was deluged by the monsoon rains. Waves of 'mango showers' swept in off the Bay of Bengal, presaging the start of the full monsoon, when massive tropical storms would turn the fields and roads into a sea of liquefied mud. They had made it.

★★★

For Ras's comrades left in Rangoon jail, the end came very differently. After the walking column had left, there was an air of unreality. On 30 April, Hudson noticed something strange was going on. The following morning, he realised that the Japanese had stolen away in the night and left them to their own devices. They had left two notes pinned to the gates one of which read: 'We hope that we have an opportunity to meet you again at battlefield of somewhere.'

Gradually, it dawned on Hudson that the Allies were unaware that the enemy had fled and that Rangoon was an open city. With a massive Allied attack imminent, they faced being obliterated by friendly fire. In an inspired move, they decided to paint two messages on the red corrugated iron roofs of the jail blocks. 'JAPS GONE' was daubed across one and 'BRITISH HERE' across another. As the last letters were being painted, an RAF Beaufighter flew over the jail at treetop height. One man waved to the pilot with his brush. They were convinced they had been seen, but early the next morning an RAF Mosquito skip-bombed the jail wall behind No. 6 block. Several men were injured, but miraculously no one was killed. The prisoners were apoplectic, and Hudson sick with anxiety. 'What can we do about it, sir?' he was asked. 'How can we get them to pull their finger out?' Hudson had a brainwave. 'That's it!' he cried, and instructed the men to paint another message on their roof, which no Japanese person could ever have devised: 'EXTRACT DIGIT'.[19]

At 2.30 p.m. on the afternoon of 3 May 1945, a huge B24 bomber loomed up in the sky on a bombing run, heading straight towards the jail. As the bomb-bay doors opened, the PoWs below froze, expecting to be blown to pieces in the very hour of their salvation. Then, suddenly, twenty-two containers of 'K' rations and medical supplies floated down by parachute into the jail. An hour and a half later, a British war correspondent and two official army photographers knocked politely on the main gate. They were given a rapturous welcome and surrounded by a mass of laughing PoWs. Their surviving photographs are a fascinating record of the jail in those first extraordinary moments.

As is so often the case, history was followed by pure farce. Two hours later, a Royal Navy party marched up to the gate. The officer, with a colour sash across his chest, knocked on the gates several times with his sword, yelling, 'The Navy's here. The Navy's here.' Hudson stuck his neck out the window and replied tartly, 'The Navy can fuck off. The Press was here two hours ago.' On being let in, one sailor complained, 'You're a rotten lot. At least you could have let us rescue you. We haven't been able to find one bleeding enemy to shoot at.'[20]

And thus did freedom come to Rangoon jail.

Above and right: Rangoon Jail, 1 May 1945, with 'British Here – Japs Gone' painted on the roof to alert Allied aircraft.

Chapter 18

The Birth of a Legend –
The Lawrence of Burma

'For some are born to do great deeds, and live,
As some are born to be obscured, and die.
Do thou the deeds I die too young to do
And reap a second glory in thine age.'

MATTHEW ARNOLD

With the outstanding success of Operation Character between April and August 1945, a wave of reports and witness statements began to circulate of the heroic exploits of the saintly British major and his remarkable exploits among the Karens. On 27 June 1945, the head of Force 136 in Burma, Ritchie Gardiner, was approached by Ian Morrison, the war correspondent of *The Times*. Morrison wanted assistance with an article he was writing on Seagrim. It had already mushroomed to over 100 pages, and he freely admitted that it was fast becoming a book. Gardiner thought Morrison 'a first-class fellow, young, modest and I should say intellectual; in fact, just the type of man who should write the story of Seagrim'.[1]

Morrison was transfixed by Seagrim's story, and even while the war was still raging he decided to concentrate his time and effort on recording it. His editor wrote to him on 13 July 1945:

'I am not in the least surprised that you should have been fired by the story of Seagrim's magnificent sacrifice, or that it should have moved you to wish to see it fully recorded. Even the brief details, which you give in your letter are stirring enough. I have, equally, no difficulty in understanding the spirit in which you would set about it and well know that your writing of the book would be undertaken simply as a service to the memory of a man of whom we should all know and should all be proud.'[2]

Morrison interviewed many of Seagrim's closest Karen comrades. He sat with Ta Roe while he was still in hospital recovering from his shocking ill treatment by the Japanese. In his endearingly old-fashioned English, Ta Roe told Morrison:

'When I think about Seagrim, I always want to shed my tears. He said, "Ta Roe when the British come back I shall look after you." When he wrote to me he would say: "Ta Roe, you may come to me." He loved me very much.

We are poor people and we had no precious things to give him. I gave him my long pants, but he was very tall and they were too short for him.

In the hills everybody knew him, even the small children …
He once said to me: "Christ sacrificed for the world. I will sacrifice for the Karens." He was always smiley-faced. I saw him many times and he was never cross or angry, no, not once. He was always speaking sweet words.'[3]

Others had the same impression. San Po Thin of the Delta Karens believed: 'He was a great chap. I think that if he had lived he would have gone even to the King of England about us Karens.'[4] Saw Willie Saw said quite simply: 'The Karens loved him. Of course. They knew that he came to save them. If it had not been for him we should all have been killed.'[5]

Official testimonies were also taken. Saw Kan Nyun, his clerk and interpreter at Pyagawpu, attested:

'During his trial by the Japs, he fearlessly said that the Karens were all innocent and should, therefore, be freed. He laid the whole blame on himself and bravely died for the cause of the British Govt. and the Karen people on 2 September 1944. Such being so, we all do hope that he has a full right to be ever remembered and recognised as a hero among the Karen people as well as the British nation.'[6]

A post-war report on the Shwegyin Karens made it very clear how much they owed to Hugh Seagrim.

'During moments of doubts and hopes, triumphs and failures, he was their inspiring idol and guiding spirit. Not having the heart to hear their cries and protestations, to see the oppression and violence inflicted on them by their taskmasters, he dedicated himself, gave up his life, a martyr for the Karens who are justifiably immortalising his name and keeping his memory in the warmest corner of their hearts. He had not died "unwept, unhonoured and unsung."'[7]

While the vast majority of Seagrim's contemporaries paid unqualified tribute to his charismatic personality and selfless martyrdom, the response of his peers was not wholly hagiographic. Some critical voices were raised. Many years after the war, in a taped interview, Colin Mackenzie, the head of Force 136 India Mission, was shocked by a conversation with Charles Cruickshank, the author of a definitive work on SOE in the Far East. When Mackenzie mentioned the enormous reputation Seagrim had among the Karens, both alive and dead, Cruickshank remarked tartly: 'Shouldn't he be accused of treason for surrendering?'[8] Cruickshank may well have been playing devil's advocate. In his book he is scrupulously fair to Seagrim, but more conventional military minds were uneasy that Seagrim had allowed his own spiritual beliefs to outweigh his military duty. In Europe and other theatres of war, for instance, often the price of guerrilla warfare was mass reprisal against the civilian population, but rarely did this trigger the voluntary self-sacrifice of the protagonists. To his critics, Seagrim was a conflicted character, an eccentric mystic, a missionary masquerading as an officer rather than a soldier. But in truth he was both. The twin poles of his personality co-existed – hence the Bible in one hand and a tommy gun in the other. Believing that suffering had a deeper purpose, he increasingly reconciled the two by allowing the spiritual dimension to prevail.

Another who formed a contrary view was Richard Lewin, part of a force sent up from Bilin to Papun as the Japanese invasion began in 1942. In a recorded interview many years after the war, he explained that while he was there he met up with 'Stookey Seagrim', who was busy raising Karen levies. When asked what impression Seagrim made on him, Lewin replied bluntly: 'He was a stupid chap. He was a very charming, energetic and intelligent person.' After a long, thoughtful pause, he continued: 'I think he was wrong to raise the levies in the Karen Hills. It brought down the Japanese on the Karens.'[9]

That was unfair. When given free rein by the Japanese, the BIA and its successors wreaked havoc among the Karens and provoked savage reprisals. Seagrim did his best to rein these in and to channel their rage into a more disciplined and coherent resistance. At crucial moments he urged restraint, specifically to avoid the risk of an escalating cycle of violence. More importantly, Lewin was ignoring the priceless intelligence that Seagrim and the Karens passed back to India and the crucial role that the Karen levies played in the Allies' race for Toungoo and victory. His views were at odds with prevailing opinion, but it is clear that not everyone viewed Seagrim's self-sacrifice in quite the same light.

However, the overwhelming view was one of unqualified admiration. It was not just the Karens who spoke out. An increasing number of British officers involved in Operation Character realised that their success had been built on the foundations laid by Seagrim. Though the Karens were cowed and fearful following Seagrim's death and their brutal treatment at the hands of the Japanese, just six months later they had risen up again as part of Character in by far the largest guerrilla campaign of the whole South-East Asian theatre. They may have fought for their freedom, but they fought also for Seagrim and the memory he was so determined to leave behind.

Captain Duncan Guthrie was parachuted into the Karen hills in February 1945 as part of Operation Character but broke his ankle on landing. Like Seagrim, for over three months he was secretly sheltered and fed by the Karens at Pyagawpu, where he heard first hand about the legendary English major. Guthrie was deeply impressed by the kindness of the Karens, who 'proved that in these Burmese highlands the Englishman's name and integrity still stand for something. In a world of cynicism in which men talk of the falling away of the English tradition, it was good to find a mountain colony which still believes in the example of our old island.'[10] On Guthrie's return, just a month after the end of the war, on 10 September 1945 the BBC broadcast a radio interview with him about Seagrim. Guthrie concluded that 'there has not been – there could not be – any more heroic act during this war. Major Seagrim was a very great Englishman.'[11]

Unfortunately, Seagrim's mother, Amabel, missed the unheralded broadcast. Shortly afterwards, she wrote to Jack:

'Dearest Jack,

I was so glad to get your letter, hear all yr. news especially about dear B. I have heard nothing yet. I look at the list each day in the D.T. [Daily Telegraph] but it is a relief to know he is really with Daddy ... and perhaps did not suffer too long from those devils. It has all been so distressing, so long. I feel so sick I did not hear the BBC broadcast as we hardly ever miss the 9.00 news and talk after, but as you say if his memory can live, help the Karennis, Burmese, as he hoped, it is far more than any medal here. I've sent 2 photos of B. ... How proud Daddy would be of all his boys; no doubt he knows it.'[12]

Other than the few surviving letters, the only other glimpse of Amabel's grief can be seen on the back cover of a family photo album, which she inscribed as:

'A tribute to the memory of so many young men who have laid down their lives for the cause. The record of their sacrifice and achievement is only once made public on the day when their names are printed in the small type of the casualty lists. As individuals they live forever in the secret heart of a proudly sad home. Collectively they swell the immortal ranks of the unknown warriors of our island story.'[13]

No one ever saw her weep at the loss of her sons. On hearing of their deaths, on each occasion, alone and grief-stricken, she went for a solitary five hour walk along the North Devon cliffs gazing out to sea to remember them and to collect herself.

On the back page of the photo album, she transcribed various elegiac poems. Perhaps sensing her own end, she gave pride of place to Tennyson's poem 'Crossing the Bar'.

'Sunset and evening star,
And one clear call for me!
And may there be no moaning of the bar,
When I put out to sea ...'

She died in 1963 at the age of eighty-seven.

★★★

While Morrison was researching his book and interviewing survivors in Karenni, official attempts were made to discover Seagrim's diaries, equipment and papers. In early December 1945, information was received that suggested that Seagrim had buried documents at one of his hiding places. An officer was dispatched to the hills to try to retrieve them. He spent a week searching a small area of barren ground at Hticlerplaw and found Seagrim's bamboo hut still standing, but after digging in six different places where he thought it likely that Seagrim might have hidden his 'box of treasures', he found nothing other than a few empty food tins. To this day Seagrim's box remains undiscovered, hidden somewhere deep beneath the blood-red loam of the Karen hills.

Late in 1946, Amabel once again journeyed to Buckingham Palace to collect a medal for a dead son. Originally Hugh had been nominated by Ritchie Gardiner for the Victoria Cross, but the lack of first-hand witnesses and the technicality that he had been executed rather than killed in action meant that the George Cross was deemed more appropriate. There was also some official confusion over whether he had earlier received the Military Cross. Several documents appended the suffix, but it appears that in the fog of war this had never been gazetted.

Rarely in the annals of the George Cross has Seagrim's citation been surpassed:

'Throughout his sojourn in jail he made every effort to comfort his men and sustained their courage by his Christian example, and the degree to which he had inspired them may be realised from the fact that they all expressed their willingness to die with him ... There can hardly be a finer example of self-sacrifice and bravery than that exhibited by this officer who in cold blood deliberately gave himself up to save others, knowing well what his fate was likely to be at the hands of the enemy.'[14]

With the award of the George Cross on 12 September 1946, a whole raft of newspaper articles emerged relating Seagrim's inspiring story: 'VCs brother said: Let Me Die For Others', blazed the *Daily Express*, comparing Seagrim's self-sacrifice with that of Captain Oates, one of Seagrim's personal role models, whose noble end he had set down years beforehand in his own private anthology with a quote from Captain Scott's diary. Many articles compared him with Lawrence of Arabia: 'Lawrence of Burma wins GC', announced the *Daily Mail*.

Morrison's book *Grandfather Longlegs: The Life and Gallant Death of Major H. P. Seagrim, GC, DSO, MBE,* published in 1947, generated intense public interest. It remains the most important source of information on what was widely believed to be one of the greatest stories of the war in the East. In its review of the book, the *Church Times* commented: 'He cut the same kind of legendary figure among the Karens as Lawrence had twenty-five years earlier among the Arabs; his courage was matched by his prudence, and even his enemies respected him. This admirable account of his life ... is an epic of devoted personality and Christian faith.'[15] *The Sunday Times* concurred: 'This is without doubt one of the epic stories of the whole war.'[16]

On 29 December 1946, a memorial service led by the Bishop was held for Hugh Seagrim and his fallen comrades in Holy Trinity Anglican cathedral in Rangoon, complete with a Karen choir and an appreciation of his life delivered by Ian Morrison. Among the hymns that day was the last Seagrim and his men had sung as they had lined up to die, 'The Solid Rock'; it was followed by 'Abide with Me' and the Karen national anthem. Six months later, in May 1947, the Bishop traversed the Karen hills and heard first-hand stories of Seagrim. When he asked a Karen villager why Seagrim had captured the Karen hearts and minds so completely, the man answered: 'Because he loved us so much.' In a village overlooking the Mawchi road, in spite of being destitute, hungry and having just lost their best houses to a devastating fire, the villagers declared to the Bishop that they would build a new church in memory of Seagrim and all the Force 136 men, both British and Karen, who had fallen in the battle for Burma.

They were not alone. A group of ex-SOE officers suggested that the cash-strapped British government should make a gift of money to the hill tribes of Burma to help with reconstruction, a tangible token of thanks for their loyalty during the war. Known as the Force 136 Memorial Fund, the plan was to support three projects. The first was to establish three scholarships for Karens at Rangoon University to help train a new generation of leaders. The second was to create the Seagrim Memorial Hospital, a forty-bed hospital that would cater for local needs and inculcate greater levels of medical awareness and hygiene. The third was to create a small model farm to provide food for the hospital and help propagate improved methods of agriculture and animal husbandry.

The impecunious British Treasury agreed to provide 500,000 rupees (£37,550), which was sent to Rangoon, but the new Burmese government drew up a document specifying how the money should be controlled. It insisted that two Burmese should be included in the decision-making. The Burmese, anxious for the rebellious Karens not to receive anything, dragged their heels. With the advent of a new Labour government in London and cutbacks in all areas of government spending, questions were raised by the Public Accounts Committee. The money was sent back to London. In spite of all their suffering and hardship, the Karens never received a penny by way of thanks from Whitehall. On 26 August 1949, the British ambassador in Rangoon reluctantly concluded that with the deterioration of relations between the Karens and new Burmese government 'it now seems unlikely that it will be possible to establish the Fund on the lines originally envisaged for some time to come.'[17]

Among his contemporaries, Freddy Spencer-Chapman offers perhaps the most obvious comparison with Seagrim. Like Eric McCrindle, Chapman was an alumnus of Sedbergh school, a pre-war Arctic explorer, mountaineer and naturalist, who was also trained to lead a left-behind party in Malaya. Between January 1942 and late 1943, working alone alongside Chinese communist guerrillas, Chapman carried out hit-and-run raids against the Japanese, blowing up trains and killing more than 500 enemy soldiers. As with Seagrim, when he finally re-established contact with the British, two Force 136 officers were dispatched to join him, John Davis and Richard Broome. Soon they too were beleaguered by the Japanese and cut off, but eventually, with the help of the Chinese communists, they managed to repair their radio and escape by submarine to Ceylon. Unlike Seagrim, Nimmo and McCrindle, however, Chapman and his two companions survived the war. Following the publication of his book *The Jungle is Neutral* in 1948, he was lionised, ironically at the very moment when his erstwhile allies, the Chinese communists, were taking up arms against the British at the beginning of the Malayan insurgency.

Although their experiences were similar, Chapman and Seagrim were very different characters. Both were very English heroes. Both were staggeringly brave. Masters of guerrilla warfare, both spent long periods cut off far behind enemy lines, perpetually in fear for their lives, and both were befriended by the indigenous peoples with whom they fought side by side. Both were wracked by hunger and privation, and both were assailed by a plethora of tropical diseases. But there the similarities end. Chapman was a freebooting adventurer, while Seagrim was a much more complex person: contemplative, spiritual and constantly seeking the deeper meaning of life. While Chapman was a constant thorn in the side of the Japanese for over 1,000 days, Seagrim laid the foundations for the most effective guerrilla operation of the war – one that played a decisive strategic role in the final victory in Burma and which at one point inflicted greater Japanese casualties than the entire 14th Army.

Seagrim's parallels with T. E. Lawrence, too, are striking. In the First World War, Lawrence raised the Arab tribes of the Hejaz against the Turks with promises of independence and the freedom to manage their own affairs, only to see the Middle East carved up cynically between the Great Powers as part of the victory settlement. In Burma, Seagrim pledged his personal honour to encourage the Karens to rise up and support the British at great cost to themselves. They did so unhesitatingly, confident in the belief that the British would stand by them and, at the very least, ensure that their autonomous status and way of life were preserved. Seagrim, like Lawrence before him, was eventually betrayed by the government he had done so much to serve. For a man of such moral integrity, perhaps it was fortunate that he did not live to see his honour traduced by politicians far away in London.

But in the wider annals of Empire, perhaps the most notable parallel is between Hugh Seagrim and Gordon of Khartoum. In 1885 Gordon wilfully ignored government orders to evacuate Khartoum and abandon the Sudan to Mahdist forces. He refused to do so and died in a Victorian war against Islamic fundamentalism. Both men were loners. Both were immensely charismatic individuals with absolute faith in a higher spiritual power that guided their actions, although not in any fanatical sense. Their spiritual beliefs were based on a highly personal direct relationship with God. This was the cornerstone of their moral integrity and the charismatic power they exercised over all those around them, including their enemies. Gordon, it was said, could quell a riot by the sheer power of his personality and his penetrating blue eyes.

Neither belonged to any established church. Neither had much time for officialdom, nor the rigid social hierarchies in which they worked. Gordon once remarked: 'I dwell on the joy of never seeing Great Britain again, with its horrid, wearisome dinner parties … I would sooner live like a dervish with the Mahdi than go out to dinner every night in London.'[18] Both had a deep respect for all religions. They believed in acceptance and the surrender of the self to Divine will: Thy will – not my will – be done. All men mattered irrespective of colour, creed or belief. All were part of the unfolding of the Divine on earth. All deserved to be treated with humility and compassion.

Both men could have escaped their ultimate fate, but to do so would have meant betraying themselves and those they loved, having encouraged them to fight against tyranny and oppression in conditions of great hardship and suffering. Both chose self-sacrifice. It is a measure of their innate moral integrity that they regarded it as their duty to share the fate of those they had pledged their honour to protect. Both epitomised the British Empire at its finest.

Although forgotten in his own country, Seagrim succeeded in his ambition of leaving a lasting memory among the Karens; a memory so indelible that he is revered to this day. Sixty years later, in 2004, the Karen General Tamlabaw recalled his childhood fighting the Japanese and his own memories of Seagrim:

'In the hills I was privileged to meet the English soldier Major H. P. Seagrim, who had stayed to organise the Karen resistance. He was the best type of Englishman: soft-spoken and very religious. He carried a Bible everywhere ... My heart ached when I heard he had been beheaded [executed by firing squad]. I hope he is remembered in England.'[19]

To date, he has not been. With Britain's withdrawal from India in 1947, and then Burma in 1948, interest in the Far East war gave way to the much more immediate threat of confrontation with the Soviet Union in Europe. A year earlier, on 5 March 1946, Churchill made his famous 'iron curtain' speech in Fulton, Missouri, while the British people, exhausted by six years of war, were preoccupied in coping with rationing, austerity and reconstruction. Burma rapidly became a forgotten country and the Allied sacrifices there regarded as a noble, but Pyrrhic, victory. Ian Morrison's subsequent death in Korea in 1950 removed the one man who might have given Seagrim the sort of legendary global reputation enjoyed by Lawrence of Arabia after the Great War. While revered among the Karens in eastern Burma as a very great Englishman, at home he was forgotten: a forgotten hero of a forgotten army in a forgotten conflict in a forgotten land.

★★★

The Karens paid a fearful price for their steadfast loyalty. After his release from prison, Ta Roe was in a desperate state, assailed by ringworm, scabies, dysentery and septic sores. Following months of intensive hospital treatment, he was eventually reunited with his family in Pyagawpu. Saw Willie Saw was in a similar condition. He needed an operation before he could return home to his old job as forest ranger at Kadaingti.

Po Hla was among a large group of prisoners from Insein jail taken eastwards by the Japanese as Rangoon was evacuated in late April 1945. He escaped from the train near Waw and crossed the British lines in early May

1945. However, suspicions lingered about his role in Seagrim's capture. As Seagrim's right-hand man and most enterprising agent, questions were raised as to why he had not been executed along with Seagrim. Ritchie Gardiner, the head of Force 136 in Burma, was uneasy, particularly because when Po Hla arrived at the British lines he appeared to be very fit and fat, and might have received preferential treatment in jail, but after being held for six months without charge, he was released in January 1946. Po Hla was certainly not guilty. He rejoined the Irrawaddy Flotilla Company, and kept in touch with his British former colleagues for many years after the war.

Saw Digay and Po Myin, who had been sentenced alongside Seagrim to eight years' imprisonment, escaped from a labour gang at Syriam outside Rangoon. They made their way home in time to fight in Operation Character, after which both returned to their old jobs: Digay as a timber contractor and Po Myin as the police officer at Pyagawpu. Over sixty years later, in September 2009, Digay's grandson Digay Htoo died fighting as an officer in the Karen resistance against the Burmese government. Although arrested, the cross-eyed, roguish Saw Darlington was never sentenced. After his release he returned to the hills to fight again in Operation Character.

The two redoubtable pastors, Thra May Sha and Thra Kyaw Lay, returned to their respective villages to rebuild their churches and care for their flocks. Saw Tommer and Arthur Ta Bi resumed their civic duties in Papun. Young Thet Wa, Seagrim's wireless operator, escaped to join Turrall's levies as part of Character and, later, Operation Nation.

Quite what happened to Saw Po Thin, the mysterious *éminence grise* behind the Karen resistance movement, and Paula, his beautiful daughter, who helped Ras Pagani escape from their house at Kyawaing, we shall probably never know; nor the fate of Ras's devoted guardian Lance Naik Mura after his release from Rangoon jail.

Father Loizeau was held under house arrest for the rest of the war and prevented from contacting the outside world. After being freed in July 1945, he wrote a full report of his experiences for the Mission d'Etrangères in Paris before embarking on the long process of reconstruction of his devastated community. Exhausted by war and recurrent bouts of malaria, and drained by the misery which the conflict had inflicted on the Karens, he died on 19 May 1950 aged seventy-four.

Jean Calmon endured months of abuse and interrogation at a concentration camp in Tavoy. The Japanese tried repeatedly to catch him out, but they never did. He was obdurate. 'The only crime I have committed,' he averred, 'is saving the lives of thousands of brave people.'[20] When he was released on 10 September 1945, he refused to be flown home to France but immediately returned to his Karens. In 1950 he became the head of mission in Papun, where he continued to care for his flock during the tempestuous post-war period before returning to Gramat in France, where he died on 14 October 1981.

After the war, Lionel Hudson, the Australian Wing Commander who oversaw the dangerous last days of Rangoon jail, became a foreign correspondent for Reuters in the Far East. He became good friends with Ian Morrison and was with him the night before Morrison flew to his death in Korea in August 1950.

Colonel Mackenzie, the heroic senior medic of Rangoon jail, who saved so many lives and miraculously survived the death march, retired to Inverness and became a town councillor.

Noel Stevenson, the doughty champion of the hill tribes, became Secretary to the Governor of Burma. He was appointed Director of the Frontier Areas in 1946. Instructed by the Churchill government to reassure the Karens that they would have a fair settlement with substantial autonomy, but not independence, he fought long and hard for their better future. The following year he resigned in disgust when the incoming Labour government reneged on the agreement. A man of honour, he refused to countenance plans that he believed would lead to civil war – a doleful prediction that sadly proved all too correct. Later he became a well-known television broadcaster and Managing Director of Scottish Television before retiring to his family home in Wigtownshire in 1965.

Jon Ritchie Gardiner, a hero of the Chaukkan Pass trek and subsequent head of the Burma section of Force 136, briefly resumed both his job with Macgregor's and his seat on Rangoon city council. When the company was nationalised in 1948, he returned to Britain with his wife, Mary, to a life of farming in Ayrshire. For a man who had defied death repeatedly on the Chaukkan Pass, his passing was peculiarly ironic. He died in 1990 after pricking his finger on a blackberry bush; the wound turned septic and caused blood poisoning.

Seagrim's close ally, Noel Boyt, the gung-ho, ex-forestry man from Steel Brothers and another survivor of the Chaukkan Pass, retired to Surrey. He died in 1985.

Arthur Bell Thompson, who led his party of officers and men on the epic 900-mile trek to Fort Hertz with Jimmy Nimmo, became a best-selling, crime writer, 'the thinking man's Ian Fleming', under his pseudonym Francis Clifford. A manuscript describing his harrowing escape from Burma in 1942 only came to light among his possessions after his death in 1975. It was published three years later under the title *Desperate Journey*.

The magnificent Subedar-Major Kan Choke, blind in one eye, who was such a tower of strength during Thompson's trek, survived both Operation Character and the war. The proud recipient of the Burma Gallantry Medal and a Mention in Despatches, he took part in the victory parade in Rangoon in 1945 before retiring to his village in the Irrawaddy Delta.

'Pop' Tulloch, the incorrigible old rogue who commanded Walrus section in Operation Character, played a major role in a post-war plot by renegade SOE officers to assist the Karens against the newly independent Burmese government. In 1952 he was remanded in custody for trial at the Old Bailey, accused of fraudulently converting £1,300 12s entrusted to him for the education of a Burmese boy. He pleaded that 'for reasons which I do not wish to make public at the moment, I do not wish to apply for bail', hinting that as a result of unofficial post-war espionage work with the Karens in Burma in 1949 and 1950 he 'had incurred the enmity of very powerful forces, who would have no compunction about doing me personal injury'.[21]

Ralf Magener and Heins von Have, the two intrepid Germans held in the New Law Courts at the time of Seagrim's incarceration, were taken to Tokyo. They finally reached home in October 1947. Magener resumed his business career and retired to Heidelberg in 1974. He died in 2000.

Lieutenant General Kimura was found guilty of war crimes by the International Military Tribunal and hanged in 1948. His ignominious flight from Rangoon so appalled his staff that the Japanese said that they would have hanged him if the Allies had not.

The enigmatic Colonel Keiji Suzuki, the spymaster behind the Minami Organ, fell out with both his commander-in-chief and the kempeitai. He was eventually sent back to Japan. When Aung San saw him during a visit to Tokyo in 1943, he found Suzuki crying with shame at his disgrace.

Captain Motoichi Inoue, who captured Seagrim, was arrested by war-crimes investigation officers – not in relation to Seagrim, who had been tried and sentenced in accordance with due process, but on charges of brutality against the Karens. So, too, was Corporal Noda, 'The Killer' of the New Law Courts. Maung Shwe, the corrupt deputy commissioner and bully, who caused so much suffering in Papun, was shot and killed leading a Japanese raid on a Karen village in July 1945.

As for the indestructible Ras Pagani, elated after his liberation with the column of PoWs outside Pegu, he was fed, and that same day flown to Poona in India, where he was admitted to hospital for medical checks and treatment and given a fresh new uniform, complete with a Reconnaissance Corps badge. Without further ado, he got an Indian photographer to take his picture in uniform, which he sent with an airmail letter to Pip, who had not heard a single word from him in three long years. He was all too aware she did not know whether he was alive or dead. Remarkably, after being grilled by an intelligence officer, Ras pressed to be sent back to the Karen hills where, fearing civil war between the Karens and Burmese, he felt he could use his influence to persuade the Karens to hand in their arms and promote peace. After over two years in prison, he was unaware that as a result of Operation Character there were now plenty of British forces in place to deliver the *coup de grâce* to the Japanese and oversee the aftermath. His frustration at being refused was soon forgotten when he received a letter from Pip, ecstatic at his survival and release, and telling him that he now had a three-year-old daughter, born nine months after his embarkation leave. Just days later, he was flown home in a Dakota. On landing, he was sent straight on leave to Colchester and the beginning of a new life with his young family.

In 1945, Ras was discharged from the Army with a 25 per cent disability pension in the rank of corporal, the Army refusing to accept his field promotion to sergeant by Seagrim. Adjusting to family life proved difficult for him. By nature, stubborn and independent, he was an austere father, who never showed his feelings or gave outward displays of affection. Although his back was scarred horribly from the wounds inflicted by the Burmese dahs when he was recaptured on the banks of the Irrawaddy, the psychological scars went much deeper. For years he never spoke about the war or his experiences. He could not abide being in bare feet or hearing a dripping tap. It was only over forty years later, in the mid–1980s, that he began to write down his life story. His private manuscript was transcribed by Robert Hamond as the basis for his book, *A Flame of Freedom*. On becoming aware of his survival, Ian Morrison added a late postscript to *Grandfather Longlegs* summarising his story, which he was keen to write up much more fully, but with his death in Korea in 1950, the chance was stillborn. This book is the first time that the whole story has been told.

Some found Ras's story hard to believe. On 18 and 22 January 1946 he was interviewed by MI9, the Directorate of British Intelligence tasked with overseeing all matters relating to PoWs. There are some discrepancies between his debriefing and his subsequent accounts. For instance, he gave the date of 16 September 1942 to MI9 for his escape from the railway, yet other sources place this two months' later. Such inaccuracies are perhaps understandable after months in the wilderness, followed by his horrendous injuries and two long years in prison cut off from the wider world. However, the most significant difference between his various accounts relates to his escape from Singapore. Both in his report to MI9 and in the letter he threw to Lionel Hudson in Rangoon jail, he refers to four other Europeans who joined him on the boat. In his own memoir, and Robert Hamond's book, they are omitted altogether – whether from failing memory or from simple hubris one can only conjecture. It is clear from the MI9 debrief that they did not get on. Ras had been very tough on them, but their omission makes little difference to his achievements. Notwithstanding some minor discrepancies, the MI9 interrogator was 'strongly inclined to give credence to the recital of Pagani's experiences',[22] which subsequently were verified by a host of other witnesses.

Shortly after the MI9 debrief, Ras received a Military Medal through the post with no citation, no mention of who had nominated him and no indication of an official presentation. Having successfully escaped from both Dunkirk and Singapore, and as the only European to escape successfully from the Burma railway, it was scant official recognition of his astonishing personal achievements – unequalled by any other soldier during the course of the war. Ras Pagani deserves to be remembered as one of the most courageous and intrepid British escapees of the Second World War.

When Ras's disability pension ceased, he pressed the Army to be allowed to re-enlist. His request was granted. He entered the Royal Artillery in

Carlisle as a driver for the brigadier. By a quirk of fate, the brigadier was posted to Rangoon and asked Ras if he wanted to go with him. Ras jumped at the idea, but with growing tensions between the Burmese and Karens, and Ras's wartime reputation among the Karens, he was rejected. The brigadier arranged for his transfer to the infantry, initially to the Royal Sussex Regiment, with whom he served at Khartoum and Suez, and then back to the East Surreys, where he became a motor transport sergeant.

In July 1959, Ras finally left the Army and set himself up in a taxi-service business in Clacton-on-Sea, which later expanded into garages both there and in Colchester. Bizarrely, one of his first taxi bookings in Colchester was Major 'Appy' Apthorp, his old commanding officer from Sumatra, whom he had last seen when he had absconded from the 18 kilometre camp on the Burma railway seventeen years earlier. Like so many who fought and suffered at the hands of the Japanese, Ras retained a loathing for them after the war. Years later, when on holiday in the south of France, he was convinced he saw one of the Japanese from the camps and had to be physically restrained from assaulting him.

In looking back over his extraordinary life, Ras rightly took justifiable pride in all he achieved, particularly his escape from the 'Death Railway'. The vast majority of people thought it was inconceivable for a European to escape successfully through a hostile oriental country, but Ras achieved the near impossible and very nearly made it clear across Burma to the

Left: Roy Pagani shortly after leaving the army to set up his taxi service in Clacton, c1962.
Above: Roy Pagani with Countess Mountbatten at the Imperial War Museum in 1995.

Allied lines. Courage comes in many forms. For Ras, his burning desire for freedom and his refusal to be cowed by people or circumstance was innate. It was part of the very essence of his being. His stoicism and self-belief in the face of unspeakable suffering bear testament to the triumph of the human spirit in the face of overwhelming odds. He simply never gave up. He was a prisoner at war rather than a prisoner of war. Having taken the King's shilling, he thought he was doing no more than his duty. He was a man of unimpeachable courage, who stands in the front rank of Britain's war heroes.

In his personal manuscript, he attributed his survival to his upbringing at the Convent of St Joseph in Crau, where he was taught self-reliance, and to his subsequent Army training as a regular in the East Surreys, which he believed instilled rigorous self-discipline. What impelled him never to give up was the promise he had made to his darling Pip that no matter what befell him, no matter how long it took, he would return. And, against all the odds, he did.

Ras twice returned secretly to the Karen hills to revisit his old haunts and old friends, and to support the Karens in their unending struggle against the Burmese government. In 1989, with his devoted Pip, he crossed the Salween covertly from Thailand. They spent over a week in Papun and the surrounding area, incensed that the Karens had been treated so badly in return for their steadfast loyalty and friendship in the war. A year later, he returned with his youngest daughter and her husband and dined with the Karen General Bo Mya, who remembered Seagrim and Ras's wartime exploits when he had been just a boy.

Whenever Ras Pagani recalled his wartime adventures, his thoughts always returned to one man – Hugh Seagrim; a man whom he believed had the rare gift of being able to inspire men of all different races to live courageously in a spirit of self-sacrifice. Seagrim was his greatest inspiration. 'I owe no other man a greater debt,' he said.[23] On 31 March 2003 the indomitable old warrior passed away from heart and renal failure aged eighty-seven … just one month before I tracked him down. There were no obituaries in the national press.

★★★

In London, beside the Commonwealth Gates at the top of Constitution Hill, is an elegant stone chattri, or Indian pavilion. High inside the dome, in raised bronze letters, are the names of those from the countries commemorated by the memorial who won the Victoria Cross and the George Cross. Hugh Paul Seagrim stands alongside Noor Inayat Khan and other heroic individuals who laid down their lives for freedom.

In far-off Rangoon, tucked away down a narrow unpaved lane off the Prome (Pyay) Road in Kemmendine, lies what was once the Japanese execution ground, now a place of quiet repose set aside for commemoration and sombre reflection. Today, it is the Rangoon War Cemetery, a peaceful sanctuary beautifully maintained by that great British institution the Commonwealth War Graves Commission. Here, on the central axis, close to the cross of sacrifice, lies Hugh Seagrim, flanked by his Karen comrades, united forever in death, asleep under the sunshine and stars. Nearby, rests Jimmy Nimmo. Sparrows dart among the graves. Bright, iridescent dragonflies hover in the limpid, heat-laden air. The plangent cries of raucous crows mourn those who lie beneath, buried far away from the cool, green grass of their homeland.

Long gone, but never to be forgotten, the bronze plaques on the headstones are cast with words of yearning, hope, faith and heartbreak.

O for the touch of a vanished hand
And the sound of a voice that is still.

★

'Who plucked this flower?'
I said, 'The Master,'
And the gardener held his peace.

★

Death is the veil which those who live
Call Life; They sleep, and it is lifted.

★

I was not there to hold your hand;
Sleep on, dear one, though in a foreign land.
Loved with a love beyond all telling;
Missed with a grief beyond all tears.

It is a place of transcendental beauty and deep sadness, a poignant reminder that ultimately we are all but feathers on the breath of God.

The lives of mortal men are like the spring flowers. They rise and fall all too fleetingly, but some men will never die. Their deeds live on long after they have passed away in the hearts of those they have left behind.

Over seventy years after his death, the name of Hugh Seagrim – Seagrim of Burma – remains a legend in the wild, untamed country between the Sittang and the Salween rivers in the far-distant Karen hills.

Above: Memorial plaque for Hugh Seagrim in Rangoon City Cemetery. The date of his death is incorrect.

EPILOGUE

In the post-war years, many felt that Britain's victory in Burma was meaningless, or at best ambiguous. Given the hardships and suffering endured by the people of Burma and the British Indian Army and the Allies, what was it all for? Within three years the British had left Burma and, on independence, the country left the Commonwealth. Politically, the British gained little.

But this is only part of the story. The Japanese offensive into Burma was a fatal miscalculation and a strategic catastrophe. It failed in its primary aim of knocking Britain out of the war in the Far East, and it failed to foment widespread unrest in India. Instead, it provoked a massive British response, which inflicted the greatest defeat ever suffered by the Japanese army in its entire history. Over 185,000 Japanese troops were killed in Burma, three-fifths of the entire force, and untold numbers were wounded – many believed more than the total killed by the Americans in their bloody island-hopping across the Pacific. British and Indian Army casualties amounted to around 73,000, of which just over 14,000 were killed. Just under 5,000 of these were of UK origin. As a result of the sacrifice made by British and Imperial troops, and their levies, Burma was delivered from an appalling tyranny and given the freedom to manage its own affairs. Tragically, that freedom was soon lost through internal dissent.

As the tide of Empire receded, those loyal Karens who had stood shoulder to shoulder with the British throughout the darkest days of the war felt a huge sense of betrayal. Not only had the British befriended Aung San; they were also preparing to deliver the Karens back into the hands of a Burman-dominated administration as part of a wider Union. Most Karens wanted to remain as an autonomous part of the British Empire in their own state, a plea that repeatedly fell on deaf ears in London. Communal violence flared as Karens and Burmese settled old scores and forged new hatreds. But it was not just the Karens who felt aggrieved. Feelings ran high right across the British establishment, nowhere more so than among a cadre of ex-Force 136 officers, who had fought alongside the Karens. Many felt that after fighting as brothers in arms, a new relationship had been forged between the British and the hill tribes, brokering what Mountbatten called 'a new spirit of Empire'.

Although during the war the British High Command had been cautious about fostering unrealistic political aspirations among the minorities, there was a clear promise that the special status of the hill tribes would be preserved. Anticipating trouble, at the end of the war a small cadre of canny Force 136 officers quietly passed over captured Japanese weapons to the Karens to store in case of future need.

On 19 July 1947, and at the most crucial moment in Burma's transition to independence, Aung San, together with some of the most promising men of his generation, was assassinated by gunmen on the instructions of a political rival, U Saw. He was just thirty-two years old. He left behind a wife, Daw Khin Kyi, two sons and a two-year-old daughter, the young Aung San Suu Kyi.

In 1948, post-independence, those in Britain sympathetic to the Karen cause mobilised support and offered both funding and assistance. Chief among them was Frank Owen, the editor of the *Daily Mail*. Newspaper funds were diverted to support the 'Friends of the Burma Hill People', a convenient cover for the Karen cause. A former Force 136 officer, Alexander Campbell, was even dispatched to Rangoon as a *Daily Mail* journalist. Just two years after it had been disbanded, a private unit of the SOE was established to help the Karen cause.

As disenchantment among the people grew and sporadic violence flared, the Karens sought help from their old friends in Force 136, not least the eccentric, monocle-wearing Lieutenant Colonel Cromarty Tulloch. In 1948 Tulloch began to organise covert drops of supplies to the Karens from secret jungle airstrips in Thailand, which not surprisingly alarmed the newly independent Burmese government. The Foreign Office, aghast at the damage to Anglo-Burmese relations by renegade ex-Special Forces officers, instructed MI5 to put an end to all the plotting. The proprietor of the *Daily Mail*, Lord Rothermere, was invited to take action against his renegade staff. Frank Owen and his foreign editor, Ewan Butler, were promptly sacked.

Burma was a powder keg. It needed only a single spark to explode. Early in January 1949, the Karens rebelled and civil war broke out. Within a month, they were at the gates of Rangoon. The Karens claimed that eighteen renegade British officers and NCOs were helping to train their forces. In direct opposition, the official British Services Mission to the Burmese government provided British advisers and aircraft to quell the revolt. In a bizarre twist of fate, British officers ended up fighting each other on opposite sides.

The Karen rebellion was never fully defeated. They retreated to their strongholds in eastern Burma and along the Thai border, conducting a sporadic insurgency that has continued ever since, only held at bay today by a fragile ceasefire. It has been the longest-running conflict of the past century.

One of the most intriguing questions is what role, if any, Hugh Seagrim would have taken in all this had he survived the war. The Karens told him repeatedly that after the war they intended to press the British government for a separate state. They wanted him to be its first governor. We do not know his reply. He never discussed it with any of his inner circle. But his deepest aspirations for the Karens were far less political: better infrastructure, better education and better medicine were his priorities. His intense religious convictions meant that he was much more likely to have stayed on as a missionary than as a political activist, but, as ex-Force 136 British renegades fought alongside the Karens against the independent Burmese government, could he really have remained aloof? How would he have responded to the chronic betrayal of the Karens by the British government? Ras Pagani had no doubts: 'I think he would have been desolated, absolutely desolated, by what's happened.'[1]

There is little doubt that Seagrim would have been a very eloquent spokesman for the Karens. He would have championed their cause with London, but whether he would have supported the case for an independent state, let alone taken up arms against the newly independent Union government, is debatable. It may well be that, had he lived, he would have acted as a voice of reason and moderation, and maybe brokered a working arrangement with Rangoon. We shall never know. It is one of the great imponderables in this story.

Aleksandr Solzhenitsyn wrote that a nation without an understanding of its past has no sense of direction for its future. Perhaps the time has come to put an end to the perpetual cycle of violence and retaliation, and for men and women of goodwill on all sides to come together in free, frank and constructive discussion, to heal the scars of the past and find an effective balance between tribal autonomy and national union. Vicious cycles of retribution have solved nothing and brought untold misery to so many. After all, what use is the pain of the past if it does not change the future? Mahatma Gandhi once said: 'An eye for an eye and the world is blind.' More recently, Nelson Mandela observed: 'Reconciliation means working together to correct the legacies of past injustice.' I suspect that Hugh Seagrim would have concurred.

With the advent of a reforming government in Burma, and the victory of Aung San Suu Kyi and the National League for Democracy in the 2015 elections, at last there is real hope for peace and reconciliation in a new democratic and pluralist Burma. The tiny two-year-old daughter that Aung San, the father of the nation, left behind when he fell in a hail of bullets on that fateful day in July 1947 is now Burma's greatest hope. The present is the child of the past. This is Burma, and Burma likes patterns.

Burma. Beautiful, blessed, benighted Burma; sublime, serene and supremely sad; an enchanted land of lost dreams and forgotten promises, but perhaps, just perhaps, one now charged with hope for the future.

APPENDIX A

Although the letter pasted into Hugh Seagrim's personal anthology has long been believed to be his last letter home, it is not. The letter was featured in *The Times* on 18 June 1940. It was written by an airman to his mother shortly before his death, but its sentiments are so similar to those expressed by Hugh Seagrim that the misattribution is understandable. It is reproduced here because it encapsulates the sacrifice of a generation who put duty before self in their defence of freedom.

'Dearest Mother,

Though I feel no premonition at all, events are moving rapidly, and I have instructed this letter to be forwarded to you should I fail to return from one of the raids which we will shortly be called upon to undertake. You must hope for a month, but at the end of that time you must accept the fact …

First, it will comfort you to know that my role in this war has been of the greatest importance … Though it will be difficult for you, you will disappoint me if you do not at least try to accept the facts dispassionately, for I shall have done my duty to the utmost of my ability. No man can do more, and no one calling himself a man could do less.

I have always admired your courage in the face of continual setbacks; in the way you have given me as good an education and background as anyone in the country; and always kept up appearances without ever losing faith in the future. My death would not mean that your struggle has been in vain. Far from it. It means that your sacrifice is as great as mine. Those who serve England must expect nothing from her; we debase ourselves if we regard our country as merely a place in which to eat and sleep.

History resounds with illustrious names who have given all, yet their sacrifice has resulted in the British Empire, where there is a measure of peace, justice and freedom for all, and where a higher standard of civilisation has evolved, and is still evolving, than anywhere else. But this is not only concerning our own land. Today we are faced with the greatest organised challenge to Christianity and civilisation that the world has ever seen, and I count myself lucky and honoured to be the right age and fully trained to throw my full weight into the scales. For this I have to thank you. Yet there is more work for you to do. The home front will still have to stand united for years after the war is won. For all that can be said against it, I still maintain that this war is a very good thing; every individual is having the chance to give and dare all for his principles like the martyrs of old. However long the time may be, one thing can never be altered – I shall have lived and died an Englishman. Nothing else matters one jot nor can anything ever change it.

You must not grieve for me, for if you really believe in religion and all that it entails that would be hypocrisy. I have no fear of death; only a queer elation ... I would have it no other way. The universe is so vast and so ageless that the life of one man can only be justified by the measure of his sacrifice. We are sent to this world to acquire a personality and a character to take with us that can never be taken from us. Those who just eat and sleep, prosper and procreate, are no better than animals if all their lives they are at peace.

I firmly and absolutely believe that evil things are sent into the world to try us; they are sent deliberately by our Creator to test our metal [sic] because He knows what is good for us. The Bible is full of cases where the easy way out has been discarded for moral principles.

I count myself fortunate in that I have seen the whole country and known men of every calling. But with the final test of war I consider my character fully developed. Thus at my early age my earthly mission is already fulfilled and I am prepared to die with just one regret, and only one – that I could not devote myself to making your declining years more happy by being with you; but you will live in peace and freedom and I shall have directly contributed to that, so here again my life will not have been in vain.
Your loving son'

What mother could not read such words and weep for her lost son?

APPENDIX B

Ian Morrison

Hitherto, Ian Morrison has been Hugh Seagrim's sole biographer, but he too was a remarkable individual. He was attracted to the story of Seagrim because he shared many of the same qualities. Ian Ernest McCleavy Morrison (1913–50) was the son of George Morrison: 'Morrison of Peking', a Victorian missionary and the first person to translate the Bible into Chinese, who later became a political adviser to Yuan Shih-K'ai, president of the newly formed Chinese republic. Educated at Winchester and Trinity College, Cambridge, at the remarkably young age of twenty-two Ian was appointed Professor of English at Hokkaido University at Sapporo, Japan, before being appointed private secretary to the British ambassador, Sir Robert Craigie. After a spell in Shanghai, he became on the outbreak of war the Far East correspondent of *The Times* in Singapore, where he married Maria Therese Neubauer, a charming Austrian girl with whom he had two children.

Among the last to escape from Singapore in February 1942, Morrison later penned a series of brilliant dispatches from New Guinea, where he narrowly escaped death in several plane crashes deep in the jungle. Beneath a rather fey, effete exterior he built a legendary reputation for endurance and toughness among the battle-hardened Australian and American troops. At one stage SOE even considered recruiting him for special operations in China. The buccaneering Peter Fleming commended him to his boss at *The Times* in the highest possible terms. He was described by his friend and fellow correspondent, Michael Davidson, in his book *The World, the Flesh and Myself* as having 'that quality of intellectual awareness mixed with physical courage that has produced some of the most remarkable British men of action and explorers'.

In June 1950, at the outbreak of the Korean War, Morrison returned to Singapore to cover the fighting. Here he fell passionately in love with Elizabeth Han, the widow of a Chinese general. At Taegu in Korea, he spent the evening of 11 August with Lionel Hudson, the former senior officer at the liberation of Rangoon jail, by then the Reuters Far East correspondent, agonising about the future of his marriage. The next day, Morrison and Christopher Buckley, the *Daily Telegraph*'s veteran war correspondent, drove off to cover a story. Both were killed instantly when their jeep was blown up in a minefield. Elizabeth Han exorcised her grief by writing a novel based on their love affair. Under her nom de plume, Han Suyin, her heart-rending book *A Many-Splendoured Thing* became one of the the best-selling love stories of all time and a major Hollywood film. To protect his wife's reputation, Ian Morrison's identity was disguised and his nationality changed to American in the film, in which he was played by William Holden.

Notes

Chapter 1: Eastern Catastrophe
1. Louis Allen, *Burma: The Longest War*, p. 44, eyewitness account by George Rodger, press photographer.

Chapter 2: Brothers in Arms
1. Charles Allen, *Soldier Sahibs*, p. 11, quote by Field Marshal Sir Neville Chamberlain.
2. Tom Bunnett, Whissonsett village archives.
3. Mary Rush, Whissonsett village archives.
4. Thomas Makins, Whissonsett village archives.
5. Dora Robbins, Whissonsett village archives.
6. Michael Seagrim, *Escaping Shadows*, p. 337, quote by Jack Seagrim.
7. Andrew Stephenson, *Eastern Daily Press*, 1944.
8. Douglas Liddell, *Eastern Daily Press*, 1944.
9. Anne Seagrim, author interview, 30 October 2003. Anne Seagrim (1914–2011) was secretary to the writer C. P. Snow for several years, where the experience she gained led to her appointment in 1950 as private secretary to the Duke of Windsor, 'the only man she would willingly have laid down her life for' (author interview). She worked on his memoirs, *A King's Story*, for four years in both Paris and London and travelled with the Duke and Duchess between their homes in Paris and New York. In 1954 she became secretary to Earl Alexander of Tunis as Supreme Allied Commander in the Mediterranean, and later as Lord Lieutenant of London and Constable of the Tower. In 1965 she became the first administrator of the Winston Churchill Memorial Trust. In retirement, she became an accomplished painter. She never married.
10. Ruby Knight, Whissonsett village archives; and author interview, 20 August 2006.
11. Monica Nelson, Whissonsett village archives.
12. Known as the Prostitutes' Padre for his attempts to save vulnerable girls from life on the streets, the Reverend Harold Davidson, vicar of Stiffkey (close to the Seagrim family home at Whissonsett), was found guilty of immoral conduct and defrocked in 1932. Afterwards, he protested his innocence in increasingly bizarre ways – as a seaside performer on hunger strike in a barrel in Blackpool, pretending to be roasted on a spit by the devil and finally, and most spectacularly, starring as Daniel in the lion's den in Skegness with a lion called Freddie and a lioness called Toto. Things did not go entirely according to plan when he trod on Toto's tail and was mauled to death by a vengeful Freddie in front of a shocked audience.
13. Ian Morrison, *Grandfather Longlegs*, p. 31.
14. Ian Morrison, *Grandfather Longlegs*, p. 20.
15. Hugh Seagrim, 'An Anthology', p. 174: Writings on Writing by Rudyard Kipling.
16. Hugh Seagrim, 'An Anthology', p. 221: De Profundis by Oscar Wilde.
17. Ian Morrison, *Grandfather Longlegs*, p. 40.
18. Ian Morrison, *Grandfather Longlegs*, pp. 38–9.
19. Neville Hogan, author interview, 20 August 2005.

20. Harold Braund, *Distinctly I Remember*, pp. 32–3.
21. Camilla Seagrim, Seagrim family papers.
22. Ann Purton, *The Safest Place*, p. 82.
23. Hugh Seagrim, 'An Anthology', p. 54a: The Leader by Giovanni Papini.
24. Hugh Seagrim, 'An Anthology', p. 214: Greatness by Giovanni Papini.
25. Hugh Seagrim, 'An Anthology', p. 10: 'Death of Captain Oates' from the Diary of Captain Robert Falcon Scott.

Chapter 3: Behind Enemy Lines

1. Ian Morrison, *Grandfather Longlegs*, p. 50.
2. Ian Morrison, *Grandfather Longlegs*, p. 50.
3. Ian Morrison, *Grandfather Longlegs*, p. 50.
4. Ian Morrison, *Grandfather Longlegs*, p. 50.
5. Cecil Smith, Report by H. C. Smith, 8 November 1942.
6. Lionel Hudson, *The Rats of Rangoon*, p. 202.
7. Major General J. G. Smyth, *The World at War*, Thames TV, interview 1973.
8. Teruo Okada, *The World at War*, Thames TV, interview 1973.
9. Bruce Kinloch, interview: www.youtube.com, 23 September 2011.
10. Neville Hogan: author interview, 20 August 2005
11. John L. Christian, *Burma* p. 26.
12. Alfred and Valerie Wagg, *A Million Died*, pp. 47–8.
13. Stephen Brookes, *Through the Jungle of Death*, pp. 111–12.
14. John Beamish, *Burma Drop*, p. 30.
15. Stephen Brookes, *Through the Jungle of Death*, p. 99.
16. Kazuo Tamayama and John Nunneley, *Tales by Japanese Soldiers*, p. 64.

Chapter 4: Grandfather Longlegs

1. Hugh Seagrim, Seagrim family papers.
2. Hugh Seagrim, Seagrim family papers.
3. Ian Morrison, *Grandfather Longlegs*, p. 52.
4. Cecil Smith, Report by H. C. Smith, 8 November 1942.

5. Francis Clifford, *Desperate Journey*, p. 117.
6. The astonishing trek of Thompson's party for over 900 miles to eventual safety and evacuation at Fort Hertz in the far north of the country is a long-forgotten epic of human endurance during the Second World War in the Far East. Pursued by a merciless enemy, they had a desperate fight for survival in the face of atrocious conditions at the height of the monsoon. *Desperate Journey* was written in 1944 after Arthur Thompson was invalided back to England. The manuscript was found among his papers on his death in 1975 and eventually published four years later.
7. Ritchie Gardiner, *Diary of a Journey from Sumprabum to Margherita by the Chaukhan Pass: May-July 1942*, BL: MSS Eur A202.
8. *Flight by Elephant* by Andrew Martin relates this long-overlooked tale of the heroic rescue of the Chaukkan Pass party by Gyles Mackrell.
9. Ritchie Gardiner, *Diary of a Journey from Sumbrabum to Margherita by the Chaukhan Pass: May-July 1942*, BL: MSS A202.
10. Ian Morrison, *Grandfather Longlegs*, p. 59.
11. Ian Morrison, *Grandfather Longlegs*, p. 59.
12. Ian Morrison, *Grandfather Longlegs*, p. 60.
13. Ian Morrison, *Grandfather Longlegs*, p. 60.
14. Kyaw Thra Lay, Letter, Nimmo family papers, 10 September 1945.
15. Marshall Saw Shwin, Letter to Major Dennis Ford, The Black Watch, 19 April 1946. Nimmo family papers.
16. Marshall Saw Shwin, Letter to Major Dennis Ford, The Black Watch, 19 April 1946. Nimmo family papers.
17. Marshall Saw Shwin, Letter to Major Dennis Ford, The Black Watch, 19 April 1946. Nimmo family papers.
18. Harry and Beatrice Cryer, Letter to Saw Marshal Shwin, 2 March 1947. Nimmo family papers
19. Peter King, Unpublished thesis, Centre of Chaplain Studies, Cardiff, 2014.

20. Ian Morrison, *Grandfather Longlegs*, p. 81.

Chapter 5: The Master of His Fate
1. Ras Pagani, 'I Did It My Way', p. 1, Campbell family papers.
2. Ras Pagani, 'I Did It My Way', p. 2, Campbell family papers.
3. Ras Pagani, 'I Did It My Way', p. 3, Campbell family papers.
4. Ian Denys Peek, *One Fourteenth of an Elephant* p.674. Gallingly, many of the troops that survived the sinking of the *Empress of Asia* were taunted and jeered by some of the Liverpool Irish stokers, who waved their neutral Irish passports at them as they were marched away in to captivity.
5. Ras Pagani, Statement by Corporal Pagani, 18 January 1946, to I.S.9: NA: WO/361/1550. In his debriefing interview in 1946, Pagani states that he escaped from Singapore with four other Europeans, who joined him on his voyage to Sumatra – one called 'Darkie' and another, 'Len'. They left him on arrival in Sumatra as he said he was 'probably too much of a disciplinarian whilst at sea conserving food and water and that they had had enough'. In his own personal transcript and *The Flame of Freedom*, which is based closely upon it, no mention is made of any companions. Whether accompanied or not, it was a terrifying experience that he was lucky to survive.
6. Robert Hamond, *The Flame of Freedom*, p. 31.
7. A. A. Apthorp, *The British Sumatra Battalion*, p. 62.
8. A. A. Apthorp, *The British Sumatra Battalion*, p. 63.
9. Ras Pagani, 'I Did It My Way', pp. 8–9 Campbell family papers.
10. Lt Colonel Nagatomo, Speech to Allied Prisoners of War at Thanbyuzayat, 23 October 1942. J. W. Turner IWM: 71/41/1.
11. Lt Colonel Nagatomo, Speech to Allied Prisoners of War at Thanbyuzayat, 23 October 1942. J. W. Turner IWM: 71/41/1.

12. A. A. Apthorp, *The British Sumatra Battalion*, p. 93–4.
13. Stanley Saddington, *Escape Impossible*, p. 108.
14. A. A. Apthorp, *The British Sumatra Battalion*, p. 93–4.
15. Stanley Saddington, *Escape Impossible*, p. 108–9.

Chapter 6: Walking with Destiny
1. Ras Pagani, 'I Did It My Way', p. 12, Campbell family papers.
2. Ras Pagani, 'I Did It My Way', p. 13, Campbell family papers.
3. Kyawaing remains a small village, which straggles along the coast road close to the railway line south of Thaton. Although it has grown since the war, some of the older village houses remain surrounded by the plantations which Ras recalled so well. When I visited in 2012, in spite of extensive local enquiries, I was unable to locate the precise house where Ras found sanctuary so long ago.
4. Ras Pagani, 'I Did It My Way', p. 14, Campbell family papers.
5. Ras Pagani, 'I Did It My Way', p. 14, Campbell family papers.
6. Ras Pagani, 'I Did It My Way', p. 17, Campbell family papers.
7. Ian Morrison, *Grandfather Longlegs*, p. 85.

Chapter 7: Lords of the Sunset
1. Ras Pagani, 'I Did It My Way', p. 18, Campbell family papers.
2. Ras Pagani, 'I Did It My Way', pp. 19–20, Campbell family papers.
3. Ras Pagani, 'I Did It My Way', pp. 26–7, Campbell family papers.
4. Ras Pagani, 'I Did It My Way', p. 28 Campbell family papers.
5. Ras Pagani, 'I Did It My Way', p. 31, Campbell family papers.
6. Ras Pagani, 'I Did It My Way', p. 32, Campbell family papers.
7. Ras Pagani, 'I Did It My Way', p. 32, Campbell family papers.

Chapter 8: Lord of the Far-Flung Battle Line
1. Ras Pagani, 'I Did It My Way', p. 36, Campbell family papers.

2. Ian Morrison, *Grandfather Longlegs*, pp. 86–7.
3. Ras Pagani, 'I Did It My Way', p. 38, Campbell family papers.
4. Jean Calmon, *The War, the Troubles and the Captivity of a Missionary*, Report to Mission des Etrangères, Paris.
5. Ian Morrison, *Grandfather Longlegs*, pp. 93–4.
6. Ian Morrison, *Grandfather Longlegs*, p. 88
7. Statement by Saw Ta Roe, 20 June 1945 NA: HS9/1334/7.
8. Jean Calmon, The War, the Troubles and the Captivity of a Missionary, Report to Mission des Etrangères, Paris.
9. Ian Morrison, *Grandfather Longlegs*, p. 94.
10. Ian Morrison, *Grandfather Longlegs*, p. 92.
11. Jean Calmon, The War, the Troubles and the Captivity of a Missionary, Report to Mission des Etrangères, Paris.
12. Ras Pagani, 'I Did It My Way,' p. 39, Campbell family papers.
13. Ras Pagani, 'I Did It My Way,' pp. 39–40, Campbell family papers.

Chapter 9: Perilous Journey
1. Ras Pagani, 'I Did It My Way,' p. 43, Campbell family papers.
2. Ras Pagani, 'I Did It My Way,' p. 45, Campbell family papers.
3. Ras Pagani, 'I Did It My Way,' p. 45, Campbell family papers.
4. Ras Pagani, 'I Did It My Way.' p. 46, Campbell family papers.

Chapter 10: Undercover in the Jungle
1. Ian Morrison, *Grandfather Longlegs*, p. 97.
2. Saw Kan Nyun, Statement by Saw Nyun Kan, NA: HS/1334/7.
3. Ian Morrison, *Grandfather Longlegs*, p. 98.
4. Ian Morrison, *Grandfather Longlegs*, p. 98.
5. Ian Morrison, *Grandfather Longlegs*, p. 98.
6. James Russell Nimmo (1912–43) was born into an old-established family of Falkirk lawyers, one of seven children – two sisters and five brothers, three of whom were destined to die in the war. Educated at Fettes and Trinity College, Cambridge, he went to Burma in 1934 with Macgregor's, the Glasgow-based forestry company, and immediately took to outdoor life, forming a close friendship with Eric McCrindle. The second son, George, was awarded the MC for rescuing wounded under fire, but was killed later in Burma serving with the King's Own Scottish Borderers. Patrick Nimmo, a regular officer in the Argyll and Sutherland Highlanders, was killed at Sidi Barrani in North Africa in December 1940. Bill Nimmo served in Burma in both Wingate expeditions, and was later parachuted into the Karen hills, close to where Jimmy had been killed. Helen Nimmo was awarded the OBE for her service as Chief Commissioner in the Auxiliary Territorial Service.
7. Eric McCrindle (1912–43) was born in Surrey but moved to Helensburgh on the Clyde at the age of two, where his father was the head-office manager of the Union Bank of Scotland in Glasgow. Educated at Sedbergh, he arrived in 1926 just as another notable alumnus, Freddy Spencer-Chapman, was being excluded. Spencer-Chapman stayed behind the Japanese lines in Malaya for over three years and survived the war. After Sedbergh, McCrindle had a spell at a school in Switzerland and then travelled to Spain, before going up to Pembroke College, Cambridge. In 1934 he joined Macgregor's and began life as a forestry assistant in Burma.
8. Ian Morrison, *Grandfather Longlegs*, p. 103.
9. Francis Clifford, *Desperate Journey*, p. 18.
10. Terence O'Brien, *The Moonlight War*, pp. 179–80.
11. SOE personnel file: report by Flying Officer King, NA HS9/1334/7.

Chapter 11: Dark Night of the Soul
1. Ras Pagani, 'I Did It My Way', p. 47, Campbell family papers.
2. Ras Pagani, 'I Did It My Way', p. 47, Campbell family papers.

3. Ras Pagani, 'I Did It My Way', p. 47, Campbell family papers.
4. Ian Morrison, Grandfather Longlegs, pp. 146–7.
5. Ras Pagani, 'I Did It My Way', p. 49, Campbell family papers.
6. Ras Pagani, 'I Did It My Way', p. 50, Campbell family papers.
7. Ras Pagani, 'I Did It My Way', p. 50, Campbell family papers.
8. Lionel Hudson, *The Rats of Rangoon*, p. 60.

Chapter 12: This Long War Beneath the Stars
1. *London Gazette*, Citation for Victoria Cross for Derek Seagrim, 11 May 1943.
2. British embassy records: Fergus Eckersley, author interview, 19 January 2013.
3. Ian Morrison, *Grandfather Longlegs*, p. 115.
4. Ian Morrison, *Grandfather Longlegs*, pp. 114.
5. Ian Morrison, *Grandfather Longlegs*, p. 115.
6. Ian Morrison, *Grandfather Longlegs*, p. 117.
7. Ian Morrison, *Grandfather Longlegs*, p. 118.
8. Ian Morrison, *Grandfather Longlegs*, p. 119.
9. Ian Morrison, *Grandfather Longlegs*, p. 122.

Chapter 13: Death in the Forest
1. Ian Morrison, *Grandfather Longlegs*, p. 142.
2. Statement by Saw Po Hla 11 May 1945 NA: HS9 /1318/ 9.
3. Ian Morrison, *Grandfather Longlegs*, p. 126.
4. Ian Morrison, *Grandfather Longlegs*, p. 128.
5. Ian Morrison, *Grandfather Longlegs*, p. 128.
6. Report on Major Seagrim by Jemadar Maung Wah 14 October 1945 NA: HS 9/1334/7.
7. Kyaw Thra Lay, Letter to Bill Nimmo, 10 September 1945: Nimmo family papers.

8. Statement by Saw Ta Roe, 20 June 1945 NA:HS9/1334/7.
9. Report on the Shwegyin Karens During the War, pp. 14–15 NA:HS1/11.
10. Report on the Shwegyin Karens During the War, pp. 14–15 NA:HS1/11.
11. Ian Morrison, *Grandfather Longlegs*, p. 138.
12. Ian Morrison, *Grandfather Longlegs*, pp.138-9
13. Susumu Kameo, *Ma no Sittan-kawa*, pp. 102–5.
14. Susumu Kameo, Ma no Sittan-kawa, pp. 102–5.
15. Susumu Kameo, *Ma no Sittan-kawa*, pp. 102–5.
16. Statement by Saw Lin Gyaw, NA:HS9/1334/7.

Chapter 14: He Who Would Valiant Be
1. Roy A. Wentz, 'The War Memoir of First Lieutenant Roy A. Wentz, US 10th Air Force', unpublished memoir courtesy of Matthew Poole.
2. Roy A. Wentz, 'The War Memoir of First Lieutenant Roy A. Wentz, US 10th Air Force', unpublished memoir courtesy of Matthew Poole.
3. Roy A. Wentz, 'The War Memoir of First Lieutenant Roy A. Wentz, US 10th Air Force', unpublished memoir courtesy of Matthew Poole.
4. Ian Morrison, *Grandfather Longlegs*, pp. 148–9.
5. Rolf Magener and Heins von Have. Magener and von Have's experiences rank among the most spectacular German escape stories of the entire war. For a full account of their daring break from a British internment camp at Dehra Dun with the legendary Heinrich Harrer, their brazen impersonation of two British officers as they journeyed openly across India to Burma, and their subsequent treatment as suspected spies by the Japanese, see Rolf Magener, *Our Chances Were Zero*.
6. Rolf Magener, *Our Chances were Zero*, p. 173.
7. Rolf Magener, *Our Chances were Zero*, p. 174.

8. Rolf Magener, *Our Chances were Zero*, p. 174.
9. John Boyd, *Tenko! Rangoon Jail*, p. 68, quote by American eyewitness
10. Ian Morrison, *Grandfather Longlegs*, p. 151.
11. Lionel Hudson, *The Rats of Rangoon*, p. 61.
12. Ian Morrison, *Grandfather Longlegs*, pp. 150–1.
13. Ian Morrison, *Grandfather Longlegs*, p. 151.

Chapter 15: The Yank from Battersea
1. Colonel K. P. Mackenzie, *Operation Rangoon Jail*, p. 88.
2. John Boyd, *Tenko! Rangoon Jail*, p. 51.
3. John Boyd, *Tenko! Rangoon Jail*, p. 52.
4. Lionel Hudson, *The Rats of Rangoon*, p. 59.
5. John Reid, author interview, 3 December 2005.
6. Alec Gibson, author interview, 25 October 2005.
7. Philip Stibbe, *Return via Rangoon*, p. 188.
8. Colonel K. P. Mackenzie, *Operation Rangoon Jail*, p. 112.
9. Colonel K. P. Mackenzie, *Operation Rangoon Jail*, p. 112.
10. John Boyd, *Tenko! Rangoon Jail*, p. 80.
11. Colonel K. P. Mackenzie, *Operation Rangoon Jail*, p. 119.
12. John Boyd, *Tenko! Rangoon Jail*, p. 85.
13. Colonel K. P. Mackenzie, *Operation Rangoon Jail*, p. 121.
14. Colonel K. P. Mackenzie, *Operation Rangoon Jail*, p. 122.
15. Lionel Hudson, *The Rats of Rangoon*, p. 84.
16. Lionel Hudson, *The Rats of Rangoon*, p. 65.
17. Lionel Hudson, *The Rats of Rangoon*, p. 92.
18. Lionel Hudson, *The Rats of Rangoon*, p. 95.
19. Lionel Hudson, *The Rats of Rangoon*, p. 144.

20. Lionel Hudson, Papers of Wing Commander L.V. Hudson 82 Squadron RAAF (Australian War Memorial PR87/204, 1945).

Chapter 16: Into Thy Hands I Commend My Spirit
1. Report on the Shwegyin Karens During the War, NA: HS1/11.
2. Address by Ian Morrison, Memorial service Rangoon Cathedral, 29 December 1946.
3. Amabel Seagrim, Letter to Camilla Seagrim, 13 September 1944, Seagrim family papers.
4. Lieutenant Colonel Ambler, Letter dated 20 October 1944, NA: HS9/1334/7.
5. Ian Morrison, *Grandfather Longlegs*, p. 154.
6. Ian Morrison, *Grandfather Longlegs*, p. 201.
7. Susumu Kameo, *Ma no Sittan-kawa*, pp. 102–5.
8. Statement by Saw Po Hla NA: HS9/1318/9.
9. Ras Pagani, 'I Did It My Way', pp. 55–6.
10. Address by Ian Morrison, Memorial service Rangoon Cathedral: 29 December 1946.
11. Major General Shiokawa, Statement, 9 November 1945 NA: HS9/1334/7.
12. Susumu Kameo, *Ma no Sittan-kawa*, pp. 102–5.
13. John Bunyan, *The Pilgrim's Progress*.

AFTERMATH
Seagrim's Legacy
Chapter 17: *Reaping the Whirlwind*
1. Louis Allen, *Burma 1941–45: The Longest War*, pp. 633–4.
2. Lionel Hudson, *The Rats of Rangoon*, p. 209.
3. Field Marshal Viscount Slim, *Defeat into Victory*, p. 572.
4. Terence O'Brien, *The Moonlight War*, p. 243.
5. Terence O'Brien, *The Moonlight War*, pp. 244–24.
6. Ian Morrison, *Grandfather Longlegs* p. 160.

7. Field Marshal Viscount Slim, *Defeat into Victory*, p. 572.
8. Major M.M. Baird, Force 136 Operations in Burma, NA:CAB/HIST/8/1/2
9. Field Marshal Viscount Slim, *Defeat into Victory*, p. 591.
10. Field Marshal Viscount Slim, *Defeat into Victory*, pp. 591–2.
11. Field Marshal Viscount Slim, *Defeat into Victory*, p. 594.
12. Ian Morrison, *Grandfather Longlegs*, p. 164.
13. Report by Lieutenant Colonel Edgar Peacock NA:HS7/106.
14. Lionel Hudson, *The Rats of Rangoon*, p. 150.
15. Ras Pagani, 'I Did It My Way', p. 56 Campbell family papers.
16. Colonel K. P. Mackenzie, *Operation Rangoon Jail*, p. 179.
17. Colonel K. P. Mackenzie, *Operation Rangoon Jail*, p. 180.
18. Colonel K. P. Mackenzie, *Operation Rangoon Jail*, p. 182.
19. Lionel Hudson, *The Rats of Rangoon*, p. 181.
20. Lionel Hudson, *The Rats of Rangoon*, p. 188.

Chapter 18: The Birth of a Legend
1. SOE personnel file: Letter to Brigadier J. Anstey, 26 June 1945 NA: HS9/1334/7.
2. Letter to Ian Morrison dated 13 July 1945, *The Times* archives.
3. Ian Morrison, *Grandfather Longlegs*, p. 178–9.
4. Ian Morrison, *Grandfather Longlegs*, p. 179.
5. Ian Morrison, *Grandfather Longlegs*, p. 179.
6. Statement by Saw Kan Nyun: NA:HS 9/ 1334/7.
7. Report on the Shwegyin Karens During the War, NA/HS 1/11.
8. Colin Mackenzie, interview, 8675 reel 4. IWM sound archive, recorded 1983.
9. Richard Lewin, interview: 12383: reel 2. IWM sound archive recorded 9 January 1992.

10. Duncan Guthrie, *Jungle Diary*, p. 51.
11. Duncan Guthrie, *Jungle Diary*, p. v.
12. Amabel Seagrim, Undated letter, September 1945, Seagrim family papers.
13. Amabel Seagrim, Photograph album, Seagrim family papers.
14. *London Gazette*, 12 September 1946, citation for the posthumous award of the George Cross to Hugh Seagrim.
15. *Church Times*, Review of Grandfather Longlegs by Ian Morrison, 31 October 1947.
16. *Sunday Times*, Review of *Grandfather Longlegs* by Ian Morrison, 18 January 1948.
17. Report on Burma Force 136 Memorial Fund: NA: TS 220/107.
18. Julian Symons, *England's Pride*, p. 156.
19. General Tamlabaw, Report in *Financial Times*, 11 September 2004.
20. Jean Calmon, The War, the Troubles and the Captivity of a Missionary, Report to Mission des Etrangères, Paris.
21. Report in *Yorkshire Post* and *Leeds Intelligencer*, 9 August 1952.
22. Statement by Corporal Pagani to I.S.9, 18 January 1946: NA: WO/361/1550.
23. Ras Pagani, 'I Did It My Way', p. 65 Campbell family papers.

Epilogue
1. Ras Pagani, TV interview for *Forgotten Allies*, BBC TV, 1997

Select Bibliography

Primary Sources

National Archives (NA):
Extensive papers, reports and signals from the following series:
HS 1/7/8/9
KV2
WO 106/172/193/203/208/220/235/311/3 25/344/345/373
FO 371/643
T 220
AIR 20/23/27/40/79
CAB 101/102 649-652/121

British Library (BL):
Dorman-Smith, Sir Reginald, Dorman-Smith papers BL/MSS /Eur E215 series
Imperial War Museum (IWM):
Tapes of BBC broadcasts from Burma sound archives
Faber and Faber archives:
Correspondence with Ian Morrison and photographs
Unpublished manuscripts:
Hudson, Lionel, Papers of Wing Commander L.V. Hudson 82 Squadron RAAF (AWM: PR87/204, 1945)
Johnston, J. A. R., 'The Story of Eleven Men's Attempt to Evade Capture by the Japanese March 15–May 19 1942 (1945)
Kidd, Flight-Lieutenant C. A., In a Japanese Prison Camp: statement. IWM 97/6/1
Loizeau, Rev. Father Paul Gaston, Reports from Papun Mission 1942–45 (Mission D' Etrangères, Paris)
Pagani, Roy, 'I Did It My Way' (original typescript c.1984)
Sammons, Alan, 'Experiences as a Jap Prisoner-of-War' (1945)

Smallwood, Lieutenant Colonel J. E. S., Operation Lynx and Character: interview 02/52/1 IWM sound archive
Tulloch, J. Cromarty, 'In the Wake of Taw-Mei-Pa', (MSS IWM)
Wentz, Roy, The War Memoir of Lieutenant Roy A. Wentz, US 10th Air Force, (courtesy of Matt Poole USA)
Wilding, R. Allen, 'Survival: A Chindit's Story' (c.1982)

Family Sources:
Campbell family papers, photographs and tapes
Nimmo family papers and photographs
Seagrim family papers and photographs

TV Sources:
The World at War: 'It's a Lovely Day Tomorrow Burma 1942–43', Thames TV
Burma 1941–1945: British Campaigns DD Video
Forgotten Allies, BBC TV
Disappearing World, BBC TV
The Karens, Everyman, BBC TV

Secondary Sources

Aldrich, Richard J., *The Clandestine Cold War in Asia,* (Frank Cass, 2000), Chapter 6, 'Legacies of Secret Service, renegade SOE and the Karen Struggle in Burma 1948–50'
Aldrich, Richard J., *The Faraway War: Personal Diaries of the Second World War in Asia and the Pacific* (Doubleday, 2005)
Aldrich, Richard J., *Intelligence and the War against Japan: Britain, America and the Politics of Secret Service* (Cambridge University Press, 2000)

Allen, Charles, *Soldier Sahibs: The Men Who Made the North-West Frontier* (John Murray, 2000)

Allen, Louis, *Burma: The Longest War 1941–45* (Phoenix, 1998)

Allen, Louis, *Singapore 1941–42*, (Davies-Poynter, 1977)

Apthorp, A. A., *The British Sumatra Battalion* (The Book Guild, 1988)

Asher, Michael, *Khartoum: The Ultimate Imperial Adventure* (Viking, 2005)

Association of Myanmar Architects, *30 Heritage Buildings of Yangon* (Serindia Publications, 2012)

Bayly, Christopher and Tim Harper, *Forgotten Wars: The End of Britain's Asian Empire* (Allen Lane, 2007)

Beamish, John, *Burma Drop* (Elek Books, 1958)

Binney, Marcus, *Secret War Heroes: Men of the Special Operations Executive* (Hodder, 2005)

Blair, Joan and Blair, Clay, *Return from the River Kwai* (Penguin, 1979)

Bowen, John, *Undercover in the Jungle* (William Kimber, 1978)

Boyd, John with Gary Garth, *Tenko! Rangoon Jail* (Turner Publishing, 1996)

Braund, Harold, *Distinctly I Remember: A personal story of Burma* (Wren Publishing, 1972)

Brookes, Stephen, *Through the Jungle of Death: A Boy's Escape from Wartime Burma* (John Murray, 2000)

Brown, Gordon, *Courage: Eight Portraits* (Bloomsbury, 2007)

Bunyan, John, *The Pilgrim's Progress* (Oxford University Press, 1998)

Calvert, Michael, *The Chindits* (Ballantine, 1973)

Chang, Iris, *The Rape of Nanking* (Penguin, 1997)

Chapman, Roger, *Beyond Their Duty: Heroes of the Green Howards* (The Green Howards Museum, 2001)

Chinnery, Philip, *March or Die* (Airlife, 1977)

Christian, John L, *Burma* (Collins, 1945)

Clifford, Francis, *Desperate Journey* (Hodder and Stoughton, 1979)

Conrad, Joseph, *Heart of Darkness* (Oxford University Press, 2002)

Conrad, Joseph, *Lord Jim* (Bantam, 1957)

Cosford, J. S., *Line of Lost Lives* (Gryphon Books, 1988)

Coubrough, C. R. L., *Memories of a Second Lieutenant* (Wilton, 1965)

Cruickshank, Charles, *SOE in the Far East* (Oxford University Press, 1983)

Davidson, Michael, *The World, the Flesh and Myself* (D. Bruce Watson 1973)

Daws, Gavan, *Prisoners of the Japanese* (Simon and Schuster, 2006)

Dudley, Ron, *The Road to Rangoon and Back* (Old Bakehouse Publications, 2007)

Felton, Mark, *Never Surrender* (Pen and Sword, 2013)

Fergusson, Bernard, *Return to Burma* (Collins, 1962)

Foot, M. R. D., *SOE: The Special Operations Executive 1940–1946* (Pimlico, 1999)

Foot, M. R. D. and J. M. Langley, *MI9: Escape and Evasion 1939–1945* (The Bodley Head, 1979)

Gavin, Denis, *Quiet Jungle, Angry Sea: My Escapes from the Japanese* (Lennard Publishing, 1989)

Gilchrist, Sir Andrew, *Malaya 1941: The Fall of a Fighting Empire* (Robert Hale, 1992)

Goodall, Felicity, *Exodus Burma: The British Escape Through the Jungles of Death 1942* (Spellmount, 2011)

Guthrie, Duncan, *Jungle Diary* (Macmillan, 1946)

Hall, H. Fielding, *The Soul of a People* (Macmillan, 1932)

Hamond, Robert, *The Flame of Freedom: Corporal Ras Pagani's Escape from the Railway of Death* (Leo Cooper, 1988)

Hedley, John, *Jungle Fighter* (Tom Donovan, 1996)

Hewitt, Anthony, *To Freedom Through China: Escaping from Japanese-Occupied Hong Kong* (Pen and Sword, 1986)

Hudson, Lionel, *The Rats of Rangoon* (Leo Cooper, 1987)

Keane, Fergal, *Road of Bones: The Epic Siege of Kohima 1944* (Harper Press, 2011)

Kelly, Desmond, *Kelly's Burma Campaign: Letters from the Chin Hills* (Tiddim Press, 2003)

Knox, Collie, *Forever England: An Anthology* (Cassell, 1943)

Lamont-Brown, Raymond, *Kamikaze: Japan's Suicide Samurai* (Cassell, 1997)

Latimer, John, *Burma: The Forgotten War* (John Murray, 2004)

Lawrence, T. E., *The Seven Pillars of Wisdom. A Triumph* (Jonathan Cape, 1935)

Leney, R. A., *'Mongoose White' Behind Japanese Lines in Burma'* (London 2005)

Lomax, Eric, *The Railway Man* (Vintage, 1996)

Lunt, James, *A Hell of a Licking: The Retreat from Burma 1941/42* (Collins, 1986)

Macarthur, Brian, *Surviving the Sword: Prisoners of the Japanese in the Far East 1942–45* (Random House, 2005)

McCrae, Alister and Prentice, Alan, *Irrawaddy Flotilla* (James Paton, 1978)

McCrae, Alister and friends, *Tales of Burma* (James Paton, 1981)

Macdonald Fraser, George, *Quartered Safe Out Here: A Recollection of the War in Burma* (Harvill, 1992)

Mackenzie, Colonel K. P., *Operation Rangoon Jail* (Christopher Johnson, 1954)

Magener, Ralph, *Our Chances Were Zero: The Daring Escape by Two Germans from India 1944* (Leo Cooper, 2001)

Martin, Andrew, *Flight by Elephant: The Untold Story of World War Two's Most Daring Jungle Rescue* (Fourth Estate, 2013)

Masters, John, *The Road Past Mandalay: A Personal Narrative* (Michael Joseph, 1961)

Merrick, K. A., *Flights of the Forgotten – Special Duties Operations in World War II*, (Weidenfeld Military, 1989)

Morrison, Ian, *Grandfather Longlegs: The Life and Gallant Death of Major H. P. Seagrim GC, DSO, MBE* (Faber and Faber, 1947)

Moynahan, Brian, *Jungle Soldier* (Quercus, 2009)

Myint-U, Thant, *The River of Lost Footsteps* (Faber and Faber, 2007)

O'Brien, Terence, *The Moonlight War: The Story of Clandestine Operations in South-East Asia, 1944–5* (Collins, 1987)

Ogden, Alan, *Tigers Burning Bright: SOE Heroes in the Far East* (Bene Factum Publishing Ltd, 2013)

Oung, Kin, *Who Killed Aung San?* (White Lotus, 1993)

Owen, Frank, *The Campaign in Burma* (HMSO)

Peacock, Geraldine, *The Life of a Jungle Wallah* (Arthur Stockwell, Ilfracombe 1958)

Peek, Ian Denys, *One Fourteenth of an Elephant: A Memoir of Life and Death on the Burma–Thailand Railway* (Bantam, 2005)

Po, Dr San C., *Burma and the Karens* (Elliot Stock, 1928)

Purton, Ann, *The Safest Place* (Wells-next-the-Sea, 1982)

Rees, Lawrence, *Horror in the East* (BBC Books, 2001)

Rivett, Rohan D., *Behind Bamboo* (Angus and Robertson, 1946)

Rodriguez, Helen, *Helen of Burma* (Collins, 1983)

Rolo, Charles J., *Wingate's Raiders* (George G. Harrap, 1945)

Saddington, Stanley, *Escape Impossible* (A Lane Publishers, 1987)

Slim, Field Marshal Viscount, *Defeat into Victory* (Cassell, 1956)

Smyth, Major General Sir J. G., *Before the Dawn* (Cassell, 1957)

Spencer-Chapman, Frederick, *The Jungle is Neutral* (Chatto and Windus, 1948)

Spurr, Russell, *Let the Tiger Turn Tail* (Mainstream Publishing, 1992)

Stevenson, H. N. C., *The Hill Peoples of Burma* (Longmans 1945)

Stewart, John, *To the River Kwai: Two Journeys 1943, 1979* (Bloomsbury, 1988)

Stibbe, Philip, *Return via Rangoon* (Leo Cooper, 1994)

Susumu, Kameo, *Ma no Sittan-kawa (Sittang: The Devil's River)* (Onishi-sha, 1980)

Suu Kyi, Aung San, *Letters from Burma* (London, 1997)

Suu Kyi, Aung San, *Freedom from Fear* (Penguin, 1991)

Sweet-Escott, B. A. C., *Baker Street Irregular* (Methuen, 1965)

Swinson, Arthur, *Kohima* (Cassell, 1966)

Symons, Julian, *England's Pride: The Story of the Gordon Relief Expedition* (Hamish Hamilton, 1965)

Tamayama, Kazuo and John Nunneley, *Tales by Japanese Soldiers of the Burma Campaign 1942–1945* (Cassell, 2000)

Tatsuro, Izumiya, *The Minami Organ* (Rangoon University, 1985)

Thomas, Vicky, *The Naga Queen: Ursula Graham Bower and Her Jungle Warriors 1939–45* (The History Press, 2012)

Thompson, Julian, *Forgotten Voices of Burma: The Second World War's Forgotten Conflict* (Ebury Press, 2010)

Tyson, Geoffrey, *Forgotten Frontier* (W. H. Targett, 1946)

Urquhart, Alistair, *The Forgotten Highlander* (Little, Brown, 2010)

Wagg, Alfred and Wagg, Valerie, *A Million Died* (Thacker & Co., 1945)

Woodburn-Kirby, S., *The War Against Japan*, 5 Vols (HMSO, 1957–69)

Newspapers, Obituaries and Journals:
The Times
Sunday Times
Daily Telegraph
Daily Mail
Eastern Daily Press
Church Times
SEAC Newspaper
Sunday Statesman
Rangoon Liberator
Rangoon Ramblings
Dekho!

Hugh Seagrim
24 March 1909–2 September 1944

Roy Pagani
23 July 1915–31 March 2003

Photographs

All the photographs and drawings are from the author's own collection with the exception of the following:

Seagrim family archives:

p.6 & 25, p.28 (above left), p.40 (top left and right), p.221

Campbell family archives:

p6 (right), p.53 (left), p.87 (left and right), p.110 (bottom), p.255 (left and right)

Nimmo family archives:

p.70 (right)

Lieutenant Pablay Singh:

p.54 (left), p.66 (far left and left), p.77(left and right), p.144 (left and right), p.172 (bottom), p.188 (left)

Imperial War Museum:

p4 & 239 (left and right), p.154 (left), p.188 (right), p.200 (left and right), p.236 (bottom), p.237 (bottom) and jacket main image

Every effort has been made to ensure that the copyright details shown here are correct but if there are any inaccuracies, please contact the publisher.